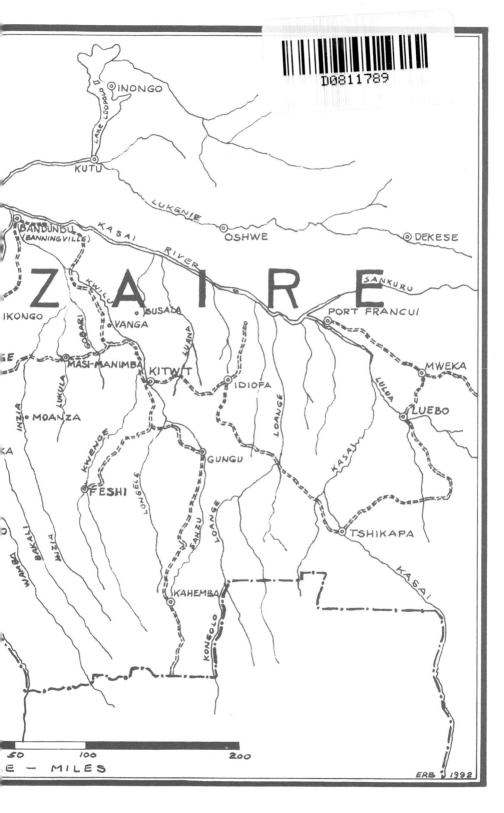

INONGO

LAKE LEOPOLD II

KUTU

LUKENIE

BANDUNDU
(BANNINGVILLE)

KASAI

RIVER

OSHWE

DEKESE

Z A I R E

SANKURU

KWILU

IKONGO

BUSALA

VANGA

LUANA

PORT FRANCUI

GOBARI

MASI-MANIMBA

KITWIT

IDIOFA

MWEKA

LULUA

LUEBO

INZIA

LUKULA

MOANZA

KWENGE

LOANGE

KASAI

KA

GUNGU

LONGELE

FESHI

BAKALI

WAMBA

INZIA

KANZU

LOANGE

TSHIKAPA

KASAI

KAHEMBA

KONGOLO

50   100   200

E — MILES

ERB 1992

Called
to Africa

William D. Scott

August House Publishers, Inc.
L I T T L E   R O C K

Published by August House, Inc.,
P.O. Box 3223, Little Rock, Arkansas, 72203.
501-372-5450

Printed in the United States of America

10 9 8 7 6 5 4 3 2 1

LIBRARY OF CONGRESS CATALOGING IN PUBLICATION DATA
Scott, William D., 1921-
Called to Africa: thirty-five years in central Africa as a missionary,
architect, builder, pilot, hunter, teacher, and friend
William Dale Scott
p.   cm.
ISBN 0-87483-297-7 (alk. paper): $24.95
1. Scott, Chester D., 1921-   .
2. Lay missionaries—Zaire—Biography.
3. Lay missionaries—United States—Biography.
4. I. Scott, William Dale, 1923-   . II. Title.
BV3625.C63S36   1993
266'.61'092—dc20
[B]   92-33473
                       CIP

Executive: Ted Parkhurst
Editor: Ed Gray
Cover design: Harvill-Ross Studios Ltd.
Typography: Heritage/North Little Rock

This book is printed on archival-quality paper which meets the guidelines for performance and durability of the Committee on Production
Guidelines for Book Longevity of the Council on Library Resources.

AUGUST HOUSE, INC.   PUBLISHERS   LITTLE ROCK

Dedication

This book is dedicated to the memory of

Lenora Scott

*Whose pride in her sons is matched only
by our love for her.*

*We thank God for her strong faith
and its influence in our lives.*

Author's Preface

This is the story of my brother, Chester D. Scott, who was an American Baptist Missionary in Zaire, a country in central Africa, known as the Belgian Congo when he arrived there in 1953.

I have been proud of him and his ministry, but it is only as I have written his story that I appreciate fully the scope of what he did and, more fundamentally, the kind of person he is. I have sought to live inside his head in order to write this book and am rewarded by knowing my brother as never before.

Three years ago we spent one solid month at his home. He talked into a tape recorder and I asked an occasional question to fill in some detail. He and Dolores had extensive correspondence and documents, which were invaluable in jogging memory and settling details. Their wealth of experiences could never be covered in a single volume, and I accept responsibility for selecting those in this book.

The first-person form was decided upon after much consideration. It gives the kind of authenticity this story demands, yet there are limitations inherent in this choice.

First, this form does not deal thoroughly with the other missionaries who worked, and often suffered, alongside Scotty. Each of their stories is equally worthy of publication. The dedication and accomplishments of his colleagues over the years stand on their own merits and no oversight on my part can diminish their luster. However, this is Scotty's story, not the record of missionary work in Zaire. I found it necessary to keep that in focus lest I wander down too many fascinating byways. So, if the reader begins to feel that Scotty is portrayed as the hub around which all mission work in Zaire revolved, please be reminded that it is only because of the form I have selected and not a lack of understanding on my part or Scotty's.

Also, more could be said about Dolores, Sharan and John, as well as other members of the family and faithful friends all over America. But to have done so would have clouded the focus of the book.

Another difficulty of writing in the first person was deciding how to recount the political dynamics going on in the country that, during their time in residence, was named The Belgian Congo, then The Democratic Republic of Congo, and finally Zaire. Like all the missionaries, Scotty and Dolores steered a wide berth to avoid any involvement or semblance of involvement in the country's politics. Yet, those events were so traumatic and of such far reaching consequences that they impinged on their lives daily.

My solution is to give a brief historical outline in the appendix. This is no more than a sketch to refresh the memory of an older generation and to set the scene for younger readers. This is the setting in which the story of Scotty's life and ministry takes place.

Yes, there are still lions and elephants and rhinoceroses and crocodiles there and, though their numbers are declining, there is not a year in which a friend or workman is not killed by one of them. There are still tribes living in grass huts, hunting with arrows and spears, who have seldom, if ever, seen a white person or heard the message of a loving God who can overcome the constant fear resulting from their superstitions. But more than anything else it is a land of human beings who have the same wishes and desires of people everywhere: food for the family, a better life for their children, and the chance to live in peace.

Wm. D. Scott
Fairfield Bay, Arkansas
1992

ii

CHAPTER 1

Santa Monica, California
1951-1953

Bob Briggs was the last person I'd have expected to have such a serious heart problem. Open-heart surgery may seem almost routine today, but the procedure was new and frightening in 1951, and the risks were high, even for a young man like Bob.

Bob and Betty were one of eleven couples in our church, all of whom shared their social life, their spiritual quest and even their economic future. We planned to pool our resources and invest in real estate in the Los Angeles area. The plan called for each of us to become independently wealthy so that we could do great things for the Lord and His church. It was a good plan; those who stuck with it exceeded their goal. But beyond all the planning, each of us had a deep and genuine love for the others.

Bob had an excellent surgeon and we had confidence that our prayers would help. We gathered at the apartment of Mrs. Brown, our Director of Christian Education, to pray while Bob was undergoing surgery. The telephone was a lifeline, connecting us to the hospital as surely as the myriad tubes connected Bob to his life-support system. Throughout the evening and into the night the calls alternately brought hope and anxiety. We felt the joy of answered prayer when the doctor called from the hospital at sunrise, telling us the operation was over and Bob was doing well. He thanked us for our prayers, assuring us they were as important as his own skill. With that reassurance we went into the kitchen for coffee and rolls.

Suddenly, Mrs. Brown said, "Quick. Everybody get down on your knees."

We all knelt to pray, not knowing exactly why. Were we to give thanks for God's intervention? Were we to ask direction for the future? Why pray now when we had already been at it for hours? But I knelt along with the others.

Suddenly, I had the sure and certain knowledge that Christ had entered the room! I experienced His presence just as certainly as I knew the others were in the room with me.

He came to me and, though I know there was no audible voice, he spoke so clearly I understood perfectly what he wanted me to hear. "Bob is going to die. I have need of him." Somehow this knowledge should have brought despair; instead it filled me with a sense of unbounded peace.

"Don't worry about Betty and the children," the voice continued. "They'll be taken care of."

I thought that was the end, but there was one more message, crystal-clear, burning in my heart. "I want you to prepare yourself for full-time Christian service. I'm going to call you."

I felt his presence leave the room as Mrs. Brown said, "All right, everybody, you can get up now." I supposed the others had experienced His presence just as I had, but it was immediately obvious this was not the case. It was further confirmed when, minutes later, the phone rang and the voice on the other end announced that Bob had just died. Disbelief, shock, frustration, disappointment hung heavy in the room.

"Our prayers were wasted."

"We prayed all night and nothing happened."

I wanted to shout, "Oh, yes it did! The most wonderful thing in my whole life just happened!" But I kept my silence. I looked at my lovely wife, Dolores. I wanted to share this experience with her as soon as possible. I knew that whatever the future held, we would face it together. My heart was overflowing with love as we left Brownie's apartment: love for my wife, love for my children, love for my Lord, and still enough left over to love everybody else in the world.

God is going to call me!

God is going to call *me*!

The thought would not leave my mind, and the prospect of such a call was as crazy as it was inevitable. Nonetheless, I began to speculate on what such a call would mean.

God *is* going to call me!

At first I wondered if I would be called to be a pastor, but I almost laughed at the image that brought to mind. That would require years of study, and I had never been a good student until after I was out of high school and took courses that really interested me: metallurgy, engineering, design, welding—the things I needed for my work. Ministers deal with ideas and I had always worked with *things*, tangible manageable things. Things like the top secret fighter planes for which I had designed tools at Douglas Aircraft. Things like Howard Hughes' "Spruce Goose," for which I was also a tool engineer. Things like the amphibious airplanes we maintained in the Pacific theater during the recently ended war. Things like the buildings I now designed and whose construction I now supervised for General Telephone Company of Southern California.

God is going to call me!

Perhaps my call would be to Christian Education. I could teach how to block a linebacker, or throw a left jab and right cross, or track a deer through the woods, but these were not a part of the Sunday School curricula. Still, Dolores and I were Sunday School superintendents at Trinity Baptist Church, and I was Scout Master of our troop so this seemed a likely possibility.

God is going to call me!

But when? And to do what? I had no idea how or why he would use me, but I had the certain knowledge that whatever it was, wherever it was, He would work it out just fine.

The Rev. Dr. Fred Judson looked across his desk at me, his glasses far down on his nose so he could see me over their top.

"You should go to Green Lake Conference Center for the Christian Education Week," Fred said. It was one of those rare times he put his droll humor aside to be totally serious. "There will be people from all over the country who are involved in all phases of Christian Education, and you can pick their brains. Find out what schools they attended. Ask them what they are doing now, what their work is. Find out what they think the needs will be in the future. Just talk and ask and listen."

"But Fred," I protested, "I've got projects under way that demand my presence here. My boss is counting on me."

"Indeed He is," the pastor smiled. I knew I would be accountable to a new "boss" from that moment. I scheduled our vacation to include the conference as well as extended visits with our families in the Midwest.

The time at the conference was inspiring and enlightening, but on returning to California neither Dolores nor I had any more sense of direction than when we had left. A mountain of work was waiting in my office. Leafing through the pile of messages, I saw that Eddy Dumont had called, saying he and some of the others from "The Couples" would pick me up at four o'clock on Friday to go to a layman's conference.

"Hey, Eddy, I got your message," I told him on the phone. "But you know I've been gone and there's just too much here for me to catch up on. I'm going to have to be in the office all week end. Sorry, but you fellows have a good time without me."

"Yea, tough, isn't it?" Eddy answered. "You should have a suitcase with you Friday because we're going to pick you up at four." There was no refusing Eddy Dumont.

Thousand Pines, a beautiful retreat center set high in the San Bernardino Mountains, lives up to its name. The stately lodge pole pines draw your eyes up to where their tops brush the heavens, and the breeze floating through the branches sounds like whispers of the spirit.

The first man on the program began by saying, "I want to read a letter to you. This may be the most important thing we do this weekend. This letter came several weeks ago and the executive committee has prayed about it. We feel sure there will be a man here who has been called to full-time Christian service and who will feel this letter is directed to him." Then he proceeded to read aloud the request from our Foreign Mission Society. They were looking for a man who was called by God to design and build buildings for our mission stations in the Belgian Congo.

This was the call I had been waiting for! It was as clear as though the letter were addressed to Mr. Chester D. Scott and personally signed, "God."

It is one thing to be called by God. It is quite another thing to be called by a Mission Society. While the missionaries must make a total investment of their lives to the Lord and His mission, there is no less investment and commitment on the part of the Society. It must be satisfied that the candidate is physically, emotionally, spiritually and professionally capable of moving into a strange culture with myriad diseases, different languages and unfamiliar expectations, and doing the job he or she is sent there to do.

So began a series of examinations and tests. People we had listed as references were contacted. Then they were asked for the names of others who knew us. Those persons also were interviewed. Physical examinations proved us to be in excellent health, but suggested that Dolores should gain weight, a suggestion that she resisted firmly. Psychiatric interviews were extensive, and the results were reported to the Society.

One day a stranger knocked on our door. "I'm Jesse Wilson from the Foreign Mission Society," he said. "I've come to stay with you for a few days."

For those days he became a part of the family. We went to see the Santa Monica High School football team play, and he was with us. He shared our pride as our darling Sharan marched with the band as team mascot, her dark beauty already striking in her fifth-grade body. When we tussled with baby John he knew the joy we had in our son.

When I left for work each morning, Jesse went with me. He was with me at the office as I did the paperwork and interacted with other staff members. He was with me as I inspected projects all over Southern California. He was with me as I argued with contractors and suppliers. He was with me the morning I went into the office of Daniel, Mann, Johnson & Mendenhal, an architectural firm I used frequently.

Mr. Mann greeted us as we entered. Without waiting to be introduced to my guest he said, "Scotty, what's all this stuff I've been hearing about you leaving General Tel and going to The Belgian Congo?"

"It's a calling. It's something I feel very deeply, and I just hope it works out," I said.

"Well, why the hell didn't you tell me you wanted to go to Africa? We'd give anything to start an office over there and you're the man who could do it for us. Just tell me what the hell they're paying you and we'll double it."

I thanked him for the vote of confidence, but assured him that my call wasn't subject to negotiation.

After we left the architect, Jesse said, "Scotty, you can take me back to the house to get my suitcase and then to the airport. I've found what I came here to learn." Then he told me about the psychiatrist's evaluation of me. "According to him no normal person would give up what you and Dolores have, leave your families behind, and take your children out of the schools here to live in a place like the Congo. He said you are a person with an inordinate and unrealistic desire for adventure.

"When I heard your response to Mr. Mann," he continued, "I knew I could go back to the Society and tell them not to worry about your motives."

5

The Board approved our appointment, along with that of other missionaries to be sent to the Belgian Congo. Later we learned that the missionaries already on the field, realizing how age, illness and retirements were decimating their ranks, had prayed that God would call twenty-two younger people to take up the work. They had prayed for pastors, doctors, nurses, educators, and for a man who could come there to design and build buildings. There were exactly twenty-two of us commissioned that year. Each had been called as surely as I was, though no two of us experienced our call in the same way.

Each missionary candidate was asked to make a statement at the commissioning service. These were dedicated men and women, but they were also humble. I listened as one after another told the Board how awed and overwhelmed they felt as they contemplated the tasks ahead of them. Finally it was my turn.

"I have no doubt that I will be able to accomplish what you are sending me out to do," I said. "I know that God has called me to the Congo to design and build buildings. I cannot believe that He would call me unless I have the ability and skill to do the job. Nor can I believe that He would send me there unless He intends to provide the resources and support and strength I will need."

Though my words were sincere, I had no idea then how many times in the next thirty-five years we would come to the limit of our own abilities, only to see God step in and fulfill the promise I had so brashly expressed.

An intensive course in French followed at the University of California. My only other brush with another language was a smattering of Spanish I picked up in my early teen years. I ran with a gang of Mexican kids through junior high school. We called ourselves "The Stockyard Wolves" because when we weren't playing ball, or having fights with other gangs, we hung out at the stockyards, often jumping into the pens to wrestle calves or ride the animals bareback. I became head of the gang through the time-honored election process: I fought and beat every other contender. But most of the Spanish I learned then held little promise of being usable on a mission field. The French we learned was much more acceptable in refined circles, but hardly enough to let us consider ourselves bilingual.

A year after the conference at Thousand Pines, we were finally on our way to the Congo. But before going overseas for our first four-year term, we wanted one last, long visit with our Midwestern families. It proved beneficial for all of us except eleven-year-old Sharry, whose cousins cautioned her at every stop along the way to be extra careful of the cannibals.

For me, the highlight of the trip came in our home town of Coffeyville, Kansas. Two of my cousins, Wynn and Bill Mace, had been outstanding football players for the local high school and junior college before going on to play for the University of Kansas. Wynn was older than I and Bill was younger, so I had never been on a team with either of them. Wynn told me there was to be a pre-season football game, the junior college alumni against the varsity. I could envision what a combination we would make: quarterback Wynn handing off the ball to Bill, the slashing, pounding runner; the defense keying on this devastating threat; then Wynn spiraling his perfectly thrown pass to the streaking end, me, for a crowd rousing touchdown. I could hardly wait to get suited up.

On my first play I was responsible for the key block to free Bill for a sweep. I remembered the feel of making a well-executed block on the man assigned to me. What I didn't remember was how I used to hunch over on the line, making myself less vulnerable to an onrushing lineman. Wynn gave the count, the ball was snapped, and the varsity player hit me high in the chest, his well conditioned body traveling at just under four hundred miles an hour. They carried me off the field with four cracked ribs. The pain was terrible, but I had played football with my cousins.

On September 22, 1953, aboard the passenger ship Maasdam, we headed for a bright new life on the Dark Continent. One thirty-two-year-old male who had as many broken ribs as usable phrases in the language on which he would have to depend. A beautiful young mother who for years had gone to her comfortable accounting office, dressed in fine and tasteful clothes. A three-year-old boy whose energy level was exceeded only by his boundless curiosity. And a beautiful eleven-year-old girl whose memories of marching as the mascot for Santa Monica High School and at some games of the Los Angeles Rams were replaced by visions of cannibals pursuing her through the jungle.

CHAPTER 2

Banza Manteke—1953-1954

The train pulled into the station called Lufu Gare late in the afternoon on the last leg of our journey. We had spent a few weeks in Brussels being indoctrinated by the Belgian government on colonial issues and policies. In Leopoldville we had a few days to be introduced to the mission and missionaries. Now we were almost to Banza Manteke, our first assignment.

The ride on the antiquated railroad had been memorable. Our first views of Africa rolled slowly past the open windows. Palm trees rose majestically over grass-hut villages. Native women fished in streams or worked in their gardens. Black faces and black bodies crowded the platform at every station along the way. Ashes and coals blew back from the wood-burning engine, through the open windows of the first-class car, and burned tiny holes in our clothes. The meal in the dining car was served by Congolese in their immaculate white uniforms. Twice, cars jumped the tracks and crewmen brought out equipment to jack up the car and push it back onto the track so the train could resume its tortuous way. Only white passengers were in first class; blacks traveled in the less expensive cars, lacking even the few amenities found in ours: a quality of travel an American hobo would have sneered at. And above all, the hot, humid air made our clothes cling to our sweaty bodies. The jarring and jostling of the train intensified the pain in my bound-up rib cage.

In the crowd waiting for us at Lufu Gare, the only white face was perched atop the chubby body of a man with a high-pitched voice. He spotted us as easily as we spotted him. "My name is Norman Riddle and I'm here to meet you," he said. "I brought the construction truck

8

over to pick you up."

As Norman, Dolores and Sharan carried our luggage to the truck, Dolores asked me quietly, "Scotty, do you think you should tell him what happened to your ribs or just let him think we carry your luggage for you all the time?"

"I picked up a load of *makayabo*," Norman informed us. "But there is room for your luggage, too." I had no idea what *makayabo* was. Norman, Dolores, Sharan and Johnny were ensconced in the cab, leaving me to ride on the back of the truck along with numerous Africans who were at Lufu Gare, waiting for a ride back to Banza Manteke. We climbed atop the cargo and Norman headed down the rough dirt road into the sunset.

Makayabo provides the main source of protein in the Congolese diet. It is dried fish and it has an odor that could never be mistaken for anything other than dried fish. Since I was a dignitary of sorts, they gave me the best seat on the back of the truck—atop the *makayabo*. Norman drove along the ruts of the road as though he were living out fantasies of being in the Indianapolis 500. Dust swirled up and engulfed us. Every bump was multiplied by the speed and transmitted directly to my aching ribs. An unbelievable stink rose from the dried fish.

For twenty-one kilometers I endured the ordeal, reminding myself over and over that God had set this up for me. But somehow, it all seemed like a practical joke.

"Oh, I've never been so happy to meet anyone in my whole life!" She threw her arms around me and hugged me with surprising strength for a woman only five-foot-two. I thought the greeting a bit effusive, but coming from the little ball of energy there by the breakfast table I accepted it as exaggeration in the cause of courtesy. Annis Ford lowered herself onto a chair and managed to balance her 180 pounds with practiced ease. Mary Bonar, at whose house we spent the night, placed a half a papaya before her and Annis dug out a bite of the delicious fruit.

"My designation here is Area School Inspector," Annis continued, "but I have also inherited responsibility for construction. You can't know how we have prayed and looked forward to this moment, because from this moment on, you are in charge of construction." Another generous bite of the cantaloupe-looking fruit disappeared into her mouth without interrupting her monologue. "Of course, that also includes keeping the vehicles running, and the electric system." She made a face indicating the electric plant would present frustrating challenges. "The water system is easier," she added as though even the mention of the electric system might discourage a newcomer and the knowledge another system functioned better would mollify things.

I wanted to protest that these added responsibilities would not be possible. My major responsibility was to design and build an entire station at Boko, deep in the interior. The stop at Banza Manteke was to allow us to learn as much of the native language as possible and to give some help to the building program there, but primarily to have time to make all the plans and preparation for building at Boko.

"Of course, we have made a beginning on the buildings here, and I would like to show you around, but I can't. Martin Engwall will have to do that. I have an inspection trip I have been putting off until you got here." By now all that remained of the papaya was an empty shell. A few more words of sincere greetings to both Dolores and me, a "thank you" to Mary, and she swept through the door.

"Wow!" I said to Mary, watching the roly-poly figure half-run across the *lupangu* (yard).

"Wow, indeed," Mary said. "You may have to see it to believe it, but she can crawl under a truck and do repairs most men would not undertake. In addition to the school here, she inspects all the schools in our *secteur*–that's a unit of the government here and it covers an area the size of Connecticut. She evaluates the progress of the students, helps the teachers learn and apply better skills, and, when necessary, oversees the building or rebuilding of the schools themselves. The other jobs she does simply because somebody has to do them and up until now there hasn't been anybody else."

"She must have to work twelve hours a day to get all that done," Dolores said.

"We all do," Mary smiled. There was no complaint in her voice. "There is just so much to be done, and so little time, and so few of us to do it." She signaled for the houseboy to clear the dishes from the table. "That's one of the reasons you will see so many Congolese working for the missionaries: cooks, houseboys, washjacks for the laundry, gardeners. If we tried to do those things ourselves we couldn't make a dent in the work we were sent here to accomplish. But that is only a part of the reason for hiring help around the house. There is so much poverty that any job we can provide is a blessing. Our cook supports seventeen people on his salary."

Mary led us into the living room. "When the teachers have to build their schools and the doctors have to build their hospitals, and the preachers have to build their churches, and whoever is handy has to build the houses, then there just isn't much teaching or preaching or healing done for a long time."

Dolores and I walked over the station later that morning. The station covered about 150 acres and had five distinctive sections, all connected by dirt pathways under the towering palm trees. At the south end we saw the hospital maternity wards, with the missionary residences standing a distance from them and closer to the church, which was set in center of the campus. To the east lay the girls' school and dormitories, and to the west the same for the boys. To the north the homes of the native teachers and workers formed a village of their own. More than eight hundred students were in residence here, plus the eleven missionaries and several hundred Congolese teachers, nurses and workers.

But my attention was focused on the work Annis had done in the last year. I knew there had been an allocation of 1.5 million francs to finish the twelve buildings in the program by the end of the next summer. She had the boys gather pebbles and small stones to be used as gravel. They had brought in sand a load at a time. All this was mixed with cement to make thousands of concrete blocks. The foundation of the school house had been dug and poured, as had those of three dormitories. Concrete blocks had been laid to the level of the bottom of the windows. This work had taken over a year and consumed over a million francs.

I was awed by what she had accomplished, yet I was concerned that so much work and so little time or money remained.

The real shock came when I examined the tools. I discovered there were two power tools of a sort: a drill press, old beyond belief, but still operative, and a planer that was used to dress the hard African mahogany boards. In addition there were some hand tools: three planes, six saws and two hammers with homemade handles. I could hardly believe that all the beautiful furniture and doors I saw were made here. Each solid mahogany door weighed about a hundred pounds, was put together with mortise and tenon, finished with dowels rather than nails, and was so beautifully crafted each would have been worth a small fortune back in America.

Our tour was interrupted by a request that we attend a wedding.

The bride and groom were teachers at the school, both dressed in white, obviously in love, and equally obvious in their Christian faith. It was a beautiful ceremony for two beautiful people. The singing during the wedding reminded me of the worship service that morning. The

Reverend Engwall had introduced me as Tata Scott, the first time I heard that general title applied to myself, and I had to "say a few words" to the thousand Congolese people gathered there.

At the reception following the wedding, the Reverend Engwall sought out Dolores and me. "You have seen one of the most dramatic changes Christianity is bringing to Congo," he said. "This woman will be his only wife; in village life a man is likely to have several. Because of our hospital, their children will have a 95 percent chance for life and health; in the bush less than half the babies survive the first year. But beyond all this, they chose each other. Without Christianity the girl is literally sold by her family to a man whom she probably never sees before they are married, and she becomes his property, his slave, really."

Martin and Ruth Engwall provided dinner for us that evening at their home, beginning a relationship that was to be unique. During the meal the Engwalls began to reminisce.

"In the early days missionaries were not allowed to raise their children in Congo," Ruth said. "They were raised in the United States in boarding homes provided for missionary children, unless some family member would care for them."

"But we certainly changed that, didn't we, mother?" Martin added.

"Indeed we did. We had four daughters and we absolutely refused to have an ocean separating us," Ruth said. "We raised them here, the first time that had been permitted. It took a lot of gentle persuasion, but we finally prevailed."

"You will soon learn how firm her 'gentle persuasion' can be," Martin smiled.

"Now, young families like yours are the rule and not the exception," Ruth continued. "It's so good to have the families together."

"But we won't be together," Dolores said. "We have to send Sharan to school at Lubondai and that's over a thousand kilometers away."

"It's relative," Martin said. "The other side of Congo is not nearly as remote as having an ocean between you and your child. And she will be home for the holidays, and for the summer break."

"You'll really be able to spend quite a bit of time with her," Ruth said. "Of course, that darling little boy of yours in the other room will be with you for several years."

"The children grow up here, but they return to the States for college and to get on with their own lives," Martin added. "Then we old-timers whose children are gone must build a new family." He looked at each of us and then added with a note of solemnity, "So that is why, as

12

of this moment, you are our children. Ruth and I have just adopted you."

There were never any documents to make the adoption legal, but the love and support the Engwalls gave us could have been no greater if they truly had been our parents.

Later that night Martin prepared me for the next day, my first day of "work." He wrote out a list of Kikongo words I would have to know and use: hammer, saw, plane, mason, carpenter, lead man. Then he helped me pronounce them so they would be recognizable to my workers. He told me about Tata Inocki, the head carpenter, a man I would come to depend on as much as my right arm. He gave me the plans that had been drawn up for the buildings. Then the fatigue of his fourteen-hour day bore down on him, and he bade me goodnight.

I lay awake beside Dolores for a while, hearing strange new sounds from the jungle, smelling unfamiliar odors, trying to convince myself that I was truly here, that my work was actually beginning. Then I went soundly to sleep with a prayer in my heart that my Lord who had brought me to this place would walk with me through the next day and all the days ahead.

The electrical system proved to be both a satisfying and a frustrating responsibility. Frustrating because it preferred to develop its problems at night, when human temperament calls for sleep. But satisfying because, considering the conditions under which it was built and the length of time it had served, it was a marvel of engineering.

Water ran down the hand-dug canal, dropped through the two-story structure to turn the turbine blades and escaped back into the river. A heavy steel grill protected the blades from floating debris and this grill caught all sorts of rubble, piling it up until it became a small dam itself, blocking the flow of water. When that happened, the turbine quit turning and the lights went off. Then someone had to go down and clean out the debris from the grill.

The gear from the turbine shaft to the generator had teeth made of wood. From time to time teeth would break off the gear and then the generator didn't turn. When that happened someone had to make new gear-teeth and attach them to the wheel.

The old transformers took the 17,000-volt output, reduced it to 240 volts, then sent it along the three miles of transmission lines through the jungle and to the station. If a wild animal knocked a pole down or a falling timber broke the line, someone had to "walk the line" and repair it.

That someone turned out to be me, and I soon began including in my nightly prayers, "Please, Lord, not tonight."

But when everything was functioning, we enjoyed the luxury of electricity twenty-four hours a day at Banza Manteke.

Over the years the concrete dam aged, and shortly after our arrival it sprung a leak, shooting a stream of water fifteen feet in the air. Drawing on all my background, a good deal of imagination, and some sheets of heavy plastic Dolores had intended for her garden, I devised a rig that could be floated out to the leak and slapped into place, plugging the hole long enough to allow us to make permanent repairs. However, the force of the current meant we had only one shot at getting it placed properly. Any mishap with a worker getting his hand, arm or leg between the frame and the dam would mean that person would become a permanent part of the dam. In view of this danger, special pains were taken to instruct the workmen on exact procedures and precautions.

Six Congolese helped Phil Uhlinger and me carefully guide the frame to the hole, and just as thousands of tons of pressure slammed it against the dam we heard someone yelling, *"Ngandu! Ngandu!"* The natives were out of the water by the time we looked up. *Ngandu* means "crocodile." Someone on the bank had seen a large croc floating not far from us.

Plastic on the sides of the frame had to be unrolled to form a seal or our efforts would be wasted. We tried to persuade our workers to return and help us, but nothing would entice them back into the river.

"No Tata Lesgo," they finally informed us. "You and Tata Uhlinger do it. Crocodiles don't eat white people. They only eat black people."

Phil and I got our guns, and we finished the temporary repairs with one standing shotgun while the other dived in the river. We saw the croc a couple of times, but it never came near us. Later, we found a nest upstream from the dam and enjoyed a huge omelet from a single crocodile egg.

The title "Tata Lesgo" was acquired on my first work day. Not having a workable vocabulary, my only option was to call out the word for carpenters and take those who responded to where I wanted carpentry done. Then back to call out the masons, get them working, and back for woodcutters and rockbreakers. During the day I made the rounds, inspecting their progress, and urged them on in the only way I knew: "Let's go. Let's go." The workmen heard it so often that before the day was over I had become "Tata Lesgo."

14

Thanks to the hour a day I spent with my teacher studying Kikongo, I was soon able to stumble through the language. All our official communications had to be in French, and we still spoke English among ourselves. Most of our workmen spoke Kibula-Matadi and a few spoke Lingala, so I used occasional phrases from those languages. During that time my speech was not unlike a salad, with bits and pieces of Kikongo, French, English, and Lingala tossed together and served up with pride. The other missionaries determined that a new language had evolved, and they named it "Kiscotty."

But from our first day together there was a rapport between me and the Congolese workmen. We were each committed to completing the buildings. I knew I could not do it without them and they knew they could not do it without me.

Difficult as the language problems that confronted us were, the problem of building materials was even greater.

Large boulders were dug out of the ground, heated by fire, then doused with water to break them into small enough pieces to be used in the foundations. Our permanent buildings were constructed of the concrete blocks, but concrete requires ingredients. Sand had to be hauled quite a distance from the sand beds we located. We were fortunate that Banza Manteke had its own convenient water supply and that the two cement plants in Congo were both relatively near our station. We were also fortunate that this station had an abundance of small, round pebbles, called *ngutu*, that served splendidly as gravel, and we paid the school children to collect them for us.

Then, when all the material was assembled and mixed into concrete, it was poured into handmade molds, one block at a time. One by one and day by day the stack of blocks grew.

We got lumber by sending workmen into the jungle, where they felled the giant African mahogany trees. As there was no equipment to remove the timber, the trees had to be hand-sawed where they fell. The men carried the large planks up out of the jungle on their heads and were compensated by a formula that recognized both the size and quality of the wood. Without the old planer the lumber would have been unusable.

The school was to be the first permanent high school complex ever constructed in our area. Prior to that time most schools were made of poles, vines, grass and thatch. In all, twelve buildings were required for this complex, and they had to be completed in just less than a year after our arrival. It seemed an unattainable goal, but we were blessed at Banza Manteke with experienced, talented and Christian workmen.

We were just getting into a routine in our work when Mary Bonar cornered us. "Scotty, I want you and Dolores to go to Kimpese and visit a little boy there. His name is Youdi. He had a lung removed and has been there several weeks." I am sure she saw the disapproval on my face. "I'm worried about him," she continued. "He's such a bright little boy and I know he must be terribly frightened and lonesome. Just tell him that we love him, that we're praying for him, and that we want him to hurry up and get well so he can be back in school."

We could have begged off, and we seriously considered it, because we did not have any allowance for the fuel such a trip would require. Every time a vehicle was driven its mileage was recorded, along with the purpose of the trip and the account to which the *kilometrage* was to be charged. Dolores was well aware that we had no account that included Kimpese, since she was bookkeeper and accountant for the project. Neither did we feel that we could take a full day away from our work. Frustrating as it was to be asked to make like a pastor just as we were getting our project moving, new missionaries do not refuse an older missionary's strong request.

The hospital at Kimpese, started just three years earlier as the dream of two of our missionaries, Dr. Glen Tuttle and Dr. Price, was fast becoming the finest medical facility in the Congo. Using their own meager funds, soliciting their friends, and drawing on a generous grant from the government, they had built three hospital buildings and more than thirty buildings to house staff and students. Yet, we were hardly prepared for what even the best of Congolese hospitals had to offer.

When a patient was brought in to the hospital, the family came along as well. The family provided food for the patient, cooking it over open fires on the hospital grounds. Family members also supplied most of the services we expect of nurses: feeding, bathing, changing bandages, attending to personal needs. The family members slept on the floor, under the patient's cot or in the hallway. The hospital beds were reminiscent of the cots we had at camp when I was a boy. Most, but not all, had some sort of bedding.

We found Youdi in the children's ward, a large room crammed with twice as many patients as it was designed to accommodate. We visited with the charming youth, barely a teenager, assured him that he was loved and missed at Banza Manteke, and prayed with him before we left.

Another child in the ward captured our attention. Minuku was a five-year-old boy who, like thousands of others, was a victim of polio, a strand of the disease that draws the legs up against the buttocks so that the child can do nothing for the rest of his life but crawl on his hands and knees. When the doctors were able to get these children to the hospital they cut the tendons, allowing the legs to be straightened. Later they would be fitted with braces and crutches, but at this stage of treatment their legs were stretched up, forcing the child to rest only on his shoulders and upper back. Dr. Price had sought out and treated nearly a thousand children in this way.

Minuku won our hearts that day as much as Youdi did, and we followed their activities through high school in the Congo.

Youdi finished his school with honors, went to the University of Oregon as a math major and remained to get his doctorate. On his return to Zaire (the country had changed its name by then) he became economic adviser to the president, a post he continues to hold. He is president of the Protestant University and has been a central figure in getting the World Trade Center built and operating in Kinshasa, yet he continues to support the mission and the missionaries, proving time and again to be a valued friend and a great help in dealing with the bureaucracy.

In the later years of my time in Zaire we were to get a new doctor at Sona Bata, a Zairian. This fine-looking young man walked in with a cane and a very bad limp. He said, "Tata Scott, you don't remember me, do you?" I had to confess that I did not.

"We first met when I was a little boy in traction and you stopped to see me when you visited Youdi."

Doctor Minuku is now director of our hospital at Sona Bata, a marvelous Christian man with a beautiful wife and lovely family. What a loss it would have been for us if we had not taken a day off from "work" to make that trip.

Another responsibility was added to my growing list when I was informed that every Tuesday morning I was to take the construction truck to Luzadi to pick up the patients who were transportable, but could not walk, and bring them to the hospital for their treatment. Luzadi, the leper colony! All I knew of leprosy was what I had read in the Bible, how lepers were outcast, required to shout "Unclean" when a noncontaminated person approached them, so I assumed leprosy was highly contagious. I supposed that when I drove the truck up, all these nice little people would climb up on the truck bed and I could take off. It didn't work out that way.

Waiting for me was the most pitiful group of people one could imagine. The ravages of the disease had cost some of them their fingers, toes, ears or noses. Some had faces so devastated they looked more like animals than humans. Others had lost use of legs, and often arms, as well. It was obvious they could not climb up on the high flat bed of the truck; I would have to lift them.

"Well, I've had an interesting life up to this point," I told myself. "I might as well dedicate it all to Him right here and now." And I began lifting men and women up on the truck bed for the trip. Later I built a stepped platform that made the task much easier for them and for me as well.

Every Tuesday morning I would drive to Luzadi, pick up the lepers, take them to the hospital for their medication, and at noon bring them back to the leper colony.

That is how I came to meet Tata Andre Kidiela.

He was a small man even before leprosy took its toll, and now he looked frail and fragile as well as disfigured. But the disease had done nothing to his mind. He was a brilliant man with a deep Christian faith and an indomitable spirit.

Andre was the son of a great witch doctor and had learned from his father all that was wise and all that was phony about the craft. The witch doctor practices a lot of mumbo-jumbo and no small amount of sleight-of-hand, but the witch doctor also is usually a man with a sound understanding of psychology, human behavior, and the curative power of native herbs. He can capitalize on fear because he understands how fear can eat at a person's reason. He relies on superstition because he understands how deeply ingrained it is in the culture. In short, witch doctors are not stupid. Andre proved early on to be an apt student, absorbing all his father had to teach him.

Then a disaster struck which no magic and no herbs could avert: Andre contracted leprosy.

He came to Luzadi, where treatment was available for his spirit as well as his body. Andre became a Christian and put away the dark parts of witchcraft while retaining the insights he had learned.

Andre's disease had been arrested, but his body had been ravaged and his features bore irreversible signs of the illness.

In addition to studying witchcraft under his father, Andre had been a carpenter for the Belgians before he came to Luzadi, so we had a mutual interest from the beginning. He also spoke excellent Kikongo, and often after my workday was over I would go to the colony and sit and talk with Andre. In no time at all, we became fast friends.

With his skill, it seemed logical to give him a job in our shop, but the other men flatly refused to have him around. The stigma of the dreaded disease blocked any and all attempts to convince them otherwise. I took some basic tools and lumber to Andre and he did custom work for me as a subcontractor. He made doors, windows, furniture, anything I asked, and his work was both flawless and prompt.

Andre's story doesn't stop there by any means, but that was the beginning of what proved to be one of the most remarkable and important relationships I developed.

The building program at Banza Manteke continued to progress in a wonderful way. Every week saw more accomplished than anyone—me included—thought possible.

The importance of Dolores' role soon became apparent, though it would be difficult to imagine the complexity of her job in keeping records straight, ordering material and especially in preparing the payroll. As a colony of Belgium, the Congo had been administered with beneficent paternalism. Workmen were assured specific benefits for specific conditions, and that is where Dolores' problems arose.

Each worker received a certain increment if married, an increment for each child, an increment for how long he had been employed, an increment for how far he had to travel from his village to the job site, and so on seemingly *ad infinitum*. With a hundred workmen there were a hundred different pay scales, and each scale had to be matched with the actual days worked. Then, when all the calculations were completed, envelopes had to be filled with the exact amount of cash for each man. Payday became a focal point around which everything else was scheduled. Payday was a month-long source of dread and one day of chaos.

Dolores also ordered materials. We had to devise a schedule and anticipate how much cement, how much steel, how much lumber would be needed and when. Then, taking into account the unpredictable delivery system, we had to have the right amount of the right material at the right place at the right time. Our budget did not allow for stockpiling.

She had to maintain an accurate and separate account for every project, since each job was funded out of a separate budget. Any material used, any salary paid, any transportation expense incurred had to be carefully monitored and charged to the proper account.

Her tools for keeping all this straight consisted of reams of paper, countless pencils and an antiquated hand-operated adding machine. It is one of God's miracles that she was able to keep all the figures and papers in order, but from the beginning she sat hour after hour, often late into the night, doing things that I would have found impossible. Like so many other men, I have received recognition for the work I did, and like so many other women who have made their husbands' work possible, Dolores' contribution has not been, nor could it be, adequately recognized by others.

But Dolores also had other responsibilities. In those early years she was Johnny's teacher as well as his mother. She maintained the home and made it both attractive and warm, a center of peace and refuge for us all. Every home we shared in the Congo soon reflected her taste in landscaping, with flowers and plants in abundance. She enjoyed getting her hands in the soil whenever possible, much to the chagrin of older Congolese trained in the Colonial mold. Dolores would be working with her flowers when such an old-timer would chance by and see her on her hands and knees, her hands covered with dirt. Soon she could expect to hear a minor commotion coming from the house,

"You no-good scamp," the old voice would carry out to the garden, berating a household worker. "Why are you in here and letting Mama Scott do your work? You should be ashamed of yourself."

Then Dolores would assure the elder that she was doing what she wanted to do, that it was recreation for her. That would settle the matter until the next time she dug or planted or pruned. Then there would be a replay of the same scene. Somehow the Congolese never seemed to realize that we crazy white people could find physical work relaxing.

Probably I didn't make the work any easier for her when my perverse humor took hold of me, as it did when I introduced her to the first cannibal she ever saw.

Ed Ferguson was teaching me how to use dynamite to blast rocks. The man who was actually setting the charges had every tooth in his head filed to a sharp point. I asked Ed about it.

"Oh, he's filed his teeth," he answered, as though that were all the explanation needed.

"But why?" I asked.

He smiled the smile one gives a newcomer who has asked a question so elementary it never occurs to the old-timers. "Because he's a cannibal, of course." He thought for a minute, deciding whether or not I was ready for more detail, then obviously decided I was. "He's always asking what we do with the arms and legs after they are amputated at the hospital."

I could hardly wait to get Dolores to meet him, so I sent a messenger asking her to come immediately. I introduced her to the man as though there was nothing unusual about him and he smiled broadly as he shook hands with her, holding her white hands in both of his black ones.

Later, she said, "Scotty, I didn't like the way that man was looking at my arm."

Growing up in the Congo was a different experience for each of our two children.

The most heart-rending thing we had to do early on was to send Sharry away to school. She was enrolled at Lubondai, a school developed cooperatively by several Protestant denominations. The students came home for Christmas vacation and during the break between academic years (which we continued to call the "summer break" even though south of the equator it occurred technically in the winter).

Lubondai is over a thousand kilometers away from our stations, too far for radio communication on our transceivers. Mail in Congo has always been delivered in a perfunctory manner, so even if the children were diligent in writing, which missionary kids are no more prone to be than any other children, it was lonesome for both students and parents.

That problem was alleviated somewhat when I became a member of the school board and was able to take Dolores to Lubondai once or twice a year for the meetings. My service on the board continued until the school was forced to close during the chaotic days surrounding Independence. After we were evacuated in 1960, Sharry remained in the States to complete her education, living with her aunt and uncle in Kansas.

Johnny, on the other hand, was too young for school when we arrived in the Congo. He received his first schooling at home on the station, and by the time he outgrew that, he attended the French elementary school at Leopoldville, much closer to our home.

Sharry's friends were primarily the children of other missionaries, whom she met at school. Johnny's playmates included the children of other missionaries, but far more of them were the children of native teachers, nurses and workers. Sharry communicated in English with a little French, while Johnny began speaking Kikongo before either of his parents. Sharry was able to spend vacation times with us for a few years. Johnny followed his father around day after day, became a friend and pest to all the workers, and began to pick up bits and pieces of experience denied to most other children.

At the age his cousins were riding tricycles, Johnny was learning to drive a tractor. While other boys his age learned to ride a bicycle, he was learning to drive a truck, albeit unknown to his father at the time.

21

When other boys began driving a car, Johnny was flying the airplane.

It is as though our children grew up in two different families. Both loved the Congo, though the ways they experienced life in that country were vastly different. We loved, and continue to love, our children equally, though circumstances dictated different relationships with each of them.

CHAPTER 3

Banza Manteke—1954-1955

By April we were under a great deal of pressure to begin building at Boko, even though we had not completed the work at Banza Manteke. We resisted leaving the project unfinished, but we did make a trip to Boko with Dr. Howard Freas.

Howard and Kay Freas had served in Congo for twenty years at that time. He was beloved by the Congolese and an inspiration to the other missionaries. Two years earlier a cult had developed that practiced a bizarre combination of native superstitions and fragments of Christianity. It was a "blood cult" that utilized the Bible in inappropriate ways as it played on the fear of death and the power of magic. Anyone who publicly disagreed with this cult automatically incurred its sentence of death.

At the height of one of the cultists' meetings, Dr. Freas strode into their midst, snatched up the Bible they were using and proceeded to set them straight on what the Bible means and how it should and should not be used. The cult leader pronounced the sentence of death on him.

A few weeks later, Dr. Freas came down with a severe form of polio that left him near death and with the prospect of losing use of his legs for the rest of his life. It was necessary for him to return to the States for treatment. This reinforced the position of the cult, as it appeared to the Africans that the curse had caused the illness.

Within a year, however, Dr. Freas was back on the field, albeit on crutches, and able to carry on his ministry. He would stand for hours at the operating table, leaning on his crutches as he performed surgery. His return destroyed the influence of the cult in that area.

23

Dr. Freas loaded his crutches, along with medicine to resupply dispensaries along the way, onto his one-ton pickup and we began the long trip to Boko. The scenery was as spectacular as the roads were deplorable, yet we were awed by the scenes around us. We drove across flat land with giant bamboo arching over us, despising the two ruts that constituted the road through the sand, then suddenly descended into a valley eroded by a river and were surrounded by jungle. There were many valleys such as this, many of them as much as twenty miles across.

As night fell we arrived at one of the mission outposts, a lovely native village of grass huts surrounding the one-room school and the grass-and-thatch dispensary. Forty patients had been waiting all day for the doctor to arrive. It was 2:00 a.m. by the time he had taken care of all of them and had inventoried and restocked the dispensary for the native medic. Our sleep was uninterrupted except for the huge tarantula that came tromping across the dirt floor and then across our bed.

Another day's drive brought us to Popokabaka and a ferry (always called a *bac* in Congo.) We would come both to appreciate and dread any *bac*. The Kwango River is broad and swift; the makeshift ferry appeared inadequate for what was required of it. Three tiny boats were lashed together, covered by a platform that seemed woefully inadequate to support the weight of the truck and its passengers. But Dr. Freas assured us he had made the crossing many times and was up to venturing it once more. We reluctantly boarded and vibrated our way across as the small gasoline engine moved us into and then across the current.

The remaining ninety kilometers to Boko provided us with yet another scene. Vast grasslands stretched endlessly over rolling hills. At times, elephant grass taller than a man's head lined both sides of the road as though we were driving through a walled canyon. Villages were of the most primitive sort. But mostly we were interested in the people of the Bayaka tribe who inhabited this area.

The Bayakas are small in stature. Most were undernourished, as their skimpy clothes, or lack of them, made evident. A few men had trousers, but for the most part both men and women wore only a piece of cloth, tied around the waist, that reached somewhere around their knees. The children wore nothing.

As we arrived in the village of Boko, Dr. Freas was greeted by about four dozen boys waiting to be circumcised. When a Bayaka boy reaches the age of twelve he becomes a man, and this rite of passage is formalized by circumcision. Without the presence of a missionary doctor the operation is a gruesome and bloody ritual performed by the witch doctor without thought of antiseptic or sterilization.

Dr. Freas began operating in the one-room dispensary soon after our arrival and continued until the light was gone from the day and only a gasoline lantern illuminated his work area. We were certain that so many operations performed on so many boys of that age, one after another, would certainly result in something just short of disaster. As he worked, Helen Robins sterilized his instruments in her pressure cooker. Bill and Helen Robbins were evangelistic missionaries and had lived at the station since they started the work there.

It wasn't much of a station, we discovered as we toured the next day, but the lack of facilities did not mean a lack of ministry. Already a school was in operation, a chapel and, of course, the dispensary. As Dr. Freas inventoried and restocked the dispensary, Dolores and I took stock of what little material was on hand and began laying out in our minds the location of various buildings.

The setting was the realization of a dream. The center of the station was situated on the grassy plateau, but the station extended through another of the jungle valleys, in this case a deep ravine whose steep cliffs dropped hundreds of feet, verdant with exotic trees and vines and ferns of countless variety. Out of the wall of this ravine a spring endlessly fed sweet, fresh water into a pool that then cascaded over the rocks as a lovely waterfall and formed a second pond. I decided this would be enlarged as a swimming pool for the children.

The abundance of rocks in the ravine, trees in the jungle and sand on the plateau boded well for a supply of raw material, but the thought of transporting truckloads of cement over the near-impassable roads and the shaky ferry dimmed our enthusiasm somewhat. We felt it would require a miracle, or several miracles, for us to translate the designs I had put on paper into actual structures that would become homes, a school, a modern hospital, and a large church.

But a small portent of miracles came to us the next morning just before we were to leave. A truckload of singers came to serenade us, and we discovered, much to our gratification, they were the young boys who had been Dr. Freas' patients just thirty-six hours before.

Back at Banza Manteke, word awaited us that we were to be hosts for a delegation of officials from our headquarters. We all wanted to do something special, so our station council meetings began to run longer than usual as each of us tried to come up with ideas.

Ruth Engwall, as I remember, said, "We've got to have something that involves the Africans. We want the officials to have a memorable day at Banza Manteke. We need something that will highlight the Congolese, and particularly the students."

I remembered frequent Field Days from my school experience.

"How about a Field Day?" I suggested.

"What's a Field Day?"

I explained that they were modified track meets for any student in the school who wanted to participate. "Our students like to run. There could be races." My own enthusiasm grew as I let possible events play out in my mind. "The students love to play soccer. They could easily do high-jumping and broad-jumping. Perhaps I could even teach some of them to pole-vault."

"That's a terrific idea, Scotty," was the response. "You get it organized." I had not said much in the discussions at previous station council meetings, and getting this assignment made me realize how wise I had been not to do so. Nonetheless, I got the plan under way.

We had trial runs for all the students and selected those with some aptitude and interest in developing their running for the various distances: 100 meters, 500 meters, 1,000 meters. The soccer teams came together naturally. I began teaching broad-jumping and high-jumping to a few of the boys. Finally, I was ready to introduce them to pole-vaulting, something totally foreign to their experience.

The workmen dug out a landing pit and filled it with sand. A splendid growth of bamboo stood in the forest near the station, and I cut three poles that seemed identical to what we had used in high school.

Safety was my first consideration. I held each pole with one end resting on the ground and threw my weight against it. Then I explained, "Always do this to be sure the pole will not break." The last thing I wanted was for one of our students to be injured.

Several of the boys who displayed an aptitude for high-jumping and seemed to have general athletic ability went into training as pole vaulters. I was particularly proud of including pole-vaulting, because the boys were learning so well and also because it gave me a chance to show off my own limited skill. On Saturday, the big day, everything came off perfectly, building to the pole-vaulting as the climax of the event. After the boys had reached the limit of their ability, I decided to give an exhibition to show to what heights they could ultimately aspire. The bar was raised after each of my vaults until it was ten feet above the ground. I made a mighty run, set the pole perfectly, soared gracefully upward, gave my body the twisting snap to throw it over the bar...but it was the pole that snapped.

Virginia Nickerson, our nurse, took me to our hospital at Kimpese, where Dr. Price, a bone specialist, examined the injury. "It looks bad,

Scotty," the doctor said as he looked at the X-ray. "I don't think there's much I can do with it. Your wrist is shattered. I count fifteen breaks. But I'll do what I can." Those were the last words I remember as I went under the anesthetic.

When I regained consciousness there was a cast from my fingers to my shoulder, there was pain in my arm, nausea in my stomach, and embarrassment in my memory. Nonetheless, I was back on the job Monday morning, giving directions and one-handed assistance.

Dr. Price proved to have outdone himself. The arm healed much more quickly and with more mobility than he had expected. But, so far as I know, pole-vaulting still has not become a part of the curriculum at Banza Manteke.

The last weeks at Banza Manteke also gave me the chance to go hunting for the first time in Africa. Since bagging that first rabbit as a boy on grandfather's farm I have enjoyed hunting. But missionaries do not hunt just for pleasure. The purpose of hunting is to provide meat for the African's protein-deficient diet. If the hunter manages to enjoy the activity, that's an extra benefit.

Like most activities in the life of the Congolese, hunting had its own ritual.

After work on the evening before the hunt I cleaned my rifle and cleaned and greased the cartridges. Then Tata Inaki came, and we drove to the village of Bete, where the hunt was to be organized.

The sun was just below the horizon, casting the grass huts in a warm pink glow from the western sky. A fire glowed in the center of the village, with all the men of the village seated around it. I greeted each of them individually, showing the proper deference to the oldest first and then to the position each man held in the village. When I was seated on the ground with the others, the chief began as though no man present had ever been on a hunt.

"The dry season is with us and the grass is brown," he began. "It is time to burn the grass and bring meat to our village. As the fire burns across the valley it will drive the buffalo and the antelope from the elephant grass, and our hunters will be waiting." He detailed how the fires were to be set, at what time, and how each man was to approach the valley to be burned. The men with dogs were instructed how to work their way toward the valley; those who were to set the fires were given careful instructions; and those who had guns were assigned specific positions from which they would shoot.

I looked at the guns laid out in a neat row before the fire. They were old muzzleloaders that would have provided a good start for a small museum, but not a decent rifle was among them.

"Let me tell you of the buffalo," the chief continued, and he recounted a former hunt with his own exploits lavishly highlighted. When he finished his tale, first one and then another stood and told of his most exciting hunt. The fire burned low and was given more wood. More stories followed, until even the seasoned veterans of the fireside ritual began to nod off. My bones were stiff when I finally rose to make my way to the hut where I spent an all-too-short night, sleeping on a grass mat laid out on the dirt floor.

Long before dawn, Tata Inaki was outside the hut calling me to the day's activities. We loaded the truck and drove out the Lazarete Road. We passed through the leper colony, and on further, until the road shrank to little more than a footpath. Then we came to a valley that only a helicopter could cross. The truck was abandoned in favor of foot travel.

The sun was just coming up and illuminated a trail that wound over a rolling hill, then dipped into a jungle valley not unlike those pictured in the Tarzan movies. Beside the trail a mass of banana and papaya trees, pineapple, wildflowers and ferns wove themselves together into a beautiful tapestry that only God could have designed. From this foundation, vines rose toward the tops of the towering trees into the lacy canopy far overhead.

Out of the forest, the trail climbed the side of a mountain, then dropped again along the long slope that stretched as far as one could see, and even further. On and on we hiked, until my feet ached and I began to wonder if the one directing us had lost his way. But just short of midday we slipped over the rim of a hill and came to the most beautiful valley I had ever seen.

All the hunters assembled and I again observed protocol by shaking hands with each of them, remembering the same order of preference I had followed the night before. And what a group of hunters they were. There was not a complete pair of pants or a shirt among them. The only shoes were those they had made from old automobile tires. Around each waist was a wide antelope skin belt that held a huge trail knife, a hollowed-out gourd filled with powder and a leather pouch for projectiles.

Each hunter loaded his gun: a careful measure of powder from the gourd, packed down with a bit of hemp unraveled from a rope, and for a projectile anything from a ball bearing to a bit of reinforcing steel cut to size, or even small nuts and bolts. The process took several minutes, and it was obvious that each man would have only one shot, and the effectiveness of that shot was highly suspect.

Because my gun was far superior to anything owned by the Congolese and also because I was a *mundele,* I was assigned the place in the line of hunters where the buffalo was most likely to emerge.

A runner joined us and excitedly pointed out where a great number of buffalo tracks entered the valley. Smoke began rising in the distance, rapidly growing into a towering cloud. As the wall of flame swept its way down the valley, new fires were started along the edge of the valley to direct the animals toward the hunters.

Waiting as the flames ate their way up the valley gave me time to recall the stories from the campfire the night before, as well as others I had heard about the African buffalo and the dangers he posed. He is a mighty beast, charges with full power and is seldom dissuaded by a fragile human standing in his way. When wounded he is twice as deadly.

By this time a wall of smoke moved before the fire and our eyes began to sting. Birds by the tens of thousands, of all sizes and descriptions, flew before the fire, feasting on insects fleeing the inferno. Soot and ashes began dropping on my clothing.

From down the line I heard the report of two guns and turned to see the antelope they had fired at escape uninjured. As I looked toward Inaki, some hundred yards away, a large antelope bounded out of the grass. The antelope took a great leap, and my shot caught him in midair, so that he nose-dived to the ground. Inaki ran to cut his throat just as a huge bull buffalo, followed by three cows, came crashing through the grass directly toward him. Inaki got off a quick but aimless shot somewhere in the direction of the charging animal. The buffalo was two hundred yards away, but my shot got him just behind the front leg and I saw him go down in the deep grass.

As the others ran to where he fell they found only crumpled grass with a smattering of blood. I had created one of the things most dreaded by the hunters: a wounded buffalo. Four natives took off in a dogtrot, following the tracks of the animal. The midafternoon sun cast stark shadows along the trail, showing he was bleeding from both sides. The bullet had passed completely through him, but had missed his heart. After an hour and a half the tracks led into a great growth of elephant grass some fifteen feet high. The men circled the growth, clearly seeing the tracks enter but failing to find evidence of any tracks leading out. The wounded buffalo was lurking in the protection of the grass.

Experience, hard won by the Africans over the years, dictated that no man should risk his life by going into the deep growth looking for the animal. By this time it was dusk and the hunt had to conclude. So ended my first hunt in Congo with both success and failure. The men divided the antelope, but the thought of the wounded buffalo and the havoc he could wreak invaded my dreams that night and for many nights to come.

That buffalo lived for many years and was recognizable by a huge blotch on his side. He was always referred to as *Mpakasa ya Tata Scott* (Tata Scott's buffalo).

CHAPTER 4

Boko—1954-1956

Our time at Banza Manteke was drawing to a close. In twelve months we completed the twelve buildings, as well as doing extra work at Kimpese, Sona Bata and several other stations. The plans for Boko had been drawn up, and we had made two trips there to get the lay of the land and look over the situation generally.

Banza Manteke was far advanced compared to Boko. The Bayaka are what we call a "bypassed tribe." Until recently they had refused help from outside, preferring to retain their tribal way of life. The men dressed in whatever they could find, with few having trousers and many in loin cloths. The women wore nothing above the waist. Their houses were poles, vines, and thatch, with the bare *lupangu* surrounding each hut. Little had changed here in thousands of years, except that now the natives were ready to move forward and welcomed us and our schools and our medicine.

At Banza Manteke I had inherited a crew of trained workmen, many of them graduates of our school and almost all of them Christians. Boko presented a labor pool trained only in native lore, totally unfamiliar with the tools or building concepts we would be using, and accustomed to having women do physical work. At Banza Manteke I had to learn the words for carpenter and mason and hammer and nail; at Boko I would have to teach the concepts behind those words. It was obvious I needed help.

Dolores and I prayed for a helper. We would be set apart from the Africans, not only because we were white, but also because we had powerful vehicles, good clothes, a comfortable house (eventually), and plenty to eat. We needed someone to whom the workmen could relate more closely, someone who could teach them the skills and also inspire confidence in themselves to learn because he could be seen as one of them. The more we prayed, the more clearly we could envision the man needed for the task. He would be tall for an African, strong, with a commanding presence and a brilliant mind. I came to picture his face with a broad smile rewarding a task well done, but turning stern when performance did not measure up to expectations. A man with the bearing and countenance of a chief and accepted as such by the Bayakas. He could be the bridge between me and my Western ways on the one hand and the Africans on the other.

On the night before we were to leave Banza Manteke, Dolores and I had our usual prayer before retiring. That night our prayers reminded the Lord that the truck was loaded and we were ready to depart at four o'clock the next morning, but our helper was still missing.

As I was preparing to crawl into bed a muffled "Ko. Ko. Ko." sounded at the front door. Since it is impossible to knock on the door of a grass hut, Congolese always announce their presence verbally. It was Andre Kidiela.

"*Mbote*, Tata Scott." He stood in the flickering lamplight as though his presence explained itself.

"*Mbote*, Tata Kidiela, it was good of you to come to say goodbye, and I am so happy to see you, but we must leave early in the morning and I need my rest."

"Oh, I know." His face conveyed his understanding of my need for rest. "God told me you needed help at Boko and He told me to go with you as your helper." He nodded to the bundle he was carrying. "I have everything I own in this world here with me." The few tools I had given him sounded a muffled "clank" as they were wrapped in the even fewer clothes he owned.

I looked at his frail body, his disfigurement. "Yes, I do need help, but..." I stumbled for the right words, something that would convey my appreciation of him as a person but clearly indicate that he was not a part of our plans. The best I could come up with was, "...but we have made no provision for you on this trip."

"Oh, that's all right, Tata Scott. The Lord makes all the provisions I need." It was as simple as that to him. "I will sleep beside the truck, and I will leave with you and Mama Scott in the morning."

"You don't understand, Tata Kid..." my voice trailed off. He was no longer there; he had settled the matter and disappeared into the night. I stood staring into the darkness for a long moment, not sure what to do, then decided the best thing to do was go to bed.

32

If I was uncertain about Kidiela's presence in Boko, that uncertainty was not shared by the Bayaka men who greeted us three days later as we pulled into the village late in the afternoon, tired, dirty and hungry. Bill Robbins had let it be known that we were coming, and an enormous crowd was gathered. Chiefs from all the neighboring villages were there, along with their entourages and most of their village. The talking drums marked our progress along the way and announced our arrival. *Luku* was prepared and a chicken had been boiled in palm oil and *pele-pele*. Dolores and I were greeted with the ritual handshakes, singing and broad smiles.

Not so with Kidiela!

The chiefs clustered in a tight knot, obviously discussing a very weighty issue, then the head chief drew Bill and me aside.

"What is that?" He motioned to Kidiela, and by emphasizing the *that* showed his refusal to recognize him as a human being.

"Tata Kidiela is my helper, my assistant. He will teach the men how to build."

"You don't understand." The chief addressed me as he might have instructed a neophyte hunter who had let an antelope escape. "We are happy to have Tata and Mama Scott here to build our school and our hospital. But that," he made a contemptuous motion toward Kidiela, "cannot stay."

"Why not?" I was dumbfounded.

"He is one of the Bakongo, and the Bayaka and Bakongo have been enemies since the first tree grew in the jungle. No Bakongo man has ever spent the night in a Bayaka village and been alive the next morning. He must leave now unless you want him dead."

Disbelief showed on my face, but the chief was as matter-of- fact as though he were telling me it would storm heavily during the night and there was nothing anyone could do to prevent it.

"Mama Scott and I are here because God called us to design and build buildings for you. The same God who called me also called Tata Kidiela to help me," I said as calmly as possible. "Tata Kidiela is my friend and if he cannot stay in your village, neither can I. If you don't want us here, we will leave. There are plenty of other tribes who want schools and hospitals and houses. We will leave tonight."

Confusion danced across his face. "We will shell peanuts," he said. This expression means a conversation is to be held, with much discussion and usually much disagreement, but one in which the extraneous is peeled away and the heart of the matter is uncovered. He motioned for the other elders to join him, and they sat long around their council fire. Raised voices pierced the twilight as first one man and then another stood to make his point, gesturing wildly.

Bill Robbins looked at me with the expression a father gives his son when the son has told the truth but told it at an awkward time. "You don't know what you're asking of these people," he said. "Not only are you asking them to go against everything they have known about their own tribe and its hatred of Bakongo, but Kidiela also has the marks of a leper and that is equally bad in their eyes."

All I could do was acknowledge their difficulty but reaffirm my position. As we waited for the men to finish their palaver, Bill told me how the animosity between the tribes had developed.

"Centuries before the missionaries came to the Congo, the Bayaka people lived in the area around Stanley Pool, where Leopoldville is now located," he began. "The Bakongo people, a much larger tribe, were around Matadi, about four hundred miles away. Every tribe in Africa raided other tribes, stealing women and children and killing the men. I suspect this was done to enhance the genetic pool of the tribes, though of course that is only speculation on my part and certainly something they would not have been aware of at the time.

"In any case, the Bakongo raided the Bayaka time after time, driving them further and further inland until finally the Bayaka settled here, where nobody else would live. I am sure you have already learned that pride in the tribe is the most central fact of life in Congo, so for the Bayaka to face such defeat could not be taken lightly. Their hatred for the Bakongo has not lessened over the centuries. In fact, it has become even more deeply ingrained as the elders have retold the old stories and traditions, no doubt enhancing already-gory details and making their enemies constantly more despicable with each retelling."

At that moment I was struck by the similarity between our situation and the native culture Bill was recalling. Oral tradition alone preserved history for these people, and now Bill was passing on to me a part of that history through the same method. His white hair and wrinkled features gave him the stature of a *Mbuta*, a true elder, and I willingly drew on his years of experience and his wisdom.

Bill continued as we waited for the chiefs to finish shelling their peanuts. He told how the missionaries' first contact was with the Bakongo, and so the mission work began with them. Then, as the missionary movement grew and expanded, contact was made with the Bayaka peoples, but the Bayaka wanted nothing to do with anyone who had worked and lived with the Bakongo. Only recently had the Bayaka people realized that they needed what the missionaries had to offer and so invited our return.

"We have reached a decision," the chief announced as he rejoined us. "You can stay tonight. You can stay as long as you like. We hope you will stay to build our school and hospital. We will accept you as our friend. That," again the nod toward Kidiela, "can stay tonight and will not be harmed. But he must leave tomorrow. That is the decision of the men. That is final. We will allow him to live only one night."

"Shell peanuts again tomorrow," I told him. "Have your men decide whether they want a school and a hospital and Tata Kidiela at Boko, all one package; or whether they want Tata Kidiela to leave and all hope for the school and hospital to leave with him."

It had not been a good start for the difficult job that lay ahead of us, and as Dolores and I settled into the grass hut for our first night at Boko, I questioned whether I would sacrifice building the Boko station because of one man. But the answer was never in doubt. The hatred expressed by the Bayaka was antithetical to everything we hoped to accomplish.

I still don't know what discussions took place among the elders of the villages the next day, but they seemed to put Kidiela on a day-to-day basis, assuring me that he could remain one more night but would have to leave the next day. I held to my ultimatum: if Kidiela was harmed, the entire project was terminated on the spot. It was a stand-off that continued day after day and week after week, even as the work progressed.

The talking drums had brought hundreds of men to Boko, looking for work, so I was able to assemble a crew and begin the project, though their rejecting of Kidiela made it infinitely more difficult for me.

Kidiela was given a hovel at the edge of the village and treated less well than a stray dog. On the job site he was ignored, treated as though he were invisible. He would come out by the fire each night where the men gathered, but none of them would talk to him. The only recognition of his presence was when the men spat on him. They tried every form of harassment they could devise, short of running a spear through him, but nothing deterred him from his cheerfulness or his continued efforts to bridge the gap. I learned later that a decree had gone out for his death, but no one was willing to carry it out. As a last resort, the Bayaka turned to their witch doctors.

Months had passed when this final solution was applied. The witch doctors had come during the night and dug a series of small holes around Kidiela's hut. They filled these holes with chicken feathers, fingernail clippings, and other magic elements prescribed by their ritual. Over these holes they poured chicken blood, then poured more chicken blood in a circle that encompassed the hut so that Kidiela could not leave the hut without crossing the dried blood. There was not a doubt in the mind of any Bayaka: as soon as Kidiela's foot crossed the darkened stain he would die instantly. The men of the village gathered outside his hut that morning, waiting for him to meet certain death.

Kidiela came to the opening of his hut and knew immediately what had been done. He recognized the holes, the trail of blood and their meaning. He looked at the men gathered and knew their expectations. He said his usual, cheerful "Good morning," and casually walked across the line.

The men waited. Total disbelief! A single gasp and then shocked silence. Perhaps it would take another minute for him to die. But Kidiela continued well, healthy and cheerful.

"Tata Kidiela, how did you do that?" one man asked. It was the first time in all these months he had been addressed directly, and now it was with the respectful "Tata Kidiela."

"There is not a man in all the Bayaka tribe who would have dared to cross that line," another said, awe evident in his voice. "Tell us how you did it?"

Kidiela could have told them that he had spent most of his years knowing nothing except suffering and the prospect of death awaiting him daily. He could have told them that leprosy's reality was more fearsome than witchcraft's superstition.

"The thing that makes it possible is the Great God who called us to come to you," he began. "He is the only one who can take away fear. I have no fear because I have a promise." He continued on with what became a powerful sermon about fear and faith and love.

From that day forward the men began coming to Kidiela for help.

"Tata Kidiela, how does one make the joints fit better?"

"Tata Kidiela, would you teach me to use this tool?"

"Tata Kidiela, am I doing this right?"

And soon they were turning to him for help and counsel for more than the work. They brought personal concerns to him and sought his advice. They brought their own fears and asked him to share his faith. He became the leader and teacher and helper we had prayed for—and much more than that. By the time we left Boko after three years of building, Kidiela was the most admired man in all the Bayaka territory, loved and respected by each of the hundreds of men who worked for us. And before the project was completed, every one of the original workmen had become a Christian and accepted baptism, learning that fear can be replaced by faith and hatred driven away by love.

But I'm getting ahead of my story.

Less than a week after we arrived at Boko, a messenger came running to our hut long after dark. "Tata Scott, Mama Scott," he exclaimed between gasps. "Mama Jorgensen needs you at the hospital."

We jumped in the truck and drove through the darkness to the hospital, another grass building with a mud floor and a tiny operating room no more than ten feet square.

"I've got a problem," Alice Jorgensen greeted us. Fatigue from a long day's work added to the wrinkles in her face. As the only medical person in the area, Alice had to go far beyond her training as a nurse, performing the duties of a doctor when time, emergency and distance required—which was more the norm than the exception. "I have a complex operation to do on this woman and I need a light. Usually after dark I use the lantern, but this woman will have to have ether, and ether will explode if there is an open flame or even a spark. Can you rig up something for me, Scotty?"

"Of course," I said before I had any idea of how I could get an electric light to work when there was no electricity on this station. But I went out to the truck, removed a headlight, jerry-rigged the necessary wiring from the truck battery, and soon returned to the operating room holding the glowing lamp in my hands.

"Oh, marvelous," Alice said. "Now you stand right here." She positioned me where the light was most advantageous, then turned to Dolores and announced, "You can give the ether."

Dolores paled noticeably, but followed the nurse's instructions and became an anesthetist faster than any American doctor would ever imagine, or permit.

"This is a difficult case," Alice said as she began working on the woman. "She just delivered a baby and the baby is fine. But something must have happened in a former pregnancy because in delivery the tissue ripped from the vagina to the rectum. We have to practically rebuild the whole area."

Since I had to focus the light on the area where she worked, there was no way for me to avoid a close scrutiny of the procedure. I had seen a few operations before, but nothing of this magnitude and certainly none that I was forced to follow so closely.

"Raise the light just a bit," she said. "There, that's better. She got here just in time; another hour and she would have delivered the baby on the road. Just a bit more ether, now." Even as she talked, her arthritic fingers flew from instrument to tissue to swab to sutures. Our presence seemed to ease the strain for her.

"We started a policy some time ago of charging the women who come to the hospital after the baby is delivered. There is no charge if they come to the hospital in time for us to give them a little prior attention, but we charge them a *pata* to encourage them to come early."

"That's only about a nickel!" Dolores said.

"Yes, but you'd think it a fortune, the way they react when they have to pay it. And perhaps it is a fortune for some," she added. "Of course, the *pata* doesn't mean that much to our budget but it does motivate more of the women to come to the hospital early. You should see some of the babies brought in after they have been delivered on the road, covered with dirt and sand. Still, that is not much worse than delivery in the village."

Already I was wishing I had come up with some kind of a lamp stand other than myself. I resolved to concoct something for her before the next nighttime emergency.

And there were many more emergencies, as well as routine procedures, for which Alice requested our assistance. At least once a week during our time at Boko we worked with her in the operating room. Dolores became her unofficial anesthetist and I assisted her with delivery. Arthritis had become painful for her, so she would place the forceps and I would provide the extracting power. Then after the birth I would tend the baby while Alice attended the mother.

That was just one more unexpected duty that entered our routine but never found its way into our job description.

What was in my job description was to assemble and train a crew of workmen who could build a complete mission station with a modern hospital, a large church, a complete school system, permanent housing for the missionaries as well as the Congolese staff, and all the ancillary buildings to go with them.

When we awoke that first morning after our arrival at Boko, hundreds of men were assembled in the open field outside our hut, and before my final crew was chosen at least two thousand Africans came to us. And not all of them were grown men.

One youngster came up to me early on and rather than asking for a job, asked me, "Where do you want me to start?" I looked at him incredulously, then recalled something of my own impertinence when I was his age—about twelve, I guessed.

"What makes you think I want you to start anywhere?" I answered. "I'm looking for men and you're just a kid."

He grinned infectiously. "Yeah, but I'm a really good kid. My buddy and I," he nodded to the more reserved youth beside him, "walked for two days from our village so we could work for you. Now, where do you want me to start?"

"What's your name?" Already I liked his spunk and admired his cocksure attitude.

"Celestine," he answered.

"OK, Celestine," I returned his smile. "You see those men over there with hammers? You get a hammer and you can break rock with them." It was the most tedious and tiresome job we had, and I fully expected he would not finish the day. But when the work ended that afternoon, Celestine was still at it and greeted me with the same engaging smile. I liked him, though I had no idea he would remain a part of our work for my entire career in Africa. He became a good friend and trusted chauffeur.

Training the workmen proved every bit as difficult as I anticipated.

"This is a nail," I explained to the men who would become carpenters. "It holds wood together. You put the nail with this end against a board and this end toward you. Then you take a hammer," I held up the hammer. "This is the hammer. Now you hit the nail with the hammer like this and drive it into the wood." So it went, step by step, detail by detail, until they grasped the concept and ultimately mastered the necessary skills.

Then I made the rounds to the other workmen with the same level of instruction: to the masons; to the lumbermen who would fell the great mahogany trees, cut them into rough lumber and carry them on their heads up out of the jungle to the veldt; to the men who would dig out the rock and break it into gravel; to the men who mixed cement and poured it into individual molds for concrete blocks; to the men who worked with shovels and hoes to level the ground and dig foundations for the buildings.

But the most difficult concepts to get across were square, level, straight and plumb, which had no relationship whatsoever to anything in their experience. They could not see why a building had to be square because they had never built a square building in all their lives. When a large rock or a tree was in their way, they just built around it. When they drove poles in the ground to support the thatched roof, they wanted the pole to go "up" but never concerned themselves that it was plumb. If their building was on a slope they let the building follow the natural terrain.

Their difficulty in understanding such concepts ultimately forced me to modify my management style. I began with the idea of collegiality, encouraging the men to share their ideas, hoping to find a balance between what they knew that I didn't and what I knew that they didn't. Instead, I found it necessary to state what was to be done, how it was to be done, and to get on with the doing without their questioning why. I could only hope that eventually they would absorb the reasons behind my orders.

That style proved to be too extreme in regard to the wheelbarrows. With the tremendous amount of rock and sand to be moved, it seemed much more sensible to have wheelbarrows for those jobs. I turned to my brother back in the States, a buyer for a wholesale hardware company, as I had done for the hand tools and a host of other supplies. Through him I was able to purchase several wheelbarrows to lighten the men's labor, and I instructed the men to carry their loads in the wheelbarrows in the future. They looked at me with the "crazy white man" expression they often used, but made no protest. I realized my mistake when I returned to find the men struggling under the weight of the loaded wheelbarrows being carried on their heads. I returned to the use of baskets for carrying materials on their heads, and we used the wheelbarrows for mixing aggregate.

Just as I was beginning to feel confident that we could meet our time schedule and our budget, we were presented with a seemingly insurmountable obstacle. The Belgian administrator from Popokabaka came one morning and sought out Dolores.

After an exchange of pleasantries he asked, "Do you have a *permit d'exploitation*?"

"Scotty would know," she told him, and then sent for me to join them.

"What is a *permit d'exploitation*?" I asked when I had been filled in on the purpose of his visit.

"You must have a permit from the government before you can cut down a tree or dig out a rock," he explained. "Unless you have the proper permit, I cannot allow you to continue your work here." I knew him to be a man of absolute integrity and great authority, as was true of all the Belgian officials with whom I dealt.

"Very well," I said, "Issue us a permit."

"Ah, *mais non*. It isn't that easy." He explained the process for obtaining the permit, and it was interminable. My heart sank lower and lower as I listened to him, his immaculate uniform and bureaucratic restrictions contrasting sharply with the primitive realities of Boko. Still, I appreciated the way the Belgians were attempting to protect the environment.

We begged. We pleaded. All to no avail. Then we began exploring with him ways in which we could be given title to the land to build the school and hospital and everything else needed there. He was both sympathetic and helpful.

"There might be one way," he said. "You could get the land under the land improvement program."

"What does that involve?" I asked.

"You would have to plant trees of value on all the land from which you wish to take any material: a fruit tree, a food-producing tree, or a hardwood tree. These trees would have to be no less than ten meters apart in each direction and would have to cover the entire area under discussion."

"Let me be sure I understand what you're asking," I said. "Obviously, we would have to clear a path through the jungle in order to get in to plant the trees. Then we'd have to move over another ten meters and cut another path, and another and another. Is that what you're telling me?"

"That's the only way you could qualify under this program," he said.

I did some quick mental calculations, ruling out the grassland on the plateau and considering only the jungle growing in the river valleys. "Do you realize we would have to clear the equivalent of a strip a hundred miles long through the jungle?"

"Only if you wish to use the land improvement program," he answered. "Otherwise, you could apply for the permit."

Delay caused by the permit process would be fatal to our project, and yet the prospect of this added work seemed almost too much. Still, this compromise allowed us to continue with the work already under way while we did the clearing and planting, and in time the trees would provide a great benefit to the station.

"We will begin immediately," I assured him.

A new crew was recruited for cutting through the jungle, and another was added to develop a tree nursery.

We grew thousands of trees for transplanting: palms for the palm nuts, mangos, bananas, papaya, orange, lemon, grapefruit, and of course hardwood trees.

Each morning I took the clearing crew to where we were working and got them started by setting up my transit and sighting the line to be cleared. A man would go as deeply into the jungle as possible, set up a stake at my direction, and the crew would begin clearing toward the stake. I could then return to the station to supervise other work, but often had to go back several times a day to extend the line the men were clearing.

Working in the humid heat of the jungle attracted swarms of sweat bees that got in the eyes, nose, ears or any exposed part of the anatomy. It was both difficult and painful, particularly trying to sight through the transit with constantly blurred vision. Dolores made a veil of fine mosquito net for me, but it proved ineffective, tending to keep the bees inside the net more than out. I didn't know which was worse, actually going into that swarm of sweat bees or just realizing I would have to go back time after time until we finished the job. But meter by meter the clearings crept slowly forward, until finally all our jungle area was neatly sliced into ten-meter tracts. By the time this was accomplished, our nursery already had fifteen thousand trees ready for transplanting, and we greeted a satisfied administrator when he came for his final inspection.

CHAPTER 5

Boko–1956

As General Superintendent of Building for all our stations in the Congo, it was necessary for me to plan, budget, lay out the buildings, employ and supervise the workers for other projects, as well as for the work going on at the station where we lived. It also necessitated my presence at the annual conference where missionary and Congolese leaders made decisions and established priorities for the entire field. The 1956 Conference was at Banza Manteke, making it a joy for Dolores and me to return and meet in some of the facilities we built there earlier; but even more cherished was the chance to be with those people who had guided us so lovingly through that first year.

The conference was an exciting but difficult time for everyone involved. Each person felt so strongly about the needs of his or her own work, yet the available resources were never adequate to satisfy the demand. Sometimes the discussions were heated. Sometimes tempers flared momentarily. But in the end each of us recognized the realities before us and accepted the final decisions.

The session on Saturday had been no less stressful than the others preceding it, and about ten o'clock that night Martin Engwall excused himself, saying only that he had to go home. Moments later a helper from the house came running, telling us that Martin had collapsed. Dr. Abell and I rushed to his house.

"Scotty, go to the dispensary for me," Dr. Abell said, rapidly listing the things he needed. Minutes later I returned to be greeted by the sad words, "I'm sorry, Scotty. He's gone."

I stared at him in disbelief. This man who had been so loving and supporting of us, so alive just moments before; how could it be?

"He had a massive heart attack," Dr. Abell said. "There was nothing we could do."

"Six months," I said. "Just six months and they were going to retire." My voice choked at the pointless words, at the futility of thinking what might have been for Martin and Ruth. Then, remembered words of scripture brought me quiet assurance because they applied so well to Martin, "Well done thou good and faithful servant. Come, enjoy the place I have prepared for you."

Dr. Abell and I dressed and prepared the body, while others comforted and supported Ruth. Then we gathered for a long prayer session, giving thanks for the love that had come to us through Martin, asking for comfort for Ruth and the rest of the family back in the States, reaffirming our faith in the resurrection and life everlasting.

The next morning I was in the shop early. My carpenters and I made the casket from the most beautiful mahogany boards on hand. Lewis Brown and Phil Uhlinger prepared the funeral service. Phil's crew dug the grave. Others decorated the church. Others met the hundreds of Congolese who came in from the villages. The funeral service was at 3:30 that afternoon and we buried the body of the Reverend Martin Engwall in the land he had loved and served so well for thirty-one years.

Death is a reality with which we all live, but in the mission field it often becomes much more immediate and personal. It reminds us that time is of the essence, and it was the death of a young Congolese that prompted me to take great risks in building the hospital at Boko.

We had been at Boko for just eight months and had finished seven permanent personnel houses, seven cook houses and the missionary residence that was our home. Plans had been completed for the other buildings the station required. Then word came that the money for more buildings could not be released until certain board proceedings in America took place, a process that I knew would delay construction for many weeks at best and could run on for months.

It was late Saturday afternoon and I was depressed over the dismal prospect of an indefinite interruption in the building program. I sat dejectedly at my drafting table, alternating between doodling on plans that might not be translated into structures for months, fuming at the frustrating bureaucracy and praying for patience and guidance. My meditation was interrupted by Muhulu Mahongi, the old chief of Luhaku, the nearest village to Boko.

"Tata Scott, please come immediately and see my son." The lines of pain and concern etched in his ebony face carried a depth of paternal concern that transcends time or race.

"Of course," I answered. "Where is he?"

"He is in the hospital and he needs you."

As we approached the hospital I was struck again by its inadequacy and the impossible demand on Alice Jorgensen to make it a place of healing rather than a place where people die, as five patients had done in the last week. It was a small stick-and-grass building, divided into six rooms, each six feet square. Stakes, driven into the sand floor, supported the native beds of woven vines and bark. There were two such beds in each room. Other, smaller grass buildings handled the overflow of patients, and these rapidly filled up with as many as six people in each small room. Depressing as it was, it was the best available anywhere in the area.

Tata Muhulu led me to where his son lay dying in the dark corner of one of the rooms, his handsome features now distorted with pain and his strong body now ravaged by the fatal illness.

"If you will pray for my son, you can save his life," Muhulu informed me.

Tears came to my eyes as I looked from the young man to his father. "Perhaps I could if I were a good enough person, or if I had enough faith." Did I say this to the chief, or only to myself? But I prayed for the dying man on the rough bed and determined then and there that I must make my own unique contribution to saving others like him.

That evening we missionaries met for our usual prayer time, and I shared my frustrations with them. There was no question in any of our minds that the greatest need at Boko was for the new hospital. I told them I wanted to start the hospital immediately, whether or not funding had been released.

"I have a thousand dollars saved," Alice Jorgensen said. "You can have that."

"I don't have any money I can give you," Rev. Robbins added, "but I can loan you a thousand dollars."

Two thousand dollars to begin a hospital that would have cost hundreds of thousands of dollars to build in the States! Yet, the absurdity never occurred to us. Rather, there was the sense of a great load suddenly lifted. Our workmen would not have to be laid off and sent back to their villages. The excellent crew we had assembled would not have to be dismantled. The hospital WOULD be built!

My oil lamp burned all that night as I completely revised the drawings to meet every existing need. I increased the size to a full forty-bed hospital and designed an operating room with luxurious space and natural light coming in through angled windows. Helen Robin's pressure cooker would no longer be needed to sterilize instruments, as we would have modern sterilization equipment and a medical environment in which sterility could be meaningful. Electric lighting would make gas lamps and jerry-rigged truck lights obsolete. Steel beds would replace the vine and bark. Reinforced concrete would replace grass and vines. Smooth plaster would replace mud. Dirt and sand would vanish in favor of sealed and scrubbable floors. A large storage room would provide a place where bandages and supplies could be kept free of termites, mice, and other unwelcome but all-too-familiar visitors.

By Sunday morning the plans were finished, and I estimated we could complete the building for two dollars per square foot, a fraction of construction costs in America and a tenth of what the Congolese government estimated as average.

Monday morning we began construction.

Ten months later it was completed, fulfilling all our hopes regarding schedule, budget, beauty and serviceability. It would have been a source of pride in any small American town; in the remote Bayaka country it was a miracle.

But the Congolese refused to be admitted to the new hospital!

On the day Alice had all the rooms ready, the beds prepared, even sheets on the beds, she announced to the patients out in the grass sheds, "You can go in now." But none of them moved.

Again she tried. "The new hospital is ready for you. Everything is nice and clean and light and comfortable."

"No, Mama, it is better out here for a while."

A woman came in from the bush in the last stages of labor. Alice immediately took her to the delivery room, gave her anesthesia and delivered the baby. It was a difficult delivery, requiring forceps, but both the mother and baby ended the ordeal in fine shape. However, just as soon as the woman regained consciousness, she dashed out of the hospital. The other women congratulated her profusely, yet still refused to enter the hospital themselves.

The next patient in the hospital was also a woman in labor. She delivered the first stillborn baby in the year-and-a-half we had been at Boko. When word of this sad affair reached the patients outside there was a general clamor, a hasty gathering up of personal possessions and a collective dash for the hospital rooms.

"What in the world is going on?" Alice asked one of the patients climbing into a freshly made bed. "Why is everybody accepting the hospital now?"

"*Mpaka*, Mama," the patient answered. "It is the tax to be paid for this wonderful new hospital. The first patient to stay here must die to pay the tax, and now it has been paid. None of us wanted to be the one to pay the tax."

Mpaka is not the only vestige of superstition so deeply ingrained in the native culture, nor was this the last time we would encounter it.

My brother, a minister, once asked me how we missionaries could learn to live with such continuing superstition.

"Do you remember our dad?" I answered. "Dad was convinced that a black cat crossing in front of him would bring bad luck. He was so certain of this that many times he would stop the car, back up and go around the block rather than drive across where a black cat had walked." I saw my brother nod in remembrance.

"Or what about grandpa?" I continued. "He knew that if you rocked a rocking chair with no one in it, somebody would die. And grandma knew that if a broom was left in the kitchen, company would come. Uncle Roy had absolute fear of walking under a ladder. This is the way they had always believed and whether or not they became a Christian didn't change it. It's the same with the Congolese. We certainly don't agree, or support them in their superstitions, but we have to face the reality that *they* believe these things."

Still, some things continue to puzzle even those of us with strong faith and pragmatic minds. Some events are inexplicable: events such as those connected with the most difficult payday I had during all the years in Africa.

We had several hundred men employed at one time at Boko, so paydays were frantic at best. On payday the men formed a line in front of our house, and one by one they came to my desk on the veranda to receive their pay. Each pay envelope was opened, the money was counted out and usually there was some conversation, ranging from "How are your children?" to "The reason there are five *makuta* less than you expected is because you got an advance on your pay day before yesterday."

One of the men, recently hired, was a troublemaker and had been creating problems among the workers. When it came this man's turn to receive his pay, the envelope was opened and the money counted. He threw it back on the desk. "I'm not going to take that money," he shouted. "There's not enough of it and it's not honest. It's not right. It's not what I agreed on. You know you are being dishonest!"

"No," I answered, "I am not being dishonest, and you know it. If you have a grievance you can go to the man who represents the workers and he will straighten it out for you."

"He is your lackey and you have probably told him to be dishonest,

47

too!" As he continued to argue I saw that he wanted a confrontation even more than he wanted his pay.

"OK, get out of here," I told him. "If you don't want your money, don't take it, but I've got a lot of work to do and I don't have time to argue with you."

He glared at me for a moment, then scooped up his money and threw it in my face. The other men standing around were watching this exchange, and I knew that such a challenge, if unanswered, would provide fertile soil for the dissension this man had been trying to create.

I took one step and was on top of the desk. The next step and I was over the desk and beside him. He turned toward the men gathered on the lawn and started screaming. He thought I was going to kill him. I grabbed him by the shoulders and shouted in his face, "You get out of here and don't ever come back! You're fired!"

He left, went back to his village, entered his hut, lay down on his bed, turned his face against the wall and died. I have no idea how he did it or what he died of.

"Tata Scott, you're in big trouble," one of the men told me the next day, "because he went to his village, turned his face against the wall and died."

"I'm sorry about it," I told him. "But everything I did was right and everything he did was wrong and all the men who were there know it."

"You're in big trouble anyway," he continued. "They are having a big trial in the village and you are at the center of it. The head of the family is a *Mbuta*, an elder statesman, and they are blaming him for not protecting this man from you."

I could follow this with even my limited knowledge of native culture. Their culture holds that when someone dies it is because some other person is responsible. It may be the fault of a relative, a friend, an enemy or even the spirit of one departed. It is important to determine responsibility and achieve some degree of recompense. There are too many contradictions in that thinking for us to fully understand. Nevertheless, it is an ingrained part of the tribal culture.

Later, I learned the outcome of the trial. The old man had defended himself by saying, "I'm just a common black man. I have no power against what Tata Scott does or doesn't do. I have no power to protect my family against him."

"Yes, you do, and you didn't use your power," he was told. "Therefore, you have to climb the palm tree."

"All right, I'll climb the tree and prove it," he said.

The designated tree was the tallest palm in the village. The procedure is simple. The person climbs to the very top of the palm tree and jumps. If he dies it is proof of his guilt. If he survives it is proof of his innocence. This man survived. He was brought to the hospital for treatment of the injuries he suffered, and his eventual recovery marked the end of the matter.

Not all victims of superstition are able to survive.

After the day was over and the evening meal, if they had one, was finished, the workmen gathered around a fire and talked. Frequently, I would amble up and join them before bedtime. On this particular night there were so few men by the fire that I knew something unusual had pulled them away.

"Where is everybody tonight?" I asked of no one in particular.

"Oh, today in the village a baby was born with teeth." The speaker, one of my older masons, assumed that was all the information one needed in order to know the whereabouts of the men.

"So! What has that to do with the men being gone?" I asked.

"Why, they went into the forest to burn the baby, of course," he answered.

Fire is often used in cleansing ceremonies, and I shuddered at the image of a helpless infant crying against the pain of a charcoal ember or a flaming branch held against its face. "That's cruel," I said instinctively.

"Oh, no, Tata Scott!" he answered, the intensity of his conviction as evident on his face as in his voice. "Animals want to come into the family so they can devour people. That is how animals get into the family."

"Through babies?" I said.

"Through babies born with teeth," he said. "Animals are born with teeth. Babies don't have teeth when they are born. The only protection is to burn the baby up before it can do harm. The men all went into the jungle, where they built a big fire, and they have thrown the baby on it to protect the family and other people in the village."

I was aghast. There was now nothing I could do for this infant, but sleep was hard to come by that night.

The next morning my workers gathered for devotions, as usual, before beginning the day's tasks. "You all know my daughter, Sharan?" I began.

Nods and a general murmur of approval swept over the men.

"Do you think she is a sweet girl?" I asked.

Again, there was the strong affirmation I expected from the men. They all thought Sharan to be one of God's special creations.

"Do any of you think Sharan is an animal?"

Had anyone other than her father even suggested such a thought to this group, he might have been torn to pieces on the spot. Their disclaimer was both loud and spontaneous.

"Well, Sharan was born with teeth," I told them. "We did not think there was anything wrong with that. All over the world there are babies born with teeth. Those babies grow up just like other babies." I labored the point through the whole of the devotions, and it must have done some good. I learned later that the Belgians had tried for a long time to put a stop to this practice, imposing heavy penalties and harsh punishment for anyone found guilty, but their efforts proved unsuccessful. Yet, after this incident, we never again heard of this happening in our area.

Another bizarre example of superstition came just before we left Boko at the end of our first term.

One evening after work, Dolores and I heard a terrible commotion coming from the building site. I jumped in the car and drove down there to find the whole station in an uproar. All the men were there, divided into two groups and having a battle royal. I waded into the middle of the fight and finally got it stopped. "OK, what's going on here?" I asked.

Inginias answered, his face still distorted with rage. "Manuel said he gave my soul to you to take back to America so you would have a slave."

"I told him he was so worthless here that you wouldn't want him to stay here anyway," Manuel said, blood from the fight now mixing with blood from a minor accident he had just before quitting time. "I told him Tata Scott is about finished here and back in America he will want a stupid little slave to work for him, so I gave Inginias' soul to Tata."

This had started the fight, and then Inginias' friends starting fighting with Manuel's friends, until finally everybody present was involved. I knew I was out of my depth, so I took the two men to Bill Robbins' home. We sat in Bill's office and explained the situation as much as possible.

"Well, Bill, since you're in charge of the Soul Department, this is your problem."

"Thanks a lot, friend," Bill said in English. Then he began preaching to both men. Bill had a great command of scripture and he was a great preacher. He exhorted both men to understand the nature of the soul, the meaning of the Gospel, the essence of creation and I don't know what all else. Frankly, I was watching Manuel glare at Inginias, and Inginias glare back at Manuel, each muttering the equivalent of, "You dirty so-and-so, wait till I get you outside." Bill was doing absolutely no good in the Soul Department that day. As he was finishing I left and found Andre Kidiela.

"Andre, I don't think this thing is settled," I told him. "Do you have any words of wisdom?"

"I might have," he smiled.

When the men emerged from Robbins' house, Andre was ready. "Inginias, what kind of a house do you have?" he asked.

"Oh, I don't have any house. I'm a single man. My mother and father have a whole bunch of kids and I'm relegated to what is no more than an outhouse."

"Inginias, what kind of clothes do you have?"

"Oh, I don't have anything. I've got this old shirt I've got on and this pair of shorts. I don't have any shoes and I don't have any socks."

"Inginias, what do you eat?"

"Food is really hard to get for our family, we've got so many. We divide up what we can find during the day, but I almost starve every night."

"Have you ever seen the pictures Tata Scott shows us of America?" Andre asked. "There are great big beautiful stores. Everybody drives a car. Everybody has a radio. Everybody dresses beautifully. Did you ever see pictures of anybody living in an outhouse, or not having clothes to wear or going hungry?"

"No, I have never seen pictures of people in America who wanted for anything," Inginias answered.

"Then what are you so upset about?" Andre said.

"I never thought of it that way," Inginias said. He turned to me with the biggest smile I had ever seen on his face. "How soon do we leave, Tata?"

That was the end of the fight, though a terribly disappointed Inginias awaited me when I returned from America and hadn't taken his soul with me.

Given such thinking, we should not have been surprised the day we stopped the truck at the edge of a village and a Congolese, whom I had seen before but didn't really know, turned and fled in absolute terror.

"What in the world is the matter with him?" I asked Duki, one of the drivers I employed.

"I will find out, Tata," Duki answered and took off in pursuit of the frightened man. Quite some time later he returned with an explanation.

"He was frightened of you because you are a *mundele a mwinda*, a white man who goes out at night with a lantern to catch and eat people!"

"What? Where could anyone get such an idea?"

"Oh, he has proof," Duki smiled. "He said he has seen cans of your food. There are pictures of tomatoes on the outside of cans filled with tomatoes and pictures of beans on cans filled with beans. His witch doctor showed him a can with a picture of people on it and the witch doctor insisted that white people capture black people and grind them up and eat them." The damning evidence turned out to be a can of chili with a picture of Spanish couples dancing.

We had been warned not to bring Aunt Jemimah pancake mix to Congo with us. The Bubecks' cook had come to the same conclusion and the Bubecks worked under a cloud for years. But chili?

Yet, there were also small victories in our struggle to replace superstition with faith.

Not long after our arrival at Boko, we were astonished to see a procession of Congolese coming down the road to the station: an entire village led by their witch doctor. He was nearly nude, with only a piece of fabric tied around his middle but with bright red and green paint forming elaborate designs over his body. Great red circles ringed his eyes. Diagonal green stripes slashed along his cheeks and across his abdomen. He carried a woven basket into the station and placed it at the feet of Rev. Robbins.

"These are all my fetishes," he explained. "They have held great *ndoki* for me and my village for many years. Now, we wish you to burn them. Give us instead this new protection which you have and which you have brought to us."

It was, and continues to be, a constant battle between the native way of thinking and the Christian perspective enlightened by knowledge. Often, and tragically, the old ways prevail.

Five years earlier, some natives brought in a five-year-old boy who was so sick and weak he had been given up for dead. His parents had both died, so he had been left to starve. Helen and Bill nursed him back to life, and then to health. They enrolled him in the school and gave him training in their home. He grew into a nice-looking lad and showed real promise.

But the elders of his village called him back soon after his tenth birthday, held some sort of heathen ceremony and presented him with a wife. She was the widow of a man who had gone to work in Leopoldville and died there. She was old enough to be the boy's grandmother.

Bill Robbins went to the village to protest to the elders.

"We have raised this boy for five years. What are you doing to us?"

"The matter is settled," he was informed curtly. "The boy has gotten the woman pregnant so she is his wife and he is her husband now. The ceremony we conducted separates him forever from any contact with you white people. *Ka diambu ko!*" ("There are no more words to be said!")

Even as we sought to combat superstition and debilitating cultural influences, a more ominous threat lurked on the horizon, though we had no indication of the terror and devastation it would bring us in the years to come. There was constant talk of "Independence," though generally the Congolese had no clear concept of what independence meant. For some it meant that pots of money would be found in their yards. For others it meant they would no longer have to work for food or clothing, which instead would be provided in abundance. But none of us was prepared fully for the turmoil and chaos it would bring to the Congo.

CHAPTER 6

Boko—1956

With the hospital completed, it was time to begin building the church at Boko. I dreamed of "Trinity in Congo," replicating our new church in Santa Monica. But the California church had required hundreds of thousands of dollars to construct, and it rose to heights that would be staggering for the Africans. Our budget for the church at Boko was a scant eight thousand dollars. Still, the dream persisted and I drew up plans for it. If all went well, there would be adequate time to finish the church before our first term ended and we returned to the States on furlough.

But, of course, not everything went well.

A Swiss prospector had come through Boko not long after our arrival and needed help to return to Leopoldville. It was obvious he had been away from civilization a long time. A scraggly and unkempt beard hid much of the leathery face, and his eyes retained a distant look as though perpetually searching the horizon for the next, best place to explore. His Doberman pinschers appeared to be his only family, but what a family they were. The male was half a head taller than the bitch, and the pup showed promise of being a carbon copy of his sire.

His old land-rover was in even worse shape than the prospector. I did some tinkering on it, got it running reasonably well, and filled his tank with gas. He showed us a thick, handwritten manuscript of a book, detailing his wanderings. He said he needed money to get it published. I thought we had given him enough, so I told him I couldn't give him money, but I would buy the pup.

It proved to be an excellent purchase. We named the pup Big Boy and he became thoroughly devoted to me, following me everywhere I went. He was gentle with me, even when we scuffled playfully, though as he attained full growth his presence intimidated the Africans.

We were working on the foundation of the church when Dolores sent word for me to come to the house because Big Boy was behaving oddly.

"He's acted strange all morning," Dolores told me. "He crawled under the desk and just lies there. He won't come out."

"What do you think?" I asked.

"I think you should go get Alice to look at him," she answered. "I'm afraid he might have rabies."

When Alice returned with me, Big Boy was still far under the desk. I bent down to turn his head so Alice could look at him, and he bit my hand.

"Stay away from the dog," Alice told Dolores. "I'd better take Scotty to the dispensary immediately." Once there, she made a quick inspection of the meager supplies on hand.

"Scotty, I don't know if this will do any good, but it's the only thing here that could possibly work at all." She opened a bottle of strong acid and poured it on the wound. The sulfuric fumes stung our nostrils, but that was nothing compared to the stinging of my hand. Then she bandaged me and we returned to the house.

"The important thing is to keep the dog isolated and to keep him alive," she said. "We must see if he develops rabid symptoms. There is no way to test for rabies here; the only way is to send the dog's head to Belgium and that takes too long for us to get the results."

There was a small shed beside the house, enclosed with heavy wire, that we used for storage. The contents were cleared out and Big Boy was carefully moved to his new lodging. He was treated to the best care and food he had ever known.

We read everything Alice had about rabies, noting the symptoms and the order in which they would appear. The book said the dog would whine at night; Big Boy did that. The book said the dog would develop paralysis so it couldn't stand; Big Boy did that. The book said the dog would avoid water; Big Boy conformed. Then we saw him frothing at the mouth. There could be no doubt that the dog was rabid.

Dr. A. C. Osterholm was at Vanga, and when we advised him of the situation he came over immediately. He brought vaccine and began what was the usual twenty-one shot series. The first one made me ill. The second injection caused a breaking out, like a bright red belt around my waist. The third made me look as though someone had wrapped a red blanket around my belly. When Dr. A. C. was advised of this, he ordered the shots discontinued.

"Another shot of the serum undoubtedly would prove fatal," he said. "Better to take our chances with rabies."

Rabies is not uncommon in Congo, and recollections of infected persons came all too vividly to mind. The suffering of the victims is beyond description, and before they die they will bite anyone who comes near them: family, care-givers, anyone within reach. The only solution is to bind the victim securely, usually with a gag as well, and not let anyone come near enough to be injured. It was a scenario into which I had to project myself.

Never in my life had I entertained a single thought of suicide, and I hesitate to use that term in connection with the soul-searching I did in those weeks and months of waiting for symptoms to develop. Still, I could not consider subjecting my family or any of the others with whom I worked to the risks involved should I indeed develop the disease. Suffice it to say that I had well-developed contingency plans and the means at hand to carry them out.

After three months Alice said, "I think we're out of the woods. I've never heard of sulfuric acid as an effective antidote to rabies, but apparently it worked. It must have burned out all the virus."

There were other scourges, equally virulent, common in that area, and not all of them were physiological by any means. The spiritual and sociological maladies took their toll as well.

Dibenzi was an orphan boy whom Dolores and I had "adopted" 2 1/2 years earlier and brought to Boko with us. He entered puberty with all the anxieties and longings of any boy at that age. One evening he went to the house of the head teacher and entered the little cook-house out back, which was the home of the *ndezi*, the young girl who does the family chores.

Dibenzi attempted to carry the relationship much further than the young girl was willing to accept, and her screams brought forth the entire household. The head teacher started beating Dibenzi unmercifully. By this time the entire village had gathered for the spectacle, including Duki, our driver. Like Dibenzi, Duki had practically been raised by us and had also come with us from Banza Manteke. Duki protested the beating.

"Please, do not beat this boy," Duki said. "You should take him to Tata Scott, instead."

"How dare you tell me what to do or not do," the teacher roared.

"You are a stranger here and are no better than this scum. You should be beaten right along with him."

Since the teacher was already occupied with Dibenzi, some of the villagers undertook to carry out the teacher's wishes by beating Duki. But a few friends of Duki were present, and in no time there was a general fight that soon developed into a riot with everyone in the village involved.

Of course, I was notified of the ruckus, and by the time the headlights of my truck lit up the area all was as calm as a placid ocean. I gathered up pieces of reinforcing steel and other such armaments, with which they had been beating one another. Dibenzi's shirt, thick with blood and lost when he made his escape, lay on the ground. I pieced together the story of what had transpired.

Dibenzi came back to his room about midnight, scared half to death. He told me a big lie, then a smaller one, and finally the truth. It was just as the *ndezi* had said.

The short night allowed me time to reflect on the situation, and by morning I had decided the teacher was as much at fault as Dibenzi. This seemed to be an appropriate time to hit at the terrible tribal rivalry which was the real root of the trouble: had Dibenzi been of the teacher's tribe there likely would have been a lesser response to the ndezi's wailing.

The *bambuta*, the head men and elders, were summoned. "When I came here I brought with me one man from a different tribe. Now we have people from several tribes. I want two things," I told them. "I want a complete apology from the teacher and I want a promise from every man on the station to be of one tribe, *Bana Ba Nzambi*, all children of God together." They looked at me in disbelief that I could make such drastic demands of them. "If these two conditions are not met within twenty-four hours I will pack up my tools, machines, family and everything else I own and I will go to another station." Without allowing time for discussion I turned and walked away from the men.

The day was not nearly as long as it seemed to me, waiting for the Bayaka leaders to respond and wondering what their response would be. But that evening they summoned us, and we were given the necessary apologies. Then we had a time of serious prayer in which all of us committed ourselves to a degree of unity previously unknown at Boko.

The following morning I called all my workmen together. "You all know what has gone on the last two days," I began. Of course they knew. Information flows throughout the community like the torrential rain flows over the dry ground, and each gets soaked up as thoroughly.

"Now, there are some things that are going to be different in our

57

working relationships," I continued. "First of all, each of you will give me your solemn pledge that you will never again put the tribe above the cause for which we are all working." There was a moment of reflection, but to my amazement every man made this pledge.

"The second thing is that all of you will clean from your hearts any grudges or hatred that you carry toward a fellow workman." This took a little longer, as the men considered the implications. Sidewise glances at former adversaries were frequently repeated before this pledge could be given with sincerity. But again, every man affirmed his willingness.

"Finally, every man who is not a church member will enter a class *minlandi*, a Christian study which is necessary for church membership." I thought this might have been pushing too far, but the response was enthusiastic and near-unanimous affirmation.

Unbeknown to me, a small group of dissenters had been employed and were planning to lead the men in a general walk-out. This last demand was too much for the troublemakers, and they got up and walked away, leaving our crew united as one group with one purpose. However, the next day even these dissidents came back to me and asked if they, too, could be considered for the class *minlandi*.

How grand it would be if the serious resolve of those days had remained perpetually untarnished. It changed the climate of Boko, and even today its impact is felt. But neither Africans nor Americans can constantly live up to the best we know or wish.

I talked with Andre Kidiela about this one day.

"We don't want to sin, to keep repeating the old ways, but we keep doing it just the same." I studied this man who had taught me much more than I ever taught him. "What is sin to you, Tata Andre?"

He sat silently for only a moment, then he began telling me a story.

"One day I was out in the bush when I saw an earth bird and a sky bird. The earth bird was sitting on the ground and the sky bird was perched high up in a tree.

"I raised my head to the sky bird and asked, 'What is the world like to a bird?' The sky bird, who can fly so high the eye cannot follow him, answered, 'The world to a bird is big and clear and beautiful beyond description.'

"'Not so,' answered the ground bird. 'The world is small and dirty and filled with danger.' The ground bird could fly only a few feet in the air before he plopped back to earth.

"The two birds fell into discussion and finally the ground bird said, 'Tell me how I could fly high into the beautiful world you know.'

"'That's simple,' the sky bird answered. 'It's those *zinzenza* (large and delicious crickets) you eat. Stop eating those big, fat, greasy *zinzenza* and you can fly like I do.'

"The ground bird stopped eating *zinzenza* and each day he flew higher and higher until, with his newfound friend, he could soar up and be lost above the clouds. One day he had been flying and came down tired but happy and, of course, very hungry. A big fat *nzenza* (one cricket) walked across right in front of him. The ground bird had a notion, but he quickly put it aside.

"The *nzenza* seemed hurt that this bird snubbed him. He marched up so close to the bird that he stumbled over his feet. He rolled over on his back and smiled up at the bird. This was too much. One peck and the *nzenza* was gone!

"Then the bird took off for the clouds and PLOP, he hit the ground.

"That is what sin is like. We know how good and beautiful life can be, but then we give in to temptation."

This down-to-earth application of the Gospel reminded me of the way Jesus used parables in his teaching, and Kidiela used it with the workmen as well. One day at chapel he invented the following parable to make his point.

"Tata Scott and I were in his big five-ton truck going to Kikongo. We met an old man walking along the road, carrying a very heavy load on his head. Tata Scott offered him a ride to help him. He got on the empty bed of the truck and when we looked back he still had the load on his head.

"Tata Scott stopped the truck and told the man he was trying to help him, that he didn't have to carry the load on his head any more, that he should lay it down on the truck bed. Then we drove on, but again we looked back and saw the man still had the load on his head. Tata Scott stopped again and gave the man the same counsel.

"The same thing happened a third time. Again Tata Scott stopped the truck and pleaded with the man, but to no avail.

"That," said Kidiela, "is how it is with God, who wants to help us if we will trust Him. Tata Scott wants to help us, but we must trust him. I want to help you with our work and you must trust me, too. And as you learn to trust us, then you can begin to trust the One who is greater than all of us."

As our crew developed a unity of purpose and unity of spirit, we saw startling progress on the church building. I watched the sand and the rock and the trees of the jungle rise up to form the church. But those elements needed a lot of help in the formation, and that help came in a variety of ways.

The pastor of a San Diego church had come to the Congo for a visit early in our term. As he left, expressing his admiration for the work that was taking shape, he asked what his church could do to assist us. After some thought I suggested that our most difficult job was sawing up rough lumber. Returning to the States, he led his church to purchase a trailer equipped with a motor-generator and a power saw. It took over a year for this equipment to clear customs, but its arrival speeded our work immeasurably.

Another great assist was provided by the village churches that were outposts of the Boko station. Bill Robbins asked for their help and they responded beyond all expectations with their labor and their love. As an example, fifty adults came from Lonzo, an area about seventy kilometers away. They walked the distance, carrying their children and all the food they would need. They carried rocks up the steep valley wall and moved many tons of rock for us in one week. Even more gratifying was the fact that at the end of the week twenty-seven of them were baptized and resumed the long walk back to their village in happiness and joy.

Construction of the church continued, but so did other responsibilities that demanded that we travel. We always took a driver with us to spell one another on the long and difficult trips. Being a driver is both a valued occupation and a status symbol for Congolese, so they are all called "chauffeur" rather than "truck driver."

Duki was not the best chauffeur one could ask for, but he had been with me since he was a youngster and I learned to put up with him, though it wasn't always easy. Most irritating were those times when he thought only of himself.

The veld is abundant with elephant grass, a tough, tall grass that grows higher than one's head. During the dry season, when the sand becomes fluffy and soft, that grass can be laid across the road in the worst spots. Without that augmentation, tires can sink into the sand. It's not uncommon to see a stretch of road covered for a quarter of a mile with such natural matting laid out by one traveler after another.

Every year the natives burn off the elephant grass. When the dry grass burns with a wind behind it, it is awesome. Intense heat is generated by the flames as the wind drives it forward at incredible speed and sparks are caught in the updraft and blown ahead of the fire wall.

Dolores and I were making a trip across a section of the veld one day with Duki at the wheel when we saw such a fire. It was sweeping toward us on an almost straight line for as far as we could see in either direction. There was no turning back; our best chance was to try crashing through the fire line.

The fire was burning on both sides of the roadway. Its heat and smoke filled the cab and stung our eyes and nostrils. We were almost through the fire when we came to a stretch of the road that was aflame. Grass, accumulated by months of travelers throwing it across the ruts, had dried and was perfect tinder.

Seeing the wall of fire before him, Duki panicked. He stalled the truck, jumped out and started running through the flames.

I slid over under the wheel, and fortunately the engine started on the first stroke. I prayed there was not the slightest leak in the carburetor or from the barrels of gasoline we were carrying on the bed of the truck. Had a leak developed either place, we would have been gone in one great flash. I eased the truck back on the road and through the fire until we reached the burned-over area. It was hell warmed over. Everything was black as far as one could see.

I checked under the truck to make sure no built up oil or grease was burning, and while lying there on my back I thought, "Well, Duki ran off and left us, but that's good riddance." I got the truck rolling again and we overtook Duki further up the road. I didn't ask him why he had abandoned us and he was smart enough not to bring up the subject again.

But that wasn't the only time Duki displayed his lack of control in a tense situation.

Dolores and I had gone to Leopoldville to pick up the new electric generator for Boko. The generator was such a large piece of equipment it left little room on the truck for other cargo and no room for passengers. We bought a few household supplies and filled the big money box with enough cash to satisfy the needs of the station for several weeks.

After the huge crate containing the generator was securely loaded on the truck, we started the return trip with Dolores, Johnny and me in the cab. Duki was stretched out atop the generator crate, dozing off and on as we covered the relatively flat road south through Inkidinga and then back east toward the Kwango River.

About twenty kilometers before reaching the Kwango, the road descends from the high plain, down hundreds of feet to the eroded river bed. The road itself winds and twists its way through the precipitous hills, carved out over millennia. The term "road" is used loosely. The road is cut into the steep hillsides, often giving spectacular vistas to the passengers as they look out over the sharp drop-off to view the jungle below. But it is not wise for the driver to take his eyes off the narrow, one-lane road long enough to justify a single "Ooooh" or "Aaaah."

The road is maintained, in a manner of speaking, by local people when they have adequate motivation. If and when the spirit, or the dictates of the secteur chief, moves them they take their hoes and shovels and baskets out on the road and scatter enough rocks and dirt around to satisfy the minimum requirements.

We were driving down a particularly steep hill with a sharp drop-off when the side of the road gave way, sending rocks and debris plummeting down the abyss. The truck lurched to the side, finally settling at near a forty-five-degree angle. I looked past Dolores and Johnny down the slope and wondered how long the truck would hang there before plunging downward. Dolores was her usual calm self—though whether in control or fear I could not tell.

"Very, very carefully hand Johnny over to me," I said. She gently pushed him across my lap as I slowly opened the door on my side and literally dropped him down to the roadbed.

"Now, carefully, carefully, crawl over my lap." She did so and jumped down.

Then I thought, "If this thing starts to go, I can jump now." But it held as I crawled out of the cab and joined them on the road.

All this time Duki was running up and down the road in a frenzy, screaming. When I got out of the cab I started putting together what he was saying. Translated into American jargon, it went something like, "You stupid idiot. I could have been killed!" Over and over, "I could have been killed!"

I had some rope that I tied to the truck and then to a large tree on the other side of the road, helping the vehicle to maintain its balance.

Just then some natives from a nearby village came by, and I asked them to get some jungle vines for me. Many of those vines are stronger than our rope. They brought the vines and started tying the truck to trees growing on the high side of the road. When they were finished, it looked like a giant spider web was reaching out from the forest to engage the vehicle.

At last I was satisfied that the truck was as secure as it could be made, and I walked around to the front to inspect the situation. Both wheels on the driver's side were completely off the ground, and the truck was leaning at more than a forty-five-degree angle. I tried to figure, particularly with all the weight of the generator so high up on the back, why the truck had not gone over the side. I know mechanics, I know physics, I know everything that's involved in this, but I know of only one reason why that truck should not have rolled down the cliff.

I knew the people back home were praying for us; that is the only power that could have kept it there.

By then Duki was somewhat in control of himself, so we started digging very carefully. We had to dig under the transmission and the differential until we could get the wheels on the driver's side back on solid ground. Then we dug a trench in the road on the driver's side, allowing the wheels to settle even lower and bringing the truck more nearly level.

By the time the truck sat solidly enough to ease my concern, it was getting late, and I had no idea what to do next. There was no way I could back the truck out of there even without the weight of the generator on it, and there was no way to get that monstrous generator off the truck bed. So, thinking of nothing more we could do, Dolores and I took time to thank the Lord that we had been spared.

Then something really strange happened.

A big diesel truck pulled up behind us. It must have been a twenty-ton truck, at least. I had never seen a truck of that size anywhere in the Congo. I didn't know there was that big a truck in Africa. Of course he could not pass us with our truck blocking the narrow road. Two Africans got out of the truck and the chauffeur said, "You've really got a problem, haven't you?"

"Not as much as if we had gone over the side," I answered.

"Well," he said, "it looks like we're stuck here as long as you are."

I thought for a moment. "The villagers gathered all these vines we've used to tie the truck to the trees." I said. "I think that we could make the vines into a cable. If you would pull up as close as you can to my truck, we could tie the cable from my truck on to your bumper. Then if you put your rig in reverse and give it everything it's got, maybe you could jerk my truck back up on the road."

"Yeah," he said, "and maybe jerk mine over the edge, too."

"What's the alternative?" I asked. "Do you want to sit here until we think of something better? Or do you want to try to back up your rig for ten kilometers?"

"Let's give it a try," he answered.

We untied the vines and I braided them into a cable, just as grandfather had taught me as a child to braid leather thongs to make a cattle whip. The other driver pulled the front of his truck as close to me as he could on the high side of the road, and I tied on to his bumper brace. When he shifted his rig into a whining mode it could be heard for miles, and when he let out the clutch it jumped back and jerked my truck up on the roadway just as we had hoped.

The village people had helped us, and we certainly wanted to compensate them for their efforts. We had the money box full of cash, so there was no shortage of means, but there was too much money. We were reluctant to open the box in front of all those people.

As often happened, I turned to Dolores for an answer. "What are we going to do? We've got to pay them in some way."

Dolores said, "I bought a case of bar soap in Leopoldville. They'd much rather have a bar of soap than money anyway." So we broke open the case and gave each of them a big bar of soap. Dolores was right, of course. They felt better rewarded than if we had given them money.

Even though our delay had caused us to miss the *bac*, that was one time we were more than happy to camp out on the river bank overnight.

Our first term came to an end and I reflected on what had been accomplished. In forty-eight months we had completed forty-eight buildings. We had learned to communicate in three new languages. Electrical systems had been installed in three stations. We had hunted buffalo, antelope, crocodile and myriad smaller animals to help feed the people. We had survived more river crossings on the precarious *bacs* than I could remember. We had made new friends who had enriched our lives more than we had theirs. Hundreds and hundreds of people had accepted Christianity and became vital parts of the church. But above all else, we left with the sure and certain knowledge that Christ had been with us every step of the way, guiding, providing, loving and at times protecting.

CHAPTER 7

Santa Monica, Cal.
1957-1958

We had spent only four years in the Congo, and yet reentering "civilization" was a culture shock. We spent delightful days in Italy, Switzerland, Belgium and England before flying back to the States. What a change from our trip over on the steamship! This time we flew in only eleven hours, the first of many trans-Atlantic flights, each faster than the one before.

Simple things can assume such importance. Imagine the thrill of turning a tap almost anywhere and having water that is either cool and safe to drink, or warm enough to wash with. How can one describe the wonder of roads that are paved and smooth, presenting no thought of getting stuck in dry sand or gulping mud? The sight of new cars by the thousands on the streets and highways took our breath away, but not as much as did the frantic driving we encountered crossing this beautiful nation.

We were met in New York by friends and relatives, and received the keys to our new 1958 Chevrolet Impala. It represented luxury beyond our dreams, but was only the first of countless expressions of love we were to share in the months ahead.

Our health was excellent, so the medical examinations in New York moved rapidly. The stops to visit family and friends as we made our way westward proved, to the surprise of many, that our skins had not turned black during our four years in Africa. Events flashed all too briefly across our calendar: Fishing in Iowa and Colorado. Golfing in

Kansas and Wisconsin. Picnic lunches in the desert. Receptions by churches and newspaper interviews almost everywhere we stopped. By the time we reached Santa Monica we thought we were ready for a bit of rest, but that was not to be.

Our home church went all out in welcoming us. Other churches across Southern California insisted on having us speak, so we were out three or four nights every week, meeting as many of these requests as possible. Our many friends wanted to share our time as much as we wanted to share theirs. In addition, Dolores and I both enrolled in college courses, as well as taking 400 hours of conversational French at the Berlitz School in Beverly Hills. It was a pace as full as we had known in the field, but the wonderful way in which people listened and responded to our message gave us excitement and energy.

Thirty-five-millimeter slides were the "in thing" in those days, and we had accumulated an abundant supply over the course of that first term to document and illustrate our work. I usually used the slides with my narration as the content of the program.

Like everyone else, my ego is fed by the people who tell me how much they enjoyed my presentation; but the thrill came for me when a man or woman, a boy or girl, came to me after a presentation, obviously moved to the point of making a significant life decision. Some found faith in Christ and dedicated their lives to serving Him. Some decided to enter full-time Christian service. And some came with tangible offers, most, but not all, of which were fulfilled. A doctor offered to pay for the construction and outfitting of a small hospital. Twin sisters, nurses, offered to serve. And one man wanted to make a movie of our story.

The film "Congo Awakening," produced by the Religious Film Foundation of Hollywood, California, was the result of that conversation. I have since been told that after more than thirty years it is that company's most-distributed film ever.

But perhaps the most personally appreciated gift I received was a custom-made Weatherby rifle, presented by the men of Southern California. It was fitted to my measurements, mounted with a precision scope, and later proved to fulfill all my expectations of what the perfect hunting rifle should be.

Before our year was up, a new GMC Carryall was presented to us to be shipped to the Congo—yet another sign of the love and concern expressed in the generosity of countless people who wanted to be a part of the wonderful work to which God had called us. We felt invigorated to know that so many were in partnership with us.

All too quickly the furlough year was over, and it was time to go "home." I reflected on the year in America and compared it with the term in the Congo. We had spoken in over two hundred churches and some fifty other gatherings. Lives had been touched and changed by our simple story of what God can do through us when we open our lives to Him. We had made hundreds of new friends, both for ourselves and the mission endeavor. We were returning with physical, emotional and spiritual renewal. It had been a year well spent.

CHAPTER 8

Vanga—1958-1959

It hardly seemed possible that we were back, the furlough year had gone so fast. But the dry heat of August and the pace of events proved beyond any doubt that we were, indeed, back in Africa.

We had missed the year in Belgium we were supposed to have spent studying French before our first term; construction deadlines at that time demanded our immediate presence in the field. We were promised that year of language study in Belgium before returning for the second term, but again new demands on us reduced that to three months at Banza Manteke. Truly, I needed more fluency than Kiscotty provided. Though the three months ahead promised to be relatively leisurely, it should have come as no surprise that this, also, was not to be.

Chet Jump, our field secretary, greeted me in Leopoldville, exchanged pleasantries, but could hardly wait to share his exciting news.

"It's wonderful, Scotty," he began. "We have just received an offer from the Belgian government to finance the construction of a totally new maternity unit at Vanga."

"Super, Chet," I responded. "I did some preliminary plans before our furlough. I can work out the final plans while I'm at Banza Manteke."

"There's just one little catch," he paused. "They have a completion deadline of August 1, next year. There's no way you can meet that schedule and take three months off the front end for language study."

Chet was right, of course. I knew what the job would entail. I would have to complete the final drawings and order material and supplies before we left Leopoldville. Dolores and I began immediately and found that material was much more readily available than it had been during our first term. We were making good progress toward our goal when Chet came up with more news.

"Scotty, guess what?" His voice exhibited an uncharacteristic excitement. "The government has approved us to acquire land for the secondary school in the Vanga area."

"Great, Chet," I said. "The next time you're in Vanga, let's do some surveying."

We kissed Sharan goodbye and put her on the plane for her school at Lubondai. Johnny was now old enough to move into the Leopoldville residence for missionary children and attend the French school there. As much as it tore at our hearts to be separated from them, we rejoiced at the year we had just spent together and took comfort in the realization that this also was a part of the life we were called to live. The secondary school in the Vanga area, when completed, would call for Congolese boys and girls to endure the same separation from their families during the course of their education.

A new red truck and the GMC carryall were picked up at Matadi and loaded with supplies. A new road had been built to Boko, allowing us to make the trip in record-breaking time of 6 1/2 hours. It seemed that everything was off to an outstanding start. But the hopes of easy travel were dashed shortly afterward as we left Boko for Vanga.

The old construction truck at Boko hadn't run for months. During the four days we stayed at Boko we replaced inserts, made a new pan gasket out of linoleum, and got the truck in working condition. Such makeshift repairs are necessary when the nearest parts supply is many miles and months away. We try to keep extra parts on hand for those things we anticipate will be needed frequently, but creative imagination enables us to augment our inventory immeasurably.

There are distinct wet and dry seasons in the Congo with August bringing the dry season to an end and September ushering in the wet. The change is not gradual. In a matter of days the country is transformed from drought to daily torrents, and those stretches of road that were dirt become a quagmire of mud. But this was the dry season and the sandy roads were powder-dry, passable in places where elephant grass had been thrown down for a base, but frequently causing vehicles to sink into soft sand nearly knee-deep.

The *bac* at Kenge was out, so we had to detour to get to the main road, using less-traveled roads that stalled our small caravan with even greater frequency. Seven-and-a-half hours to go sixty miles! Then more of the same on the main road. Finally, late at night, after we were all near the point of collapse from pushing the trucks an inch at a time, we left the trucks in their latest sand pit for the night and drove on to Vanga in the carryall. It was ten o'clock at night, the end of a trip that began at six that morning and would have taken perhaps two hours in the States. We had spent an entire day and an inordinate amount of energy unnecessarily, it seemed to me. The projects facing us did not allow for such a waste of time, and I decided that a better way must be found if our work was to continue. What all that would entail, I had no idea at the time, but a resolve crystallized that night.

The rainy season came with a vengeance and produced one of the most devastating series of storms in the memory even of the old men. Moanza was the first station hit, taking the lives of several Congolese and leaving not a single building untouched. It took us eleven days to replace roofs, repair serious damage to the church and replace the concrete base for the 10,000-watt electric plant. Then another storm hit Kimpese station, with several deaths and similar damage. We had been at Vanga for a month and still had not been able to begin building.

To complicate matters further, serious disagreement arose as to where the maternity hospital should be located on the station grounds. From my perspective, there was only one suitable location. For years a maternity clinic had been conducted under a great tree, arching its branches protectively over those beneath it as though giving reassurance that here was a place of security. The level land there and the closeness to the rest of the hospital left no other reasonable option, as far as I was concerned. However, the tree would have to be removed, a step strongly resisted both by native leaders and some of the missionaries. They felt as strongly about their choices of location as I did about mine. Innumerable meetings of the station council produced more heat than light as we debated this issue, resolving it only by a final confrontation that produced more agreement than harmony.

Harmony on the station was also hampered by the drive for Independence. Many of the older, more experienced missionaries were fearful of turning over the destiny of the country to people whom they felt to be totally unprepared for such responsibility. The Belgians had been beneficent in their government but had done little to develop native leaders. No more than a dozen Congolese had a college education, and these had been encouraged and sponsored by the various missions. A well-educated Congolese was one who had completed high school. All the missionaries were careful not to get involved in the politics of Independence, realizing that, ready or not, the Congolese would have to resolve their own future.

Nor was the situation easier for the Congolese. There was a movement to make a separate nation of the district of which Vanga was a part. Leaders of this movement were relentless in their efforts to promote their idea, and many of the meetings of Congolese dealing with Independence took place on the mission stations, the only meeting facilities available. The Congolese leaders who did not agree with this popular movement were hard-pressed: they wanted to disagree but knew that to speak against it would brand them as lackeys of the Belgians.

The tensions growing out of this climate expressed themselves in subtle ways daily, though not to the point of open discord. There was more an air of malaise, though the morale of my workmen did not seem to be affected. Thus, the construction finally got under way on the maternity hospital, and Chet and I decided on the location we wanted for the secondary school.

By early December many of the foundations for the buildings of the maternity unit were completed, and the supplies ordered in August from Leopoldville arrived by river barge. Work was progressing well, and we began anticipating the joy of Christmas and having our children home with us. We experienced days of warm satisfaction and anticipation as the holiday season approached. We had purchased a few Christmas gifts for the children, but nothing had come through the mail.

Then on Christmas Eve, just as we were deciding that this Christmas would be even less gift-filled than normal, we heard the sound of the steamer's whistle on the river. The black face of the stevedore who unloaded boxes for us did not resemble Santa Claus', but no sleigh with reindeer could have brought more joy to our children than was contained in the gifts and remembrances from home.

Christmas is always a special time, mixing as it does the singular holiday for the family and the deepened awareness of the miracle of the birth of our Savior. We spent that season warmed by the presence of family and celebrating the even more wonderful presence of Christ in our lives.

But it was too soon over and time to return Sharan and Johnny to their schools. We left Vanga on Saturday, January 3, for Leopoldville, spending the night at Boko. On Sunday a tie rod on the vehicle was badly bent on the road, and the time we spent repairing it delayed our arrival in Leopoldville. Duki had come with us, so we turned off the main artery and detoured to a side road that we had never been on before in order to take him to his family in the *cité*, as the native section is called. We were tired when we finally got to the Union Mission Guest House and went to bed immediately, but we had little sleep that night because of the unusual noises that punctuated the darkness.

"What was all the noise last night?" Dolores asked the next morning.

The other missionaries were surprised at the question, and each vied to give information.

"The military was firing machine guns into the mobs."

"A riot started on the main artery yesterday evening. How did you avoid it?"

"Probably we would have been caught in it," I said, "except for the time we spent with that tie rod, and then turning off through the *cité* to take Duki home."

"Many people were killed, including the *Commissar de Police*, a Catholic priest, a group of Belgian people and several children."

"Many Catholic churches and schools were sacked and burned. The railroad station has been destroyed."

"Gasoline drums at filling stations exploded in the fires all night long."

"Makala Prison was damaged and all the prisoners escaped."

If the communication to us was garbled and confusing, it was no less so than the situation itself.

Military reinforcements continued to arrive in Leopoldville all day Monday, setting up barbed-wire barricades around native sections where trouble had erupted or was suspected. Stores quickly sold out of food as people made a frantic rush to lay in as much supplies as possible. Many automobiles and buses were burned on the streets. Few people, other than the police and the military, were on the streets, but most of the white men (except missionaries) who ventured out that day were armed. All day long the rioting and fighting continued. The military imposed a 6:30 p.m. to 5:30 a.m. curfew on all citizens, black and white alike.

That afternoon we had a meeting at the Jumps' house on our compound.

"Nobody seems to know exactly what the situation is," Chet explained. "But we have been in contact with the American embassy and they will continue to keep us informed as well as they can. They have sent a special courier with this message I want to read to you:

'Rioting has occurred and is continuing within the entire African City making that whole area unsafe for the white population. The area has been cordoned off by the police and

Force Publique. There appears to be no immediate danger of the disturbance expanding into the European sections. Americans are strongly urged to remain in their own homes to the extent possible until the disturbances are fully under control. If the rioting continues and there is apparent danger to persons or property, American citizens may seek refuge at either the American Consulate or at the official residence of the Consul-General. The Consulate General will continue to keep citizens informed of subsequent developments and make appropriate recommendations.'

"Those of you from the interior stations may not know much about the political situation here in Leopoldville. The strongest party here and to the south is ABAKO, led by Joseph Kasavubu. Apparently, there was a meeting of ABAKO yesterday, and a conflict erupted between ABAKO supporters and the police," Chet continued. "From there it spread over the whole native city, turning into a full-fledged riot."

"I heard that some Congolese were planning a massacre tonight, but the government intercepted the plan for it," one of the missionary wives interjected.

"Some of the Congolese told our children that Phil Uhlinger had been killed and that they would kill the children if they were not good," another offered.

"Phil is perfectly all right, as you all know, but rumors are everywhere," Chet said. "That's why we must depend on the embassy for our information."

"Nevertheless, I think we should send our children back to the States now," Dolores said. "I think it is going to get worse, not better."

"That may be necessary," Chet said, "but I think we should wait a bit before we take that step. However, the school here will close, and we must get the children out of Leopoldville and back to their parents as soon as possible."

Even in stressful times there is occasional opportunity for a chuckle. Chet Jump and I decided that since there seemed to be nothing productive we could do, we might as well get in a round of golf. The one golf course in all of Congo was in Leopoldville, adjoining a military installation. There are always at least two caddies for each player, one to carry the bag and one to go ahead and spot the ball—sometimes even to keep the ball from being carried off by monkeys or adventurous boys. Our play was proceeding nicely when we came to a long par four running parallel to the military installation. I got off a nice long drive, straight down the fairway. Chet wanted to show me up with his tee shot, if possible, so he gave it just a little extra effort. The ball took off like a bullet, headed down the fairway, then began that dreaded and dreadful arc known to all golfers as a slice. Walking leisurely along under the trees to the right of the fairway was a solitary, uniformed soldier. Paying no attention to protocol, the ball hit the unsuspecting man squarely between the shoulder blades.

"What a time to hit a soldier!" The look Chet gave me was not one of panic, but there was no trace of either serenity or mirth in it. "With this country about to explode, I have to hit a soldier with a golf ball!"

Before I could reply, we saw his caddie run over to retrieve the ball. He picked up the ball and faced the soldier. "You lout! You oaf! You no-good!" he screamed at the startled soldier. "How dare you interfere with Tata Jump's golf shot! Don't you know that these are important men? They are honored guests in our country. How dare you interfere with their game! You stay out of the way of their golf balls!" The caddie turned abruptly and walked back to the fairway, placing Chet's ball on the turf with such an exaggerated show of care, one might have thought him a jeweler returning a costly diamond to its case. The soldier was as shocked as we were, having never before confronted a civilian who reprimanded him with such authority.

"What now?" I asked.

Chet stared down the fairway, glanced quickly at the soldier, then back to the fairway. "I'd say probably a three-wood from there."

The military slowly gained control of the city in the following days, and on Friday we put Sharan on a plane for her school at Lubondai. We received permission to leave Leopoldville on Saturday and, taking Johnny back with us, felt a great relief to be on our way, safely out of the turmoil.

Outside Leopoldville and all the way back to Vanga we were welcomed, as always, by the Congolese who knew us from the many trips we had made back and forth. We were stopped at a roadblock where the carryall was searched for "Dependence," the word often heard misused for independence. One would never suspect how much hatred and frustration existed only a few miles away.

Johnny was enrolled in the native school in Vanga, an easy transition for him since he spoke Kikongo as well as he spoke English.

We were ready to resume the work we were called to do.

CHAPTER 9

Vanga—1959

Kasavubu, Lumumba, Muliele, Tshombe, Mobutu. Names of Congolese leaders captured headlines throughout the world as Congo moved toward Independence. We followed political events with varying degrees of interest, but our attention focused on the work we were called to do, and the tide of history flowed past.

Work on the hospital complex continued day by day. Walls rose from the foundations. Roofs stretched over the walls. Doors and windows were hung. Interior walls and ceilings were finished. Plumbing and wiring wound through the structures. Medical equipment was purchased and installed. Housing was built for personnel. Gradually the hospital rose from the ground as a symbol of new life and hope for these Congolese. The work was nearly finished when a delegation from a neighboring village sought out Norm Riddle and me.

"Tata Scott, Tata Riddle, we have a grave problem but we know you people at the mission can take care of it for us." The speaker was an old man, dressed in a brilliant red skirt that signified high status. His bare feet matched the bare chest, and above that was a smile almost too broad for his wrinkled face. "I am Muzubi, chief of Luzubi village, 2 1/2 hours across the river. Our village mourns the death of two of our women. They were working in their garden when a crazed buffalo charged and trampled them. Other women and children have been terrorized by the beast." A murmur of assent rippled among the men, indicating that indeed women and children had been frightened, and implying that men had not.

"Has he the *rage* or has he been wounded?" Norm asked. Either the dreaded *rage* (rabies) or a serious wound could make the animal violent, attacking without provocation.

"We are sure he has been wounded," the chief answered. "But he might have the *rage* as well. We know for certain that it is a crazed beast. The women can no longer work in their gardens except in the terrible heat of the day, when the heat drives the buffalo into the jungle and away from the clearings."

"Let's have a go at it," Norm said to me. It took no more persuasion to enlist me for the hunt. We told the chief we would be at his village the next morning.

We understood all too well the need to destroy rampaging animals. A pair of lions had invaded the work site of the secondary school recently and killed one of our workmen before we were able to dispatch the male. The female was still prowling the area.

Norm took my twelve-gauge-automatic shotgun and I had the 300 Weatherby. The Weatherby was my pride and joy, a custom-built weapon and in my opinion the finest gun made. It was fitted with a fixed telescopic sight, even though I had suggested a flip scope.

The chief gave us three native guides and we set out at midday, searching over miles of grassland and through jungle paths. We saw wild guinea fowl the size of turkeys, a dozen in a group, and monkeys as large as small men in the upper reaches of the trees. By early evening we found fresh tracks of the wounded buffalo and followed them into a large clearing surrounded on three sides by jungle. A garden grew in the clearing and grass-land stretched for miles from the open end.

"Better we should wait for morning," I suggested to Norm.

"Right," Norm agreed. "I don't want to encounter him when he can see us better than we can see him."

We returned to the village and slept that night in a grass- and-mud hut. Early the next morning we made our way through the jungle, back toward the clearing, and found new buffalo tracks.

"He's been here in the garden this morning, eating manioc," Norm said.

"Sure enough," I said, "but he apparently got a scent of us and took off this way." I motioned toward the grassland. He was easy to track through the high grass, and in forty-five minutes we were so close behind him that several times we saw trampled grass springing back to position. In fact, we were so near our prey that the guides dropped back—way back.

We entered a small clearing in the buffalo grass, perhaps thirty yards long and no more than ten yards wide. We saw where he had entered the clearing, circled several times, then moved off into the heavy cover to our right. As we were looking at his trail, a twig snapped at the opposite end. The buffalo had circled us to attack from the rear. Immediately we released the safeties on our guns, and for several seconds we saw nothing but green shrub at that end of the clearing. Then, in an instant, the buffalo charged head-on from the spot where he had lain concealed.

I raised the Weatherby, but through the scope all I could see was buffalo hair. I couldn't tell if it was head, haunch or leg, so I decided to hold fire until he was too close for me to chance missing with the only shot I would get at him.

Meanwhile, Norm raised the shotgun and fired from about nine yards. The heavy buckshot caught the buffalo's face and left eye, turning him sideways. This brought the animal into perfect position for me, and I squeezed off a shot that caught him just under the ear. He was dead before he hit the ground.

"That buffalo crashing to the ground was the most beautiful sound I've ever heard," Norm said.

I agreed.

The eighteen-hundred-pound carcass provided a bit of fresh buffalo meat for three hundred appreciative people in the village. The natives thought us brave, rather than stupid enough to track a crazed buffalo through the grass. Norm and I appreciated that.

The elaborate plans for the dedication of the maternity complex included dignitaries from the government, the mission and the surrounding villages. I made a short speech and presented the keys to the medical director. I still have a copy of my remarks, which recalled our discussions regarding the location of the complex and touched on the recently established timetable for Independence.

At another time, I stood here and when I looked I saw only a big tree. It was a very good tree. It gave good food and cool shade. A baby-clinic was held under the tree. Many sick people came to Vanga, but the buildings were not adequate to hold them all.

The only place large enough and level enough for such a new building as this was where the tree grew. The good tree became a bad thing, and we had to remove it.

When the tree was removed it left a hole deeper than I am tall, two meters. We couldn't just throw in loose dirt and build a solid foundation on it. We had to build the rich cement and solid rock foundation from the bottom of the deep hole, so that we could build a building on a solid foundation that would hold a good building. It was hard work! It cost a lot of money! But there was no other way

Some people said, "Just fill it with dirt. Do it the cheaper way." We did it the hard way! We spent the money and paid the price. Now the building has a solid foundation. I have the keys to this new hospital. It is finished. We workmen are proud of our work. I will turn the keys over today to those who will save lives and protect the health of many people. That is why the money was given. That is why this hospital was built.

The Congo is building a foundation now for a new nation. I believe the Belgians were like the tree. They were good, but they have to go to make room for growth. The Congo must build a strong foundation of durable material. They can't build it on loose dirt or mud and expect to have a strong nation. You of the Congo must pay the price; you must work hard. There is no short or easy road. Some day you must stand and hand the keys of a new nation to your children. If your foundation is strong and on solid ground you will have good schools, good hospitals, good government.

There is only one solid ground on which to build. Go deep into the love of Christ. Throw away all the trash. He will strengthen everything you do.

With the maternity complex completed, I assumed that things would slow down a bit, though I should have known better. Everyone even remotely connected with the mission came up with the same story... Now that the maternity is done, you can (a) fix this thing you have been promising, or (b) build this facility you have been promising, or (c) start this project we have been waiting on, or (d), or (e), *ad infinitum.*

It was time for a vacation!

Congolese leaders grew impatient with the slow process promised by the Belgians and began making demands for immediate independence. Patrice Lumumba issued an ultimatum demanding that the Belgians leave and turn over the reins of government to native leadership. But this seemed to center in Leopoldville, so we were not uneasy about leaving the station and making our way to Kasai province, far into the eastern interior. There we could see Sharan at Lubondai and vacation at Lake Munkamba, where many missionaries had built vacation cottages. The Reverend Norman Riddle and his family joined us.

We crossed the Longi River in the usual manner. The river, some three-quarters of a mile wide, had shifting sand bars that made it necessary to drive out into the water, following the Bapendi natives who waded ahead searching out the shallower spots. Their bodies, covered with red camwood powder, and their hair, done up in heavy mats of mud, seemed like something out of the old Frank Buck movies, but they led us successfully into the middle of the river, where the water was deep enough for the ferry to operate. It was always a memorable two hours, crossing the Longi.

The second night we stayed at Tshikapa, which bills itself as "The Diamond Capital of the World," an impressive title for the few houses and company-owned hotel, store and filling station. The third day we drove through Luluabourg and reached our lakeside retreat late in the afternoon.

One recreation in that area is hunting crocodiles.

Two Presbyterian missionaries, John Miller (a doctor) and John Davis (an agriculturalist), invited us to share in this excitement. Dolores didn't much like bugs, let alone crocodiles, but she joined us about eleven o'clock at night as we took a small motorboat down the Lualuaba River.

We men wore headlamps powered by a twelve-volt battery that Dolores tended in the bottom of the boat. The lights shone across the water, catching and reflecting a crocodile's eyes. Miller and I stood in the boat, he with a high-powered rifle and I with a harpoon-type contraption. Davis maneuvered the boat slowly toward an immobilized croc hypnotized by our lights.

"When we get up to the crocodile I will shoot it, and at the same moment you must harpoon it," Miller reminded me. "Even with a good shot they take quite a while to die, and unless the harpoon is set, that's the last you'll see of that croc."

I looked at my equipment. My harpoon was a length of gas pipe fitted with a detachable head. A wire cable was attached, linking the harpoon head to the boat. "This certainly should hold him," I said.

"Crocodiles don't take kindly to being shot and speared," Miller continued. "They do a lot of thrashing around and make deep dives. That's when we need to be careful that he doesn't overturn the boat. Being in the water with a wounded crocodile is no fun."

"Maybe I should have stayed at the cottage with the Riddles," Dolores murmured.

I was bending over the edge of the boat, ready to set the spear when Miller fired. Water and various crocodile parts splattered over my face, and I could not see where to throw the harpoon. The croc quickly disappeared from sight.

"That's a croc all right, buddy," Miller said to me. "Maybe you should handle the gun and let me have the harpoon."

After we exchanged responsibilities we continued on the river until I spotted a real monster. I could tell by the distance between his eyes that he was far larger than any we had seen up to that point. I directed John Davis slowly toward the glowing eyes, until we were no more than ten feet away.

"Get the blazes out of here!" Johnny Miller shouted. "That's a hippo, not a crocodile!" I surmised that I was rapidly losing status as a crocodile hunter.

We did bring in two crocodiles that night, and gave them to the natives. They relish the meat, and the hides brought a good price at that time. But as much as they appreciate the feast, the natives are overjoyed at the loss of even one of their most dreaded and deadly enemies.

The only part we did not give them was the gallbladder. This is prized by the witch doctors, who attribute great potency to it and use it in their magic. We made sure they were removed and destroyed.

We spent three delightful weekends with Sharan on this vacation. Central High School at Lubondai was only fifty miles away. We drove in to pick her up each Friday and left the lake at five o'clock on Monday mornings to return her for 8:00 A.M. classes.

On our last scheduled weekend we kissed Sharan goodbye at the school and drove back to our camp. All along the way we saw natives with their faces and bodies painted, carrying bows and arrows and spears. We supposed they had been having a tribal dance, so we waved and spoke to the men, and they responded with equal friendliness. The true cause of the war paint was revealed to us when we returned to the lake.

"Oh, there was an all-out war," the buxom Belgian woman who ran the store there told us. "The Lulua tribe attacked the Baluba, burning several of their villages. As near as anybody knows there were about four thousand people killed."

"Is this related to the Independence movement?" I asked.

"It may be, or it may have grown out of their longtime animosity," she said. "In any case, travel is unsafe and the authorities are trying to restore order."

I knew a little of the history of these tribes.

Generations before, the Baluba people had been sorely harassed by other tribes, and fled to this area. The Lulua allowed them to stay only on the condition that they become virtual slaves, a circumstance which the Baluba reluctantly accepted in preference to returning to their homeland. Later, when missionary schools started, the Lulua held themselves aloof from such contamination; only children of the Baluba attended. The natural result was that the educated Baluba gained positions of authority in the local government and in the sparse industry in the area. So the Lulua resented the prosperity of what they considered the low-class Baluba, and the Baluba still harbored ill feelings over the way they had been treated over the years.

"All the roads have been closed," the storekeeper told us. "You'll have to stay here at the lake until things settle down."

"We didn't plan to leave until Wednesday," we told her. "It should be all right by then." But, of course, it was not all right by Wednesday, or the following Wednesday or the Wednesday after that.

The fighting continued. The Lulua were still on the rampage, and the Baluba were making them pay a heavy price through their own determined defense. Daily the Lulua sent word that we shouldn't be there and should leave. They said they were going to come to the lake and burn everything because it belonged to the missionaries, who were the real cause of the trouble.

"How can they blame us?" Dolores asked.

"Because the missionaries really are responsible in a way," I said. "When the missionaries came to this area they insisted that the natives send their children to school. The Lulua wanted none of that, so they said, 'Send the Baluba kids; they don't matter anyway.' Then the educated Baluba became the nurses and teachers, the government employees, everything. One day the Lulua woke up and said, 'These people are our slaves and here they are, running our lives.'"

"The Lulua should have gone to school themselves," Dolores said.

"Of course they should," I said. "But you've been here long enough to know that these people don't always make the wisest decisions. Now they are convinced that there is no way they can reason with the Baluba; the only way they knew to handle the situation is the way they did. They planned this attack and thought they could kill all the Baluba at once."

"What are we going to do, Scotty?" she asked.

"Norm and I have talked it over and decided that the first vehicle that comes through will be our signal that it's time for us to leave. We're going to load up the carryall so that we can make a run for it at a moment's notice. Is that all right with you?"

"Whatever you decide," she said. This was not just acquiescence on her part, but a pattern of our lives. On certain things she trusted my judgment totally, and on other issues I had the same confidence in her.

We packed the carryall and it sat for days, awaiting the moment we would call it to action. That time came on a Thursday afternoon, some 2 1/2 weeks after the fighting broke out. It was a very scared Belgian who related driving through an area of burning villages and hundreds of frightened refugees jamming the roads. But he had gotten through!

We threw the last-minute things in the carryall and headed for Luluabourg on the same road by which the Belgian had come. Within a few kilometers we came to the first military roadblock. The soldiers reluctantly gave permission for us to continue at our own risk.

From this point on, it was as though we were driving through a Hollywood set for a motion picture on tribal warfare. People were grouped everywhere. Every man and boy had a weapon: knives, spears, bows and arrows, and a few old muzzleloading rifles. One burned-out village was still smoldering, red sparks flying from what had been the heavier timbers in a roof.

Every village had sentinels walking in lines around its circumference. The tips of their ancient weapons had been freshly dipped in deadly poison. If a man carrying one of these weapons accidentally scratched himself with it, he probably would die.

By four o'clock that afternoon we arrived at the mission headquarters at Luluabourg. It looked like a refugee camp.

"My advice is to get as far from Luluabourg as possible and do so as quickly as possible," Mr. Haverstadt, the mission secretary there, advised us.

"But we've just gotten out of Lake Munkamba. Certainly this couldn't be any less safe than there," we protested.

"No," he said, "you'd be in far greater danger here. We are positive that tonight they are going to hit our mission."

"Which side?" we asked.

"It could be either side," he answered. "They're both mad at us because we've been helping anyone who came here injured. Now both sides think we're favoring the other."

"Any suggestions as to where we should go?" we asked.

"Try to make it to Tshikapa if possible. They have a hotel there, and probably there is no fighting in that area. That's largely Bapendi area over there. With the diamond mines there you can be sure that they'll have plenty of security, anyway."

"Can we at least get a drink of water?" we asked.

"Certainly," he said, "but I wouldn't suggest you take time for anything else."

We hadn't even gotten out of the vehicle at the location where we had intended to spent the night. Later we learned there had been a major action that night in which many men died, many women and children were taken and more than fifteen hundred homes burned.

As we made our way through the night's darkness toward Tshikapa, I noticed that the roads were even worse than usual. I saw one particularly bad hole ahead and a lot of junk in the road—logs and rocks. I began to slow down so as not to break a spring. I had no more than touched the brakes when both Dolores and Von Riddle screamed, "Don't stop! Don't stop! Keep going!"

Safely past the hole, I turned briefly to them. "I had no intention of stopping. What's the matter with you two? Are you flipping out?"

"No, we're not flipping out," was the answer. "But we're not so sure about those wild-eyed natives on both sides of the road. Didn't you see them?"

"No," I said. "I didn't see anything. I was watching the junk in the road."

"The headlights picked them up," the women said. "They had spears and everything ready to throw at us."

I passed it off with a laugh, but the next day we learned that one of the leaders of the Lulua tribe had been ambushed and slain at that same spot. Apparently when they saw our vehicle on the road, they thought it was their target.

The next day we thought we were out of the area of conflict, but discovered conflict of a different and less traumatic sort. Norm was driving and ran over a pig that was accustomed to sharing the road only with goats and chickens, not motor vehicles.

Immediately our carryall was surrounded by frenzied natives who banged on the fenders and screamed that their world had come to an end.

Norm and I got out of the car and saw two men lying in front of the wheels of the carryall. "Go ahead. Drive over us, too," they wailed. "We might as well die that way. Without our pig, we certainly will starve to death."

By this time the whole village had assembled.

"Who does the pig belong to?" Norm asked.

They looked around and picked the most pitiful, scrawny little man in the village. "It belonged to him," they insisted. Then the designated owner sat down at the side of the road and began an outstanding performance of a man crying his eyes out.

"Without my pig we are doomed," he wailed. Then he looked us directly in the eye and informed us that doom could be forestalled if we paid him the equivalent of fourteen dollars.

"You know the regulations," Norm said. "The driver of a vehicle is not responsible for an animal killed in the road. We offer you nothing."

Needless to say, the negotiations carried on for a good hour, and at the end of that time we had negotiated a much lower price and were the proud owners of a freshly slaughtered pig carcass. We shared the good news with the women.

"You're not putting that pig in this car!" Dolores was emphatic.

"The bargain has been made," I told her. "We get to keep the pig, and we'll roast it tonight or when we get back to Vanga."

"You can just go back and bargain some more," Dolores said in the tone of voice I had long ago learned to recognize as ultimate finality.

So the bargaining started all over again. After three-quarters of an hour they happily settled for one dollar and the pig. They were already planning a village feast as we left. We parted the best of friends.

Back at Vanga, it seemed that settling into the routine again would be our real vacation.

At my desk at General Telephone in 1952.

Our family shortly after arriving for our first term in Africa.

Dolores helps find clothing for the children.

Johnny enjoys his new life and new friends.

Johnny's 'Companion' taught him many new skills.

Our sand pit at Boko.

Some sand came from the river.

All lumber was cut by hand saw before it could be carried out of the forest.

Rocks were carried up from the ravines.

The large rocks were broken up by our workmen.

Mixing aggregate for making concrete block.

One more block is done.   The block is laid in the sun to dry.

One by one the supply of blocks grows.

Clay bricks form their own kiln before firing. After five days of burning, the bricks are red and beautiful.

89

The first building we finished was the High School at Banza Manteke.

Graduation ceremonies at Banza Manteke.

The muzzle loaders would have been a good start for a small museum.

At the end of the hunt a portion of meat is placed on each gun, whether or not that gun was fired.

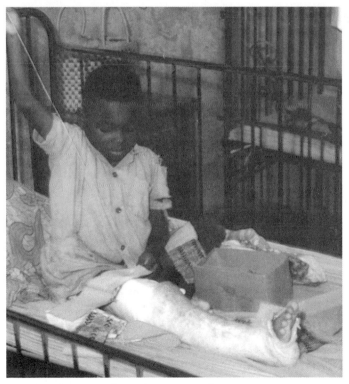

A polio patient in the pediatrics ward at Kimpese.

A *bac* on the Kwango river. Every trip required many river crossings.

Chief Ndinga making an official visit to Boko.

This was the hospital at Boko when we arrived.

Johnny began learning building trades at Boko.

Trinity in the Congo was copied from our church in Santa Monica, California.

An interior view of *Trinity in the Congo.*

The DC3 which evacuated us in 1960 was uncomfortable, but no one complained.

Musiti Paul's wife and the baby he delivered by Caesarian section.

CHAPTER 10

Vanga—1960

Fighting in Kasai province intensified. Mr. Shepard, the principal of Central High School, decided in November that conditions warranted sending the children home early for Christmas vacation. And what a holiday season it was!

We brought out the artificial tree we had used for years, and decorated it. The angel with its fiberglass wings finally looked comfortable in its place on the uppermost branch. We missionaries rejoiced in the certainty of our faith and the camaraderie of kindred spirits. Then, on New Year's Eve, all the women and older girls dressed in their formals, the men dressed up as much as possible, and we welcomed in 1960 with joyful celebration, much prayer and even more concern for the future.

"For all the challenges we have had in the past, 1960 very well might prove to be our biggest challenge yet." Wes Brown looked over the small group of men as though he were beginning a sermon on evangelism. "It isn't just the usual things we'll continue to do and the usual problems we encounter in getting them done. As Belgium grants independence to Congo next June 30th, it will affect our work in ways we can't imagine now."

"If we can't imagine what the future holds, then let's just concentrate that much more on the work at hand." Dr. Osterholm, like most of our physicians, was more pragmatic than philosophical.

"I agree with Dr. Osterholm," I added. "Whatever trouble we have to face, we'll deal with when the time comes. Doesn't the Bible say something like, 'Don't worry about tomorrow until it gets here'?"

"Not exactly," Don Deer answered. "It says, 'Take no thought for your life, what ye shall eat, or what ye shall drink; nor yet for your body, what ye shall put on.' But that deals more with materialism than it does with planning." Don was a linguist, translating the Scripture into the Kituba language, so none of us questioned his accuracy.

"There's no way we can plan for a future we can't define, and there's no way we can go into the future without planning." Norm Riddle, as usual, put into words the dilemma we all recognized.

So we discussed the work before us in the coming year: a year shaped by momentous events over which we had no control.

But the days of our lives are not filled with momentous events. Rather it is the succession of countless routine and seemingly insignificant happenings that continue on until their flow is interrupted...

Duki arrives with two truckloads of supplies: 130 sacks of cement and 6 1/2 cubic meters of lumber to be unloaded and stored.

The native leaders decide that two midwives needed at the Boko station will not be given permission to leave Vanga.

Both trucks have to be repaired before they can be used again.

Twenty desks for the school are taking shape in the carpenter shop.

Two residences for teachers are completed this week.

Amid an epidemic of snakes, we kill five around our house in four days.

Dolores is teaching Johnny at home—not so easy when he prefers to be hunting with his pellet gun.

Nlandu George comes in the middle of the night, telling us that his wife has miscarried, so we take Dr. Osterholm to his house in the village.

Sharan returns to school at Lubondai.

Don Deer wants his front porch screened in.

Emily Keyes wants six new classrooms for the elementary school, but has only $140 for the project.

The native leaders at the council meeting demand to know when the missionaries are going to quit shirking their duties and dig toilet holes for them.

The malaria medicine, *aralen*, has a bad effect on me and I vacillate between despondency and unexplained anger, until I realize the cause and switch medicines.

The diesel generator quits functioning, so I take it apart and find the cylinders are frozen. I repair it and put it back together, but it doesn't work.

Johnny is baptized by Pastor Pambi along with 330 others.

Kamitatu, organizer of the P.S.A. party, and his entourage come to

Vanga, where they hold a daylong political rally.

Trees are cleared and the foundation poured for a new eighty-bed hospital ward at Vanga.

We buy two sacks of potatoes at Kikwit, and for the first time in three weeks we have potatoes.

Mail is delayed this week. The truck carrying it speeded onto the *bac* at Leverville, hitting a pickup truck, which was knocked off the front of the *bac*. Then the mail truck went off the back of the *bac*, sinking the ferry. A second truck was dispatched, picked up the mail, but overturned between Leverville and Vanga. A third truck picked up the load, but the chauffeur got lost and has not been heard from.

The diesel generator is taken apart and reassembled again. I don't know enough about diesels, but this time it works.

Kibungu hands me a letter he has written out in longhand. The letter says he needs an advance on his salary to buy his family out of slavery.

What was that again?

The Congolese think an important message should be put in a letter and handed to a missionary, as there is a supernatural power to written words that spoken words do not carry. The letter Kibungu handed me read:

> Mister:
> Much trouble to me and little happiness this day. I beg you. This day I come a little bit to you, mother and father, for I am your child. I have come into difficulty this day. There at the village they are torturing us, or our women, because we are in slavery to the center of that village. And now we must take ourselves from slavery. They demand from us $220 and a sewing machine. But among us there are only three men. The situation gives us terrible trouble. We can see no happiness.
> I beg you - you can help in this matter. You can help by giving me a salary advance of $24. If God, my chief, is with me in three months I will finish this obligation.
> You can help please.
> Your child,
> Kibungu

I looked at this tall, handsome young man before me, feeling a mixture of shock and doubt. My workmen used all kinds of ruses to get advances on their salaries, but Kibungu was different, and had been

97

different from the first day I met him. I trusted him, and yet this story was so far-fetched it stretched my credulity.

"Kibungu, we are friends," I said. "If you have a problem you can talk to me about it. You don't need to give me a letter."

"I know, Tata," he said. "But it is difficult to talk of."

"Well, for Pete's sake, try," I said. "How could you be a slave to anybody when you work for me?"

"Many years ago when my grandmother was a child her father owed a debt of six dollars which he could not pay." Kibungu's eyes roved over the dusty ground as though he could read his family history in the dirt. "So to settle the debt he gave my grandmother to be a slave."

"But that's your grandmother," I protested. "Your letter says that you are all slaves."

Kibungu looked up at me with an expression that seemed to suggest that a white man was very dense when it came to understanding certain things. "That is the center of the problem," he explained. "Grandmother has twenty-one descendants and we are all healthy and strong. Her owner has only seven descendants and they are weak and sickly. He had decided that my grandmother put a curse on him and his family because he owns her and her family. Now he wants to kill her because of the curse."

"Then why the money?" He was right: certain things are very difficult for an American to understand.

"My brother and my cousin and I went to him to beg for grandmother's life. Finally he agreed that he would spare her and give us all our freedom if we would pay him the equivalent of $220 and give him a sewing machine."

This was too bizarre for me to handle. "Let me shell peanuts with Pastor Pambi," I said. At least that would give me a little time to think and digest this incredible tale. As I was leaving I turned back to Kibungu. "You work for me and I pay you a salary. What happens to that?"

"Tata Scott," his eyes were again on the ground at his feet, "all the money I make and all the money my brother makes and all the money my cousin makes belongs to the man who owns our grandmother. He provides us the food he thinks we should have."

I shuddered at the thought that what Kibungu was saying might possibly be true.

"Tata Pambi," I began as I sat in the pastor's study, "I have a problem. Kibungu is one of my most valued workmen. He is unlike any of the other workers. The rest of them are content for me to tell them what to do, and they do it. But Kibungu always wants to know why things are done in a certain way. He wants to know why we use reinforcing steel and why we mix cement in the proportions we do. He wanted to learn drafting, so I set up a table on my veranda where I could teach him after work."

"Yes," Pambi smiled. "I have seen him sitting there, bending over the table, long after the others have returned to their villages."

"He wanted to learn accounting, so Dolores taught him simple accounting. He wanted to learn about laying out buildings, so I taught him that. Now he can lay out a building exactly as I want it, and when I check his work it is always perfect. I trust him completely when I give him a job."

"Then what is the problem?" Pambi smiled.

"This," I said, handing him the letter. "This I have trouble believing."

As Pambi read the letter his expression changed from its usual warm and friendly mien to that of a person who sees a family secret finally coming to light. His voice was flat as he handed the letter back to me. "Yes. This is true."

For a moment I sat speechless. "But why...? How...?" I stammered.

Pambi returned my stare, his eyes now saying what his voice could not, and I realized anew that there are depths to the African culture that no foreigner could truly penetrate.

"Why would he give the whole family their freedom when they are giving all their salaries to him?"

"Independence," Pambi answered. "It is rumored that when Congo gets its independence all the slaves will be free. This man is not so dumb. He is putting pressure on the family now so that he doesn't lose everything."

"But would he actually kill her?" I asked.

"You know he would," Pambi answered. The sadness in his eyes spoke for itself.

We were able to buy Kibungu and his family their freedom, and he continued to be my valued helper and friend for years. Later, he went into business for himself in Kinshasa as a contractor and was as successful as I was sure he would be.

Freedom for slaves was not the only expectation accompanying Independence.

The graves of family members were decorated with the expectation that Independence would bring about their resurrection and those raised from the dead would be on hand to fight their enemies.

Some natives buried pots and cans filled with leaves, having been promised by aspiring politicians that when Independence came the leaves would be turned into money and they would all be wealthy.

Rumors circulated that all white people would be killed, even that certain people had been chosen to carry out specific assignments. One such story had a cook assigned to kill the woman he worked for. When she asked the cook about the truth of that story, he was purported to have answered, "Oh, no, Mama, I couldn't kill you! Tata Minu will kill you."

Whether or not that story was true, any doubt about the seriousness of the situation was dispelled when one of my workmen came to tell me I was in big trouble.

"What do you mean, 'I'm in big trouble'?" I asked him.

"They had a trial at the village last night and you were found guilty."

"Guilty of what?" I asked.

"Oh, you killed a goat."

"I never killed anybody's goat," I protested.

"But you were found guilty last night of shooting a goat."

I searched my memory and drew a blank. The nearest thing I could come up with had happened months earlier, when a goat strayed into Dolores' flowers and I used Johnny's BB gun to drive him out. I asked if that was the incident.

"Yes, Tata. You shot the goat, and you *could* have killed him."

I tried to find out more about this, but all I could learn was confirmation that a trial had indeed taken place and that the guilty verdict was in. Beyond that, nobody was talking.

As usual, when events didn't make sense to me, I turned to Kidiela. "Can you find out what happened?" I asked him.

"I know what happened," he answered. "They had a trial at the village last night and each of the missionaries was found guilty of an offense."

"But why?" I asked.

"Because if there is trouble when Independence comes and the people are not able to protect you, they will be free of guilt. They will do their best to keep you safe, but if they can't then the fact that you have all been tried and convicted will relieve them of responsibility."

"That doesn't make sense to me," I said.

"But it makes a great deal of sense to them," Kidiela answered.

The intertribal war in Kasai proved to be the first of many such outbreaks. Longstanding rivalries and hatreds intensified emotions fanned by impending independence. Rioting in Stanleyville resulted in the death of some twenty people. A military patrol in Leopoldville was ambushed, leaving several people dead and the city again under martial law with a dawn-to-dusk curfew. But the bloodiest and most gruesome fighting continued to be in Kasai, where frequently people were dismembered before they were killed.

Without discussing it between ourselves, Dolores and I each decided independently that Sharan should be sent back to the States for her senior year in high school. When Sharan returned from school in May, we learned that she also had been thinking along the same lines.

I wrote to my brother, Leon, in Hutchinson, Kansas, to explore whether or not he and his wife would allow Sharan to live with them and finish her last year of school there. Of all the people in the world, he was the one who could be the role model I wanted for her. Leon's reply was enthusiastically positive, and we made plans for Sharan to return in August.

Independence was set to take effect on June 30, and before that, elections were held across the Congo to choose leaders for both local and national councils. Patrice Lumumba was the most popular spokesman for an independent Congo, as far as we could tell, though his obvious ties with the Communist Bloc gave us great concern. The next most popular candidate for national leadership appeared to be Joseph Kasavubu, a Bakongo who was more inclined toward the West.

Two men on our Vanga station were running for minor offices, and they almost drove me crazy wanting vehicles to take them to one village or another for their campaigning. We could not disregard such requests completely, but these distractions were a real nuisance.

For those of us raised in America, with our long tradition of voting booths and secret ballots, the Congo elections were a marvel to behold. In this election the officials went from village to village recording the votes of the electorate. They assembled the people of the village and called out the tax number for each man and boy on record. Each voter had been given a slip of paper. Since few people could read, each candidate's picture was on a separate box. If a person was present when his number was called, he dropped his slip of paper into the box of his choice. His preference was noted in a book carried by the officials. Given the general illiteracy of the population and the inexperience of the country in holding elections, it was probably the best method at that time. Yet we wondered if the process did not open itself to all kinds of abuses. Still, we were gratified that the party of Kasavubu made such a strong showing.

We missionaries went to bed on the night of June 29, committing ourselves and our work to the Lord's keeping with even more immediacy than usual. Over half of the missionaries on our station had received notices that they would be killed during the night and the station would be sacked. Unbeknown to us, our Congolese leaders placed guards around the houses of each missionary, and throughout the long night of uncertainty they stood their posts, prepared to defend us with their lives if necessary. But, thank God, such sacrifice was not needed. The threats proved false, and Vanga ushered in Independence Day with great joy, relief and celebration.

The church service marking Independence Day was overflowing with people in the beautiful spirit of the day. After church was dismissed, a huge crowd gathered at the house occupied by the single women, singing and praising our missionaries. It was a happy day for us, with no reports of incidents anywhere; but news comes slowly, and we prayed that the rest of the new nation experienced as much happiness and no more trouble than we had.

The Congolese leadership declared a six-day holiday in celebration of Independence. The politicians announced that the workers would receive full pay for these days, and all we had to do was come up with the money to fulfill their promise.

CHAPTER 11

Vanga—July, 1960

We resumed construction on the hospital wards as the Independence holiday ended. It was an X-shaped building with twenty beds in each wing, providing maximum attention to the patients with the most efficient use of the staff's time and energy. I was pleased that we were still on schedule in spite of the distractions. Reports of serious trouble in other areas came in over our radio, but nothing seemed to be developing around Vanga. Perhaps, I thought, we had overrated the dangers Independence posed to us and we could maintain a normal routine. Still, to be on the side of caution, we kept our radio working overtime.

When mail is unpredictable, telephones nonexistent, and travel torturous, radio becomes the primary means of maintaining contact with the world beyond the station. Each station had a transceiver, and we always had a scheduled time in the morning when the stations would "check in." It was not unlike a morning coffee klatsch where business, general information and benign gossip was shared throughout our whole community of missionaries at all the stations. Our talk was relaxed and varied from missionary to missionary, some trying valiantly to adhere to the proper protocols of shortwave transmission while others were as casual and "gee whiz" in their style as though rules for the airwaves had never been developed. Our transceiver was powered by a generator made by the Manerheim Motor Works in Germany—a good machine but one intended for light use, not to be run for days on end. We certainly needed all the power we could get, as our station was on the edge of radio range from Leopoldville.

Chet Jump kept us posted on developments in Leopoldville and as much other news as he was aware of. He told us that expatriate women and children were leaving the Congo by the thousands. He informed us that Moise Tshombe, the newly elected premier of Katanga, had seceded from the Republic of the Congo and declared Katanga a separate nation. Situated in the southeastern section of the Congo, Katanga had more mineral resources than the rest of the nation combined. Shortly thereafter, King Kalonji led his tribe to secede, also. Such fragmentation reminded me of the Civil War period in America.

Less than a week after Independence, the Voice of America broadcast brought news that the military had rebelled in Bakongo and had overrun a Protestant mission station. This was the area in which Banza Manteke was located, where Dolores and I began our work, and it was the first violent incident involving our mission in the western Congo.

That afternoon Chet Jump came on the radio with instructions that missionaries at the three stations in the interior (Vanga, Kikongo and Moanza) go to Boko, where we could be evacuated by helicopter. He suggested that we each call in our African headmen and go over such details as were necessary to turn the work over to them. Then he gave us the news we were all praying we wouldn't hear.

Our station at Banza Manteke had been attacked by a band of drunken, renegade soldiers who beat the men and violated a couple of the women. None of our people were killed, due to the courageous intervention of some of the young Congolese men on the station. They confronted the military at the risk of their own lives. Chet informed us that all the missionary personnel in the southern Congo had been evacuated to Leopoldville by helicopter. Not only did we share the shock and sorrow of our colleagues there, but this was the first attack on one of our stations, and it brought home to me, in a way nothing else had, the likelihood that a similar attack could be imminent at Vanga.

Soul-searching is such an overworked term it has lost its impact, yet no other word exists to describe the agonizing conflict inside me. I knew that if drunken soldiers came to our station we men would be beaten up, but that was not important. What was important was that our wives, the two single women, and the young girls would face far worse than a beating. Sharan was sixteen at the time, the oldest of the girls on our station, but none would be too young to escape assault.

During World War II I had served in a forward unit and we were proficient in combat, from the defense of our base to hand-to-hand. I had my .300 Weatherby rifle and an automatic shotgun, with hundreds of rounds of ammunition for each. I had no doubt that I could hold off two truckloads of drunken, undisciplined Congolese military. I lacked neither the means nor the restraint to kill as many men as necessary to protect the women and girls.

But...

Ah! There's always a "But."

For more than seventy-five years, our missionaries in the Congo had sacrificed their lives for the cause of Christ and His church. They suffered tropical diseases, endured separation from their children and loved ones, saw their wives and husbands through agonizing deaths, and yet they had kept coming, these giants of the faith who had planted where we were now reaping.

One shot fired by a missionary at a Congolese, no matter how justified, would undo everything that sacrifice had accomplished. Could I take that responsibility upon myself?

But on the other hand, could I stand by and see our wives and daughters ravished without doing everything in my power to prevent it?

Each of us who had responsibility for a particular area of the work called in our headman for consultation. We explained that we would be evacuated and that they must take charge of the work. I chose Tata Zaya not only because of his abilities, but also because he was a native of the area, whereas Kidiela was of the Bakongo tribe and so might be in danger himself. I showed Zaya where we kept the money for the payroll and gave him the key. Dolores showed him briefly how the records had to be kept. We asked him and his family to move into our house after we left, use the food on hand, the clothes we were leaving, and the chickens in our backyard. Whatever we left—everything except one change of clothing for each of us—was his to use as long as we were gone.

Then I asked Duki to take Tata Kapini and Tata Ngunza in the 7 1/2 ton truck to Kikwit to buy food for the Congolese on the station. If Duki could get to Kikwit and back, we would be able to evacuate to Boko in the morning. I also gave him a letter to mail, a copy of which is still in my files:

Dearest ones:

Five days have passed since our last letter. Not much chance of this letter getting out, but we want you to know that as of now and during these days our only trouble has been just like yours.

Worry about loved ones. We know you have been anxious. We have listened almost continually to the radio stations of all the Congo missions. To the best of our knowledge all have been safely evacuated except the American Baptists and British Baptists. It has been a dramatic, very emotional time for us to listen to all these things and not be able to help where help is needed. Our friends John Davis and Mark Poole of the Presbyterians were able to move most of their missionaries to large airstrips, where they were picked up and taken out by Navy and Air Force planes from the good old U.S. Our stations have no landing strips and of course road travel is out of the question, because all our stations are set in this vine-work of rivers where there are no bridges... We cannot help but feel very sorry for those who have left not only their life's work but also everything that they have in the world. As of today 20,000 whites have left Congo during the last week. We missionaries want to do whatever would be best for the work and the Congo Church. This terrible decision with all its ramifications can only be made here and by us. If we leave, the work could and would suffer greatly. However, if we stay and are forced into uncompromising situations, the work might suffer even more.

At noon today the Belgian military forces took control of Leopoldville and in so doing had to kill one or more Congolese soldiers. The result of this action for the average Congolese was an immediate and most frightful release of hate against the Belgians. The Congolese have had this hate stored up in their hearts, seeking any likely reason for release. Today's action gave them their reason, and so now we are even more concerned than before. Of course, what this means is the first giant step toward black against white.

We are very happy that the United States did not send troops as requested. This would have been a great mistake. The United Nations can possibly help in this situation and keep the Congo from becoming a pawn. If you have been trying to follow the thinking of these leaders, you can see what we have been up against for the last seven years and can probably understand some of the things we have told you.

...Our mission radio transmitters are the last ones on the air. We are able to follow closely the developments by means of our radio. We have all the crew at work on the new hospital. It's going pretty well. All we know is that worrying will not help even the least little bit. This is a mess and everybody involved,

106

Congolese, Belgians, or whoever, needs all our prayers and yours.

We are attempting to send a truck to Kikwit today in order to get some food for the Congolese. If the truck can get through, this letter can get at least that far. We understand the postal department is not working.

Love,

Us

Duki and the others returned empty-handed.

"The roads are closed by large trees, which they cut so as to block off all traffic," Duki said. "We will have to go out with saws and cut the trees up so we can remove them and clear the road."

"I think not," I said. "If we stopped the vehicle and got out to saw up the trees, we would be totally vulnerable to anyone who attacked us."

That night all the missionaries on the station met and agreed that we should remain where we were for the time being. But that forced us to think through how we would respond in the event renegade military invaded our station.

I proposed that we put the girls and the single women in the attic of one of the houses. This house had an attic door that swung down from the ceiling and was opened and closed by being pulled on with a rope. The refugees would be instructed not to make a sound, regardless of what might happen below them. I knew that if the rope was pulled up out of sight, the soldiers would never guess that a hiding place existed right over their heads. We would leave our wives and ourselves at the mercy of the military and in the care of the Lord.

"You think I'm going to allow myself to be used as a sacrificial lamb?" one of the mothers screamed at me.

"Think of the girls," I replied.

"Never!" She shuddered from the terror of her thoughts. The tension of these days was brutal for all of us, and it was obvious that she would never be able stand up under such debasement. It seemed to me the only solution, but I had to recognize the sacrifice I was asking the women to make.

We could not reach a consensus as to what we would do in the event of attack. The thought was never far below my consciousness, and it became unbearable as I cradled Dolores in my arms that night.

Any remnant of optimism was shattered as the radio picked up conversations from Kasai province. A Catholic station had been overrun, the priest murdered and the nuns raped. Units of the military were rebelling against their Belgian officers, and all discipline vanished. Freed from all control and intoxicated as much by this strange Independence as by the alcohol they consumed, the soldiers went berserk. They had been promised that after Independence they would have everything the white man had, and to them this included the white man's houses, cars, possessions, and women. One native newspaper had carried a story suggesting that after Independence it would not be a crime to rape a white woman.

We also monitored a radio network from a mission in Kasai run by a different denomination but with the same purpose and problems as ours. We would hear them go round-robin with their reports:

"We're finally organized here and we're going to leave in ten minutes and try to make it to the border. We're going off the air for the last time."

"'Visitors' just arrived on our station, so if you don't hear from us in fifteen minutes you probably won't hear again at all."

One station always came on with the same concern. "Well, now, have you read the missionary manual? What are we supposed to do in a situation like this? What does the manual say?"

One by one the stations went off the air as the missionaries fled. The last voice we heard from that network was the station still asking, "Is there anybody out there who has read the missionary manual?"

As other reports of slaughter, rape and rampage came in from the interior, the Europeans, and particularly the Belgians, accelerated their exodus from Leopoldville across the Congo River to Brazzaville. But these were mostly the families of merchants, managers, industrialists: people who had been attracted to the Congo because of the economic incentives it offered them. We believed that the missionaries were viewed in a different light.

Then, Vanga radio went off the air. The overworked generator had held up valiantly but finally reached the limit of its endurance and quit on us.

"Leopoldville will think we've been overrun, won't they?" Dolores asked.

"Probably," I answered. "But since we didn't alert them of 'visitors' on the station they may guess we have transmission problems." I dug into the problem, overhauling the generator, but the hours of radio silence dragged on menacingly. When I finally had it reassembled and gave the 'Go' signal, it sputtered back to life with a reassuring rhythm just in time to bring in the voice of a stranger calling us. We acknowledged his call.

"This is Monsieur Leo. We have been concerned about your

silence." The voice was distinctly American, cultured and precise. He obviously wanted to broadcast no more identification than the phony name.

"We're nervous, but so far everyone is well and healthy," we assured him.

"Your uncle has been concerned about you," M. Leo said. "He wants you to know how urgent it is that you come visit him."

"We love our uncle and miss him terribly right now. We want to see him as soon as possible, but we just can't get away at the moment," we said.

"Let me talk to your uncle and see if there is any way he can come to you. I'll be back on the air as soon as I can."

Soon M. Leo was back on the air, telling us that a bird with many wings would fly to our station but that the bird only liked people, not things, so we should say goodbye to anything that would not fit into one carry-on. We understood the message: a helicopter was coming in to pick us up but no luggage! Each family hastily packed a carry-on and we waited for the helicopter.

We waited and waited.

The only news we got that day was discouraging. Fighting had broken out all around us and all the *bacs* were under rebel control. Moanza and Kikongo stations informed us that they were leaving for Boko. They could do this since neither had to cross a *bac* to make the trip.

The next day M. Leo was on the air again, telling us that the bird eats too much food for the trip. We understood his message: we were out of range for the helicopter to fly from Leopoldville to Vanga and back without crashing in the jungle when it ran out of gas.

"I feel like a bride who has been left stranded at the altar," Maurice Entwistle bemoaned.

"Well, stay at the altar and your lover will be there as soon as earthly possible," M. Leo said.

These days were like no others I had ever experienced. Work on the hospital wards continued. Someone was monitoring the radio twenty-four hours a day. The women, realizing we would have no long-term need of our food stores, one way or the other, dug deeply into their hoarded treasures to fix the most exotic meals possible. We shared these scrumptious meals with little appetite. Dr. Osterholm brought sleeping pills for everyone, knowing the terrible tension we were under.

"Scotty, I'm not going to take any more of those sleeping pills," Dolores told me the morning after taking her first one.

"Why not?"

"Well, they make you dopey and groggy. If something happens, I want to be alert enough to deal with it," she answered.

Each day brought news of the fighting drawing nearer and nearer. And each day brought its promise of evacuation, only to be followed by disappointment. Our connection now was with Radio Blue, a collection of British, Americans and Belgians in Brazzaville.

We were told that a helicopter on its way to us had been shot down by rebels.

One day I was informed that a sea plane could be brought in from Germany if there was a place to land on the Kwilu River. Radio Blue asked me to measure how long a straight stretch of river was available for landing and to get a reading on the current. However getting the sea plane from that distance proved impractical.

The Congolese devised a last-ditch solution, if needed: they would take us by canoes across the Kwilu River and inland to Tata Kapini's farm, where we could be hidden.

In the midst of this, I received a delegation from a neighboring village. Heading the large procession was the village chief in his finest regalia. His worn, black suit coat extended well down the ceremonial cloth draped around his waist.

"Tata Scott, there is a buffalo with the *rage* which is terrorizing our village. We know of your prowess as a great hunter and you will come with us to kill the buffalo." The banality of the chief's request struck me as humorous, coming at such a time.

"I'm sorry, but it just isn't possible for me to go now," I told him.

"You don't understand, Tata Scott." The chief gave me the steely glare that had no doubt served him well over the years. "I did not come here to ask you to accompany us. I came here to tell you that you will accompany us." He smiled to take some of the bite out of his words, showing four gaping, yellow teeth that had never had dental attention.

"No, it just isn't possible," I insisted.

"Look, Tata," the chief said patiently, "I am a chief of the village and I have walked this distance to summon you. If it were not a matter of the utmost importance, I would have sent a messenger for you. If I come this far and you refuse me, I will lose face with my people."

I understood all too well the importance of maintaining face. "You are a chief, but you have a chief higher than you, don't you?" I asked.

"Of course," he said.

"And you must do whatever your higher chief orders you to do?"

"Of course."

"Well, I also have a higher chief, and he has told me to stay here until he comes to take me away."

"Ah, yes," the chief smiled again and the wrinkles in his forehead gave him a corregated look. By using his position on the status ladder, I had allowed him to save face.

Another day two trucks drove up filled with shouting Congolese. This was normally the first warning of trouble with the military, so I told Dolores to stay inside while I went to see what was going on. Maurice Entwistle was already on the radio anouncing, "We have visitors." I had no more than stepped outside when I was joined by Pastor Pambi. If there was to be trouble, he would not allow me to face it alone. However, on approaching the trucks I recognized some of the natives from a village not far away.

"What in the world are you doing here?" I asked.

"Oh, all the *mindele* (white people) have fled our village and they left the trucks, so we are just out joy riding."

The radio continued to report intensified fighting in the population centers, and we kept those centers posted on the reports we got from the interior. A blood bath swept across the country as tribal hatreds, personal grudges, individual thrill-seeking and long-simmering resentments against the colonialists found expression in the most barbaric forms of violence.

One woman was raped repeatedly by a band of soldiers while her three companions were held helpless. A fourteen-year-old girl watched her sister being ravished by another band. Another woman was attacked while she held her three-month-old baby in her arms.

Stories of evisceration of live captives made the rounds. No form of humiliation prior to mutilation was too obscene or too brutal to be omitted in this frenzy of savagery.

Each report made me waver just a bit more in my resolve that the future of the mission must take precedence over our welfare.

Then, after some two weeks of uncertainty, Radio Blue informed us of a final plan to evacuate us. A C124 from a U.S. military base in Germany was bringing one of the largest helicopters made. The helicopter would be reassembled in Brazzaville, then make a hop to an intermediate point between Brazzaville and Vanga, where it could offload fuel. Then it would return to Brazzaville, refuel and take extra fuel on board to make the trip to Kikwit. Meanwhile, a DC3 would fly over Kikwit with Belgian paratroopers, who would drop and secure the airport. The cargo plane would bring in more fuel for the helicopter and then take all twenty-eight of us to Brazzaville. The helicopter would bring us from Vanga to Kikwit, but its load limit had to be strictly observed and would necessitate at least two trips to take us all. We were instructed to determine everyone's weight and be sure that the load limit was not exceeded.

I designed a form on which to record each individual's weight and started making the rounds.

"We need to know how much you weigh," I told the wife at one of the missionary houses.

"You must be crazy," she bristled. "I'll never tell you how much I weigh."

"I don't give a hoot how much you weigh, but I've got to have it for this," I said, holding up the form.

"Well, I'm just not going to tell you."

The solution was to take a pair of scales to each house and have the occupants record the total weight of the family and the weight of the luggage. This produced the following:

Trip #1	Kilo
A. C. & Peggy Osterholm	149
Mrs. Entwhistle & 4 children	165
Rev. Brown, Wife & 4 children	218
Rev. Deer, Wife & 1 child	160
Luggage	65
Total	757

Trip #2	
Rev. Riddle, Wife & 3 children	230
Engwall & Nickerson	137
Mr. Scott , Wife & 2 children	213
Rev. Entwistle	63
Luggage	108
Total	751

That evening I made a most difficult decision. I took the firing mechanism out of my Weatherby and put it aside, where it could not be found by the military should the weapon fall into their hands. But neither could the weapon be fired by me.

There was little sleep that night as we awaited evacuation, and the next morning a jubilant air of expectancy pervaded the compound. The joy drained from us when we heard a transmission from the helicopter.

"Vanga, we're going to have to divert our mission. We are being fired on by rebels with high-powered rifles." It was pushing human patience to the breaking point to be this close and face another disappointment, yet it was essential to remain calm on the radio: we never knew whether a band of rebels might be listening, and we dared not show weakness or lack of resolve.

One of the missionaries standing by the radio began shouting in Kikongo, "They're shooting at our helicopters. We'll never get out of this alive. We're all going to die." I grabbed him and put my hand over his mouth.

"Shut up!" I ordered. "We don't want that kind of thing going out where it could be monitored."

Meanwhile, Maurice was speaking into the microphone as calmly as though it were the most routine communication imaginable. "Yes. We understand that message. Come back on the air when it's convenient."

The station radio was located in a small room I had built under the water reservoir. Maurice manned the transceiver twenty-four hours a day, Judy bringing meals to him in the cramped quarters.

While we were waiting for our people with the helicopter to make a decision, Musiti Paul, Dr. Osterholm's male nurse, called the doctor to the hospital to examine his wife. She was overdue in her pregnancy and Musiti was worried.

Musiti Paul was one of those truly exceptional men found in every culture, with insatiable curiosity and outstanding intelligence. Over the years he had stood beside Dr. Osterholm during surgery, assisting as directed and absorbing all that the doctor taught him. It was said that when they operated, it was as though a pair of white hands and a pair of black hands were connected to the same brain.

Dr. Osterholm determined that an immediate Caesarean section was mandated. Musiti's wife was being prepped as the helicopter finally landed.

"This is our only chance," Dr. Osterholm looked into the face of his friend and colleague. "I must go now or I can't go at all."

"But my wife," Musiti pleaded.

"You can perform the surgery, Musiti. You've been through it enough times."

"She will die if I operate on her," Musiti said.

"She most certainly will die if you don't." The doctor turned, left the hospital and was the last to board the helicopter, not knowing when or if he would see his friend again.

When the helicopter returned for the second load the pilot asked me, "Is there anyone here who has any high-powered rifles?"

113

"Yeah, I've got a .300 Weatherby back at the house that I sure hate to leave," I said.

"For God's sake, go get it while I'm gassing up," he said. "When those guns fall into the rebels' hands they wreak havoc with us. They use them to shoot at the helicopters."

I turned to go but had another thought. "Since I'm going down there, Don Deer has a three-hundred-year-old cello that means the world to him. It doesn't weigh much but it's bulky. Do you suppose we'd have room to take it, also?"

"Sure," the pilot said.

Barbara Deer had told me that she left her wedding and engagement rings at their house above the sink. "If you happen by the house, would you pick them up for me?" she said.

I couldn't think of anything that better summed up the haste with which we made our last-minute preparations, nor could I imagine a better way of putting "things" in proper perspective.

I looked down at the station for the last time as this angel of mercy carried us on the first leg of our flight to safty. The buildings that had occupied us for these two years seemed somehow smaller and less significant. What was the value of the buildings without ministry going on inside them? Would they still be standing when we returned? Would we ever be able to return to this turbulent nation? If God called us back, would we be as ready to respond as when we first came?

Then my eyes swept over the jungle surrounding the station, its treetops looking like an endless display of broccoli. If there had been a landing strip, I thought to myself, we could have flown out by light plane. If I had had a plane, I could have evacuated the station myself. If it is God's will, we will have landing strips at each of our stations, and we will have a plane. A plane would turn wasted days of travel into a few hours in the air and allow us to do the work we came here to do. I knew then beyond any doubt that it was God's will for us to have a plane available.

Brazzaville had hosted a flood of refugees, overtaxing its resources to care for them. Since we were the last group of expatriates to leave the Congo, the only food available was K-rations, which the plane crew shared with us. We slept on the Tarmac under the wing of the C124 that night. Then we were flown to Casablanca, where we were reunited with other of our missionaries. For all the discomforts, not one complaint was heard.

The newsmen were awaiting our arrival and took dramatic pictures of disheveled and haggard missionaries disembarking from the plane. We had not bathed or changed clothes for three days. The men had not shaved and the women wore no make-up. As unkempt as the photographs portrayed us, we felt even more so.

The next leg of our evacuation took us to the Azores. The military wives at the base did everything possible to help us, from cooking meals to entertaining the children so the women could get some rest. Our wives used the self-service laundry and washed the clothes we had worn. We were fed, rested and put back on the cargo plane for our final leg to Andrews Air Force Base at Washington, D.C.

Our experience with the newsmen at Casablanca was not pleasant, so we determined that we would not arrive in the U. S. in the same condition. There were no restrooms on the C124, only a bucket curtained off in one corner of the cavernous interior. There were jerry-cans of water and a supply of Dixie Cups. The women performed their cosmetic rituals with these limited facilities, and the men shaved with cold water in the paper cups. All the men put on ties; the women wore the best they could manage; and the children each received a last-minute hair-combing. We felt much more presentable for our homecoming.

As we were on our final approach to Andrews, the plane suddenly gained altitude and veered away from the landing strip. "What now?" we wondered. "Is it possible that after all we've been through we have a problem with the plane just as it's getting ready to land?" But the only problem was that the newsmen did not have their cameras set up properly, and the control tower instructed our pilot to make another pass at the airfield to allow them more time.

CHAPTER 12

Santa Monica, California
1960-1961

"Home" took on a new meaning for us all. Visits with families followed, to reassure them where possible and to comfort them where necessary. A sense of security seeped back into us, though we avidly followed the tragic news from the Congo. Gradually, life resumed its more normal rhythms, and we returned to Santa Monica to await developments.

One of the first things I did was to write a detailed proposal for our board, explaining the many reasons why we should have light aircraft on our mission field and detailing the way in which landing strips would be built at each of our stations. The response from headquarters was a flat and outright rejection of that idea. Years earlier, a mission in the Congo had a light plane, and two missionaries had been killed when the plane crashed in the jungle. Unlike the United States, there are few alternatives for emergency landing areas. Either the plane reaches its destination or it crashes in the jungle. Our officers did not deem it prudent to accept such risk.

I said, "OK." Then I enrolled for flying lessons to get a private pilot's license.

The Mission Aviation Fellowship came to my attention. This wonderful organization provides aviation services in third world countries where missionaries are located. I sought out their offices in Fullerton,

California, and met Grady Parrott, the man who could make something happen if anyone could.

"We're always open to survey the needs and possibilities of serving on any field," Grady said. I sensed a warmth to his personality that matched his commitment to this phase of the Lord's work.

"Grady, you have to be there to believe how difficult travel can be. We waste days and days making trips that are absolutely essential but which turn into nightmares." Memories of harrowing travels flooded my mind as I talked. "Medical emergencies are a real concern in areas as remote as Vanga, particularly. If someone needs attention beyond what can be provided on the station, they are subject to the torture of a truck ride. It's brutal."

"Let's get some details down on paper," Grady said. In addition to giving him all the names, addresses and locations he asked for, I continued to pour out our needs. It was well beyond the intended interview time when I finally left his office, confident that I had made a friend and that Grady would take my concern seriously. I was correct on both counts.

Before the year was over MAF had done its survey, arranged for a landing strip to be built at Vanga, and stationed Wes Eisemann and John Strash, their pilots, at Leopoldville. Of course, MAF served the missions of all denominations, not just ours, so there was more than enough to keep them busy. Within months their services were expanded until they finally had three planes and pilots in service there. Their contribution to the success of the mission endeavor can never be overstated.

Dolores and I shared a great concern about the famine that so often plagued the Congo and the malnutrition that was a constant part of life. The protein-poor diet consisted mostly of starches. Generations of inbreeding the few goats and pigs the natives raised produced animals that were woefully inadequate by American standards. Crop failures were frequent. There were many crops that would grow well in Congo but had never been introduced there. Other crops, such as pineapple, avacado and citrus, grew well but were not produced commercially.

The culture also militated against improved practices in food production. Gardening was women's work; the men devoted themselves to hunting, thinking and talking. When food was grown it was grown to be eaten by the family, not by some animal that should be out fending for itself.

Medical services and agricultural support were the two greatest needs for these people. The medical aspect received considerable attention, but little concern was evident for food production. We made it a continuing part of our prayers that a way be found to alleviate the hunger permanently. We did not anticipate much of a building program if we could return, so perhaps we could be involved in this.

Then we learned of an organization called Congo Polytechnic Institute, referred to as CPI. This was the outgrowth of a crash program instituted by the council of all Protestant churches in the Congo, and was in the process of pulling together several million dollars in support of a variety of programs. With the loss of European expertise in all fields requiring technical knowledge, it was imperative that Conoglese be trained immediately. Doctors, lawyers, scientists, technicians and, yes, even agriculturalists were needed.

This was encouraging, and we rejoiced in a program designed to be implemented across the whole of this new nation. But we had little hope that it would have any immediate impact on the remote areas where we had struggled to find enough food to nourish our workmen and their families, let alone the entire deprived population. Still, we brought this organization to the attention of our headquarters and prayed that it would be successful.

Not long after we returned to Santa Monica, The American Baptist Men of Southern California asked me to serve as their executive director. I agreed to fill in until they could select a permanent leader. We had no idea how soon we could return to the mission field, and this provided an excellent way for me to use my time in the interim. The training would help me in working with the men in the Congo, and at the same time I could interpret missions for fellow laymen here in the States. The work proved to be one of the most satisfying experiences I have ever had. It involved a great deal of travel and speaking, as well as administrative responsibilities. The staff, the board of directors and the men in the local chapters were delightful to work with and were responsive to my suggestions. They raised no objections to my continuing with flying lessons, even though it occasionally conflicted with the job. Still, considering the number of nights and weekends taken up by the work, the job received more hours per week than our agreement called for. When we were ready to return to the Congo, after almost a year as interim executive I was asked to accept the post on a permanent basis. But many men could provide effective leadership for the organization, and there was no one else ready to pick up our work in Africa.

Events in what was then called The Democratic Republic of the Congo flooded the daily news. President Joseph Kasavubu urged the

United Nations to help stabilize the situation, and the U.N. sent in troops from countries that were not represented on the Security Council. Patrice Lumumba, the premier, resented the U.N. troops, criticized the West and was dismissed by Kasavubu. Lumumba fled to the Equatorial Province, where Antoine Gizenga had set up a secessionist government supported by the U.S.S.R. Joseph Mobutu led military forces to put down that revolt. Lumumba was arrested and later sent to Katanga Province, where he met his death. Moise Tshombe, president of that secessionist state, had declared a temporary truce with the central government and was suspected of arranging Lumumba's murder. The great powers of the East and West were maneuvering both overtly and covertly to influence the political, military and economic direction of the Congo's future. UN Secretary-General Dag Hammarskjold died in a plane crash while trying to ease the crisis. Fighting, violence, rebellion, slaughter, pillage and mutilation continued to flow like toxins through the veins of this nation being born. Yet there was never the slightest question that we would return as soon as possible.

For us that event came in early August of 1961, as we flew from the comfort of America back into the turmoil of the Congo.

CHAPTER 13

Vanga—1961

The first Congolese we saw on our return gave indication of the changes that had taken place and to which we would have to adjust if we expected to remain and work there. He was the customs inspector, a youth no more than seventeen years old who obviously held the position because he was the son or nephew of some official. His manner was officious and totally ineffective. He took pains to demonstrate that the Belgian working with him was his flunky.

But far more than work assignments had changed.

The road from the airport into Leopoldville had been a beautifully landscaped boulevard. Now it was unkept, littered with debris. Along the parkway squatters had built shacks from cardboard, scraps of wood and anything else they could find. The former European section had contained elegant houses with manicured lawns, but now these houses were taken over by families of Congolese who built their cooking fires on the front lawns and gave no attention to upkeep of the homes. The native sections of the city had suffered even more.

The main bridge on Boulevard Albert, leading to our mission station, had washed out almost a year earlier, and no repairs or replacement had begun.

UN troops, mostly Swedish, were everywhere in their blue berets and white vehicles. Nigerian soldiers directed traffic downtown. Not many vehicles, other than military, were on the streets. Congolese soldiers wore a variety of uniforms ranging from the ragtag to the elegant.

One of the first small tasks demanding attention was getting our driver's licenses. We heard horror stories of the unbelievable delay and confusion of the Leopoldville bureaucracy. One of the missionaries applied for his license, and when he finally got through to the official who would actually issue the permit he was asked for his former Congo license.

"It's still in The Kasai," he said.

"Then, give me your American license," he was told.

"It's in Texas."

Undaunted, the official began to fill out his form. "Give me a picture of yourself," he said.

"I don't have one."

"I can't give you a license without a picture on it," the official said. He thought for a moment, then opened a drawer to his desk, revealing bundles of photographs. "We have lots of pictures here. Pick out one you like."

The missionary finally convinced the official that he would prefer a photograph of himself on his license.

Changes were not restricted to the official bureaucracy. The Congolese police stopped motorists for the slightest violation and imposed a fine on the spot. Of course, no receipt was given, so it was obvious where the money went.

One of our colleagues was stopped for not using his turn signal.

"That is a most grave offense," the policeman informed him. "You will have to pay a fine for that." He named a sum that was the equivalent of thirty dollars, American.

"That's outrageous!" the missionary roared. "I'll not pay such a fine."

"Don't get excited," the policeman said. "That's just the starting price." By the time the missionary drove off, the price had been negotiated down to eight dollars.

Shopping in Leopoldville was the biggest shock of all. In stores where I had spent thousands of dollars no more than a dozen items were in stock, and none of it was building material. In the big American-type supermarket, *Libre de Service*, an entire row of shelves was filled with one case of food, all forty-eight cans spaced evenly along the long shelf. The prices were as high as the merchandise was scarce. The official exchange rate was sixty-five francs to the dollar; merchants would gladly give 100 francs per dollar for a check; and on the street 120 francs per dollar was normal. Chet told us that things had improved greatly over what they had been earlier. We were happy to spend only two weeks in the city.

No change in the city could compare with the wonderful change we experienced on the trip that took us back to Vanga.

Wes Eisemann, the MAF pilot, had already set up operations in the Congo. We boarded his Cessna 180 and flew out of Leopoldville. Forty minutes later we were over Boko, a distance that would have required one trouble-free day of travel by car or truck. Another forty minutes and we were making our approach to the airstrip at Vanga, formerly a tortuous and lucky day's travel by road. Our elation in saving at least two days of travel dispelled any apprehension we might have felt over the tight landing at the primitive airstrip.

Leopoldville had been depressing; returning to Vanga was heart-warming. Another missionary family, Morris and Judy Entwistle and their three children, had left Leopoldville by boat five days earlier and arrived at Vanga just hours before us. The Congolese at first did not believe that the women had come to stay; and when they finally accepted the permanency of their return, there was a second celebration.

Tata Zaya escorted us to our house. He saw the look on Dolores's face as she surveyed the living room, noticing the wear that had occurred in our absence. "We had a lot of company while you were gone, Mama," he explained. "Many times the soldiers and government people came and I asked myself what Mama would do if she were here. So I sat them down in the living room while I went to the kitchen to make coffee and fix refreshments for them."

Our bedroom, however, was exactly as we left it—except that our clothes had been freshly washed, ironed, folded and laid out neatly on the bed. Zaya had slept in the children's room, guarding our bedroom from any intrusion because African tradition does not allow anyone to enter the chief's bedroom. Zaya had gone without pay for many months, yet when I looked in a dresser drawer I saw a significant number of bills lying there in plain sight, money that had been overlooked in our haste to evacuate.

In the kitchen, Dolores asked if there was any boiled water.

"Oh, yes, Mama," Zaya said. "It's right here in the refrigerator, just the way you left it." Sure enough, the water she had put in the refrigerator more than a year earlier awaited her return. Nevertheless, she chose to have fresh water boiled and cooled before she had a drink.

Zaya retrieved the things he had hidden in the jungle soon after our departure. My automatic shotgun had been wrapped in oilcloth and was in good condition except for a broken spring. A barrel of kerosene and a propane "gas bomb" were also recovered from long concealment.

Other missionaries, on their return, reported similar care and protection of their possessions. It was the greatest affirmation we could have received from the Congolese of their confidence that we would return and their gratitude when we did so.

Only one truck on the station was operative, and except for the two gallons of gas in its tank there was no gasoline. The generator had broken down months before, so there was no power for the radio transmitter. Not that electricity would have helped the radio, because it also was broken and inoperative. Had it not been for MAF, we would have been totally isolated.

Work on the hospital wards had continued until the crew ran out of materials, so they stood, arrested in time and awaiting completion.

Musiti Paul was in the operating room. His wife and child had survived beautifully, as had the hundred or so other mothers and the children he brought into the world through Caesarean section during our absence. Nor was he limited to maternity procedures. He had accurately diagnosed cases of appendicitis and performed the necessary surgery. He amputated limbs and dressed wounds from battle, bottle and machete. He stood as the embodiment of all Dr. Osterholm had hoped he would become—and more!

Word of our return was spread by the drums, and hundreds of men were on hand the second day, ready to begin work. They didn't understand that work could not resume without supplies and that supplies were not immediately forthcoming.

Thus began our initiation into a new Congo. We experienced a mixture of joy, frustration, hope and hopelessness, but underlying all else was a renewed confidence that God had become real in the lives of these people, and we were called to bring that reality to many more.

Three nearly simultaneous arrivals gladdened our hearts; Dr. Dan Fountain and his family, the Reverend John Marshall, and the rainy season.

Dr. Dan, as we were all calling him within hours of his arrival, was certainly not an imposing figure at first meeting. He was scarcely larger than most of the Congolese, and it took some time to notice the strength in his hands and arms. An illness had left some of his facial muscles paralyzed, so his grin came out as more of a smirk than a smile; and the humor within him caused him to grin often. His dark wavy hair looked almost combed. Only his eyes provided an initial clue of the unfathomable depths and innate humanity in this man. His quiet and unassuming manner would not lead one to suspect that he

123

was soon to be named one of the Ten Outstanding Young Men of America by the U. S. Junior Chamber of Commerce.

John Marshall, on the other hand, erupted onto the station. He was a bundle of physical and nervous energy that I initially took for bluff and blunder. His new wife remained in Leopoldville while John completed an assignment for Chet Jump. John had gone all over Congo, inspecting and analyzing the agricultural situation before his last stop at Vanga.

"I came to Africa as an agriculturalist, Scotty," he said, fidgeting in his chair as though there must be a comfortable way to sit but that position constantly eluded him. "But it's hopeless!"

"Why do you say that?" I asked.

"I've been in Kasai, in Katanga, all over, and I haven't found anything to give me hope that the Congolese can ever become productive farmers. The Belgian government set up twenty-two agricultural training stations across the country, and out of all the men they brought in and trained not one returned to his village to apply what he learned."

"Gardening is women's work," I reminded him.

"I'm not talking just about the gardens. These people need livestock and grain crops."

"Are you going to continue your inspection around the Vanga area?" I asked.

"Of course," he said. "But I don't expect to find anything different than I've found everywhere else. When a tree dies they never ask why it died; at best they just plant another one. When a cow dies they look for the person who put a curse on it; they never look for the real cause."

"Those attitudes are deep in the culture," I said, "and you'll find them around here, also. But you'll find something else here. Our Christian men are willing to work their land. There are some pretty good farms and some fair herds of cattle—small but good."

"Oh, I'll look, but I'm sure not expecting much." His mouth tightened and the shake of his head tossed his wet-straw-colored hair in all directions. "Meanwhile, I need transportation. Do you have a vehicle available?"

"Of course," I said. "I'll give you a truck and a driver. William, the chauffeur, knows every road, rut and tree in this part of the country, so trust him when he says, 'You can't get there from here.'"

The rainy season began without prelude the night of Dr. Dan's arrival. Thunder rolled across the jungle like the sound of artillery and reverberated within our houses and our heads. Lightning split the darkness with blue-white tongues of fire. The rain poured from the sky faster than the parched earth could absorb it and then it kept on falling, cutting gullies in the yards, across the roads and over the landing strip.

We lay in bed, hoping the lightning would not strike our station, anticipating the work required to offset the erosion, but rejoicing that the dry season had ended and the greenness of new life was only days away.

Dr. Dan had been on the job for two whole days before he exploded. He had a difficult surgery that took late into the night, and he was still furious the next morning as he discussed it with us.

"I can't work with those mosquitoes," he said. "I spent as much time trying to keep them out of my eyes and off my sterile instruments as I did operating. Insects are everywhere. Bedbugs, sand fleas, you name it and they're there. There's no telling how much disease they are spreading in the hospital. We've got to have better screens and we've got to spray for all insects. Preventative medicine is far better than curative. I've got to have some DDT and a way to spray it."

Those of us seated around the table with our coffee smiled knowingly. Only one of the older missionaries had the personal prerogative to address the issue. "You'll find a spray that Dr. Leslie got when he was a young man here a long time ago. Then there's one that Osterholm ordered soon after he arrived," the old-timer said. "And there's the one that Carrie and Allan Stuart left here."

Dr. Dan was not perturbed. "Preventative medicine is both more reasonable and more economical than curative." He began a discourse that was to be repeated, enlarged and acted upon over the next decades. Before the day was over, DDT was sprayed throughout the hospital as never before.

John Marshall took off early in the morning in the truck, was gone all that day and returned the next afternoon expecting sympathy when he told his tale of woe. "We got stuck in a sand hole the other side of Bagata and broke an axle on the truck," he began.

"Oh, yeah. We know that place," we replied. "We've been stuck there before. It happens all the time."

Undaunted, John resumed his inspection trip the next day, taking a food box, an army cot, selected tools and a replacement axle out into the bush for the days necessary to study the agriculture around Vanga. He returned with an enthusiasm which, added to his normal effervescence, made him seem almost manic.

"There's nothing like it anywhere else in Congo!" he enthused. "These people lack a lot of skill, but they are already further along than anywhere else I've seen. More than that, they have a different attitude. The men are willing to work and they are eager to learn."

"So, what else do they need?" I asked.

"The best thing would be an agricultural school for them," John began. He went on to talk about new crops that could be introduced, experiments at the school that could improve the crops already grown, training in animal husbandry, even courses for the wives while their husbands were at school.

Our conversation went on far into the night, and as John talked I doodled on the paper before me, writing down snatches of ideas and sketching buildings and layouts. It was a beautiful dream but, of course, it was only a dream. Such a project would require more money than I had spent on all the buildings I had built in the last eight years combined. Much later we put the papers and the dream they represented in a desk drawer, blew out the kerosene lamp and went to bed.

Scrounging materials as best I could, we resumed work on the hospital wards. The walls were up and the roof was on; but we still had to have windows, doors, fixtures and furnishings, as well as perform all the finish work on the interior. If ever there was a time when we felt God's intervention, it was then. We would come to the very end of our materials, and somehow, somewhere we would get just what we needed to continue the work. A shipment would arrive unexpectedly by river barge. We would learn of available needed material in time for us to purchase and transport it. We were able to continue the work without interruption during a period of the most acute shortages imaginable.

But my presence on the job was interrupted frequently. With MAF providing air service, it was easier for me to get to Leopoldville and for Leopoldville to get Dolores and me there. Thus, when the school year began for our children and the houseparents had not yet arrived on the field, Dolores and I were "volunteered" for temporary duty. Not that we minded, as it gave us almost another month to be with Johnny.

Fighting, pillage, molestation and robbery still were rampant across much of the Congo, and the missionaries deemed it wise to educate their younger children on the mission compound in Leopoldville. There were seven boys that first year, and we set up two classes for them. I enclosed the carport on one of the houses and made it into a classroom. Another class was held in the Sims house. I rearranged space and built partitions for a hostel so there would be two boys per room with desks, bunk beds and closet space. From this modest beginning evolved the American School.

Even as I worked on the mission school in those weeks, I continued to think of the dream John Marshall and I had shared. I found myself fleshing out plans in my mind, arranging and rearranging buildings, adding and removing facilities. When I spoke with John, he indicated that he had been doing much the same. On returning to Vanga, it was only natural that we shared a bit of our dream with co-workers. When the Congolese learned what we had been dreaming of they became even more enthusiastic than we were. They insisted we come look at a parcel of land they thought would be ideal for the agricultural school.

The site they showed us was outstanding. Located just downstream from Vanga, it was bordered on three sides by river. By dugout canoe on the river it was only fifteen minutes away from the station, and if a road were built it would be only half an hour's drive. The land was fertile and would lend itself perfectly to farming.

John and I began drawing up a set of detailed plans. Of course, there was no funding available, and the project had never been suggested, let alone approved, by the powers that be. Still, we felt such a compulsion that I drew up a cost analysis of the project.

CHAPTER 14

Vanga—1962

Much as we might dream of building an agricultural school, other projects demanded our immediate attention.

The new hospital was nearly completed.

Miriam Fountain dropped her lipstick down the drain of the kitchen sink, and in trying to retrieve it for her I discovered that the plumbing had deteriorated to paper-thin dimensions, requiring a complete re-plumbing of their house.

Trucks continued to break down and demand repair.

A seemingly endless series of jobs, ranging from the trivial to the demanding, presented themselves almost daily.

But one job I undertook simply because I thought it was a good idea: I began building an airplane hangar at Vanga.

Chet Jump was returning to New York for a meeting of our Board of Directors with my renewed proposal that they purchase a small airplane for use in our program. MAF had proven the value of air transportation for us beyond any question, as far as I was concerned, and I was optimistic that our board might reconsider its policy. Word finally came back from Chet that the Board's decision was negative. They were adamant that they would not authorize the purchase of a plane. I had already begun building a hangar.

I had barely started this personal project when John Marshall suggested we go to Leopoldville. He wanted to explore the possibility of getting enough funding from the Protestant Council to make our dream of an agricultural school a reality. MAF flew us to the capital city, and we checked in at the Union Mission House. Two other men were already at the U.M.H.

"I'm Bill Carlsen and this is Dr. Hartzler," the younger of the two responded to our introduction. "We'd be delighted to have you join us for dinner if you have no other plans. We just arrived from the States today and would appreciate visiting with locals."

"We're meeting with the Protestant Council tomorrow but have nothing to do until then," we replied. "We'd enjoy talking to anyone who has stories we haven't heard a hundred times already."

"What brings you to the Congo?" John asked as we were seated for dinner.

"We're both Methodist laymen," Dr. Carlsen said. "We're here on a scouting expedition for an organization back in America."

"You both look too old for the Boy Scouts," I said.

Carlsen smiled. "It's a different kind of scouting we're doing. The Methodist Church set up a program called Agricultural Aids and it received excellent support across our denomination. Another of our laymen, Keith Smith, became very interested and through his leadership we have been able to plug in to government funding as well. Of course, we had to spin off from the denomination to receive the U.S. AIDS grant, so we are now called IPOC, *Institut Politechnique de Congo*. We are going to set up three agricultural schools here in the Congo and we're scouting out locations and facilities." John and I looked at one another with shock evident on our faces. "Did I say something wrong?" he continued.

"Not at all," John said. "We can help you with an ideal location near Vanga."

"Where is Vanga?" Dr. Hartzler asked.

"In Bandundu Province," I said. "About two days travel by surface but only an hour and a half by plane."

"Oh, that's out of the question, then," Dr. Hartzler said. "We are already committed to one school in the Equatorial Province and one in Katanga Province. We've made some promises for the other and it's definitely not in the Leopoldville area."

"Why not this province?" John asked.

"There are several reasons," Carlsen said. "Many of them boil down to politics, both within the Congo and within our organization. Another major factor is that we think we can rent facilities more readily in the other provinces."

"You plan to begin agricultural schools in rented facilities?" John asked.

"We have plenty of money for the three schools, but we also have a deadline to meet and it doesn't allow time for construction if we had to build from the ground up," Carlsen said.

"I wouldn't try to tell you how to run your business," I said, "but I doubt that you're going to find facilities to rent that will meet your needs. Beyond that, I'm a builder and I think you can build for less than you might think. In fact, John and I have talked about just such a school and I have a pretty good idea of what it would cost."

Now it was our visitors who looked surprised. "We'd like to hear your thoughts," Dr. Hartzler said.

"I've been all over the Congo examining the agricultural situation," John began. "The area around Vanga has the best, most fertile soil I saw anywhere. The people are aggressive in their attitudes. It's the only place I've found in all of this country where the men are willing to do the physical work demanded by farming."

"We have a major church center at Vanga." I picked up the conversation in what was beginning to sound like a prepared sales pitch. "The people there are responsive. We envision a school where young men from seventeen different tribes could be taught. Most of those men would be married and their wives would come with them to be trained in home economics."

"There must be training in management also." John's enthusiasm was beginning to feed on itself. "It isn't enough just to learn how to grow crops; farming is a business and we have to teach the business end of it also."

We continued sharing our vision with them and discovered that we had incorporated many ideas they had not yet developed, but which impressed them. Finally, Dr. Carlsen said, "Could you sketch out some plans and meet with us tomorrow at the IPOC offices here in Leopoldville?"

"I think I could have something ready by then," I smiled.

When John and I were alone I asked him if he knew these men were coming to Congo. "I not only didn't know they would be here," he said. "I didn't know such an organization existed."

"It's all fitting together too well for me to call it a coincidence," I said.

"Whoa," John cautioned. "Remember, they have already ruled out this area."

"Wait and see, John. Just wait and see."

The next morning at IPOC I unrolled the plans for the buildings while John brought out the written design for curriculum. Both were discussed in detail, and it was obvious that our planning put us months ahead of IPOC. Impressed as they were about our plans, they were even more impressed by the cost estimates I had so carefully worked out. I designed the buildings as I always had, saving every penny possible without sacrificing quality. The total dollars required seemed staggering to me but was a fraction of what they had anticipated. Still, I had a track record of building in the Congo that they could not question.

Two days of discussion left us at what appeared to be an impasse: They wanted to use our plans in developing their schools but were not inclined to develop a school in Bandundu Province; we were willing for them to have the plans, but we had a dream of our own that we would not readily forsake. As a compromise, we invited them to come to Vanga and inspect the area and the work being done there, and particularly to see the site we had selected. If, after their visit, they were still unconvinced, then we would be more open about letting them use our plans.

Again, MAF made it possible for us to move with the dispatch necessary. The single visit to Vanga sold our visitors on the desirability of that location. A quick return to Leopoldville via MAF, and the IPOC men had only to convince their headquarters to accept their decision. In less than a week we had authorization to build the Ag School.

The prize we won was miraculous, but the promises we had to make were frightening. IPOC would provide the funding for the buildings; they would provide all the machinery we needed, including tractors, trucks, tools, whatever was required; when the school was operational they would provide teachers for all the different fields on the curriculum and pay them for five years; they also would provide all the cattle, chickens, pigs, sheep and goats we needed. We happily allowed them to use our plans for the other two schools, but we also had to commit ourselves to have the school in operation in six months.

I realized only too well the magnitude of that promise. There was no road to the site, so we would have to cut a road through fifteen kilometers of dense jungle, building a bridge across the Masangu River in the process. Workers could get to the site immediately by canoe or jungle trail, but the road would have to be finished before we could begin construction that required machinery. Then we must complete forty-four buildings in the time remaining before the deadline. I had achieved a small miracle by building forty-eight buildings during the first four years in Congo; now we had to complete almost that many in less than six months during one of the worst material shortages we had known. My usual optimism was stretched to its limits, and only my faith sustained me. On the positive side, I recognized the value of the experience I had gained, the excellent crews already trained and the availability of as many willing workers as I wanted to employ.

We began work on the road immediately.

But I also continued building the hangar. The concrete floor cured, the side walls came up, and the roof grew protectively over the structure. On the day it was completed, I stood back to survey this strange building. Strange because it held so much empty space to shelter a plane that did not exist. Strange because even then I could not explain why I had the compulsion to build it. Strange because... My reflection was broken by the sound of an approaching plane. It was not the MAF Cessna; this was smaller, with a higher-pitched voice. It came into view, circled the strip, made its approach, landed and out stepped John Davis, our friend from Lubondai. I admired the way he handled the little Piper Super-Cub, but it was a dejected man who greeted me.

"Hey, John," I called to him. "Man, you look tired. Let's go up to the house and find some refreshments."

"Thanks, Scotty," he said. "I'm more than tired. I'm beat!" When we were seated on the veranda, a cold tea in his hand, John began pouring out his troubles. "The fighting in our area has been fierce. The rebels have destroyed some of our mission stations. Federal troops mounted an offensive against them, and because I have a plane the rebels think I was a part of the action. Of course I had nothing to do with it, but that doesn't cut any ice with them.

"Then I was in Leopoldville recently and got mugged by four men. They stole eight thousand francs while they held a knife to my throat. That experience by itself was almost enough to make me want out of the Congo.

"But the real crunch came just today. You know we had a beautiful herd of cattle for my agricultural program, almost five hundred head. Well, the local big shot stole all the cattle. When I made an official complaint, he accused me of being an enemy agent and gave me forty-eight hours to leave the country."

"That's a crock," I said, and John smiled for the first time since arriving, remembering the crocodile hunt and the last time we had shared that expression. "But that's the new Congo. What are you going to do?"

"I don't have any choice," John said. "I'm leaving. That's why I flew over here. I want you to have my plane. It was ordered by Air Brousse for the Belgian mosquito-spraying program before Independence, but that program fell apart, of course. So they used it as an 'executive plane' and put just 160 hours on it before they sold it to me for a third of what it cost new. I've flown it for seventy-six hours since I got it. If you can manage it, I'll sell it to you for just what it cost me."

"Let me check on something," I said, and went into the house. A quick look at our personal checking account showed that we had just barely enough of our own money to pay for the plane. For the first and only time in our married life, I made a major decision without consulting Dolores beforehand. I drained our personal funds with the check I handed John, but within minutes I was the proud owner of my own plane. After John left I told Dolores what I had done, not quite sure what her reaction would be.

"That's OK, Scotty," she said pleasantly. "If you feel it's the right thing to do then I'm sure you should have bought it." I looked at this woman from whom I had asked so much over the years and who had not only stood by me but had carried a heavier load of her own than anyone would ever know. I realized anew that my understanding of her would never be as complete as my love for her.

One afternoon, a few days after I got the plane, Wes Eisemann flew in with the MAF plane. A severe storm was developing between Vanga and Leopoldville, so we invited Wes to spend the night and depart the next day in safer flying weather. He accepted the invitation readily.

"Since we've got some free time," I said, "how about helping me with some takeoffs and landings? I haven't tried to fly my plane yet, hoping you could check me out on it. I learned on a plane with a tri-pod landing gear and this Piper is a 'tail dragger.' I'm sure there's a lot of difference, especially with these rough dirt landing strips."

"More difference than you know," Wes said. "You have to learn how to get the tail up and the weight balanced on the front wheels soon enough to be airborne before you run out of real estate The same thing in landing, too. It's tricky, Scotty, and it's easy to make the kind of mistake you won't be around to repeat."

"Great, Wes," I said. "I knew you would help me."

Wes frowned at me. "I didn't say I would help you, I only warned you how dangerous it is."

"I don't get it, Wes," I said. "You tell me I could crash and then you won't help me avoid it."

His frown deepened. "I'll level with you, Scotty. Your Board wouldn't buy a plane because they know how risky flying is out here, but there's nothing they could do to keep you from buying your own plane. The powers-that-be have made it clear that we are not to check out any private pilots, and that policy was specifically reinforced in your case." He pursed his lips with the distaste of what he had to say.

"Sure, Wes. I understand. You've got your own rules you have to live with, and I wouldn't ask you to break them." I hoped my tone of voice was warmer than the chilling fingers of disappointment tightening in my guts. "I'll do it on my own." I walked off toward the Super Cub.

"Don't do it, Scotty!" Wes shouted. "You'll kill yourself!"

"Yeah, I sure might," I answered without turning. I climbed into the cabin, went through the pre-flight check, turned over the engine and began my rollout for takeoff. As I revved the engine up to max, I looked down the runway to see Wes walking toward me, directly in my line of flight. I cut back the throttle as he neared the plane.

"You're a flaming idiot," he said, opening the door and climbing into the back seat. "I ought to let you go ahead and kill yourself, but I don't want to see such a beautiful little plane smashed up."

Wes had been absolutely correct: takeoffs and landings on such a primitive strip in this plane bore little resemblance to those in the Cessna on the Tarmac back in Santa Monica. I would never have mastered it without his help, and I owe him a debt of gratitude for the risks he took that day, not only in flying with an inexperienced pilot but also in jeopardizing his own position with MAF. Time would justify both our decisions, but on that day he was moved more by compassion for me than concern for his career.

I had earned a U.S. pilot's license during our evacuation, and before the end of the year I cleared all the hassle to get a Congo license. The following spring I had my Congo mechanic's license so that I could do my own maintenance.

There is no way the rest of this story could have unfolded as it did without that plane. Securing materials in the face of severe shortages and the bungling of an inexperienced bureaucracy required frequent trips to Leopoldville. Were we still limited to ground transportation, it would have been impossible. With the plane, I could get my crew started in the morning, fly into Leopoldville and take care of business, and still be back in Vanga in time to inspect the day's work. But other events concerning the plane transpired that had little to do with construction but everything with advancing the cause of Christ.

December was a month of incomparable problems interspersed with moments of exhilaration.

In laying out the road to the Ag School and beginning the clearing, John Marshall and I both came down with severe cases of malaria. This should have consigned us to bed rest for several weeks, but it only made us ineffective and disagreeable to be around. I lost twenty-five pounds that month, and John fared no better.

Reports of atrocities throughout the Congo increased as local and national factions sought to gain power in the only way their culture had taught them. One of the Vanga nurses came begging for a truck to go rescue his brother. Disciples of Patrice Lumumba were holding the brother in chains in a village no more than seventy kilometers away. The clouds of violence were closing in on us again.

A delegation of dignitaries came to Vanga for formalization of the land agreement for the Ag School. A great deal of preparation is required for such people as Kamitatu, president of the province, and Ngalisi, president of the National Assembly. All work came to a halt during those days.

Christmas was a celebration never to be forgotten. The forced abandonment of materialism only enhanced the joy of experiencing the true essence of this most holy of days.

Leopoldville Province received more rain and flooding than anyone could remember, completely disrupting river freight and cutting off supplies by that route.

Then lightning struck the hangar.

As usual, I began the day with the crew that was clearing the road to the Ag School. Around noon, Tata Zaya and I started for the hangar to check on a crew I had working there. On the way, seeing that one of our trucks had broken down, I stopped to help the men repair its broken spring. We paid little attention to the rain. During the rainy season one comes to accept downpours such as we had that day as a normal part of the daily routine, though the lightning was crashing and cracking even more sharply than usual.

We had just finished with the truck and were again headed for the hangar when a runner came hurtling through the torrent toward me.

"Tata Scott," he gasped. "The hangar. Lightning. Many dead."

The scene that greeted us at the hangar was ghastly. The bolt had struck the hangar and the men in it, throwing bodies around with no regard for human frailty. Had we not stopped to help with the truck, Zaya and I would have been stretched out on the floor with the others. As always in times of crisis or near-crisis, the air was filled with the screams, shouts, moans and curses of the Congolese. Men, women and children were running every which way, aimless but unyielding in their pursuit of chaos.

We had driven by the hospital to pick up Dr. Fountain before going to the hangar, and he quickly surveyed the havoc. A twelve-year-old girl was pronounced dead, apparently killed instantly. Six of my workmen were injured, with Tata Taba the most serious, unconscious but alive. We loaded the injured onto the bed of the truck, shielded them from the drenching rain as much as possible, and hurried to the hospital. Most of the afternoon was spent working with Tata Taba, and by late afternoon we felt we could leave him in the hands of the

Congolese nurse. But just before dinner we grew concerned, so, along with Dr. Fountain, we returned to the hospital to check on him. His bed was empty. His clothes were gone. Taba was nowhere to be seen!

"Where is Tata Taba?" Dr. Dan demanded of anyone and everyone in sight. No answer was forthcoming. It was as though Taba had never been seen in the hospital. Finally, one of the natives caught Dan alone.

"They came and took him away to his village to treat him," the informer said. "They got a ladder from Tata Scott's shop and used it as a stretcher. They will give him the native cure for lightning."

We all jumped in the truck and drove to the village where they were preparing to "cure" Taba. One man had a hand-powered bellows, with which he was fanning a white-hot bed of coals. Stacks of wet, green leaves were placed over the coals. On the bed of leaves they placed a wicker chair, and on the chair they placed poor Taba. The natives were kind enough to bring chairs for us, so we had front-row seats for the proceedings. Smoke and steam rose from the leaves, encompassing Taba in a sweltering, smoky steam bath. Shortly, they broke a raw egg in his mouth and forced him to vomit. Suddenly, Taba sprang from the chair and was halfway through the village before being caught. We visitors decided that the function of all this was to make the victim so miserable he will swear he has been cured just to escape the treatment. At length, Taba had all he could take and avowed that he was cured. They then took away the chair and made him stand on the leaves, holding on to a frame above his head. The hospital gown billowed from the heat as his skinny legs and ankles directed his large feet in a new war dance.

A few days later, I was presented with a bill from the village witch doctor. According to the witch doctor, they had done the work Dr. Fountain should have done in curing Taba, so they wanted to be paid. Dan said that while what they did to Taba didn't hurt him and may even have helped in some way, Taba was out of danger before he left the hospital. In any case I was glad to pay the hospital and give the village wise man his fee: a chicken and fifty cents. The New Year began with at least something to smile about.

Cutting a road through the jungle and building a bridge over the Masangu River under those primitive conditions would stretch the credulity of most Americans. A crew of over one hundred men struggled daily against the jungle, with only axes and jungle knives for clearing and shovels and wicker baskets for moving tons and tons of earth. Yet by early January half the road had been cleared. Another crew of fifty men had sunk the pilings and built the abutment for the bridge.

Other crews were working to clear the site itself, to dig rock and break it into gravel for concrete blocks, to find and cut trees for lumber. Daily they made their way along the jungle path, carrying pitiful hand tools to accomplish their tasks. We had some five hundred workmen on the various crews, including those working at Vanga on the hospital.

It was most gratifying to see the progress but frightening to be reminded of the timetable. Paradoxically, for years I had been building in the Congo and operating on a shoestring, barely having enough funds to meet minimal demands. Now we had a project where funding was no problem, but we found it nearly impossible to purchase supplies. As many as four hundred men at a time showed up demanding work, but we couldn't use manpower without tools and materials. The men who did work for me proved over and over again their dedication to the project, their desire to learn, and yet also the impossibility of overcoming deep-seated cultural elements that too often proved counterproductive.

One Sunday morning as we returned from worship, a messenger was waiting to tell us that a barge was docked at the river, carrying twelve hundred sacks of cement for us. This was wonderful news because, as usual, we were nearing the desperation point with our cement supply. The prospect of having cement on hand for Monday morning's work was an answer to prayer.

I sent for Tata Norman Zaya, one of my headmen. "Tata Zaya," I said, "I want you to go to Songo village and round up the workmen. Have them come over and unload the cement. And you are to take charge!"

"You will be at the docks later, Tata?" he asked.

"No," I answered. "You are to be responsible for everything. You can direct the men. You know what needs to be done and how to do it. You are totally in charge." His broad smile showed his pride in the new authority I was giving him.

After Sunday dinner was finished, John and Gloria Marshall joined us for a relaxed afternoon. I was especially anticipating what I call *un jour à faire rien*, "a day to do nothing." Rare as such days were, this one held special promise of fulfillment.

John and I seated ourselves on the veranda, and the scene before us inspired me as it always did. Across the river the jungle rose rich and green, contrasting sharply with the swift and muddy water of the Kwilu River. The frangipanis were in bloom, and a gentle breeze engulfed us in their fragrance. Across our lawn, the land dropped off sharply toward the river, and looking down we saw the two huge barges and the tug that had moved them slowly up the mighty Congo River, then up the Kwilu to our dock. I envisioned it stopping frequently along the way at various villages, towns and stations to discharge or take on cargo.

We watched as Tata Zaya drove the big truck up to the dock and began a beautiful job of organizing the men. Even from this distance his lean, muscular body seemed to radiate his new sense of authority.

I leaned back in my chair, put my feet up on the railing and smiled. "John, this is a whole new day in Africa. You and I have worked together for a long time and we've gone through a lot of chaos. But look at this!"

"Yeah?" John grunted in reply, his own gangly legs draped on the banister as casually as mine.

"Sure! Here we are, sitting comfortably on the veranda. My crew is down there doing a job, supervised by Tata Zaya. This is the first time in all these years I haven't felt the need to be right down there in the middle of it. The men are completely organized. Look at them! They can take care of it."

"Yeah, they sure can," said John. "Take another look!"

My feet came down from the veranda rail and I was off and running down the hill as fast as I could go. Even on the way down I could see some busted heads and the bone sticking out of the broken arm of one of my men. On the deck of the barge men were fighting with fists, feet and anything else handy. Only the curses and shouts of the men drowned out the "thumps" and "whumps" of the blows landing. The captain of the tug wasn't trying to stop it, he was trying to help his crewmen. I waded into the middle of the melee, throwing my arms and fists in such a way that I may have bruised a few heads myself.

I was swinging away, trying to get the men separated and the fight stopped, when my feet hit a slick spot from spilled oil and I went sliding across the deck on the seat of my pants.

Back at the house, John saw me go down and assumed that I had been decked. He was at the barge in nothing flat.

I got up, found Zaya and John, and we finally got the combatants divided: our workmen on one side and the bargemen on the other, with us in the middle.

The captain was bruised and scared, and so were his men. No wonder! There were about ninety infuriated Vanga men against fifteen bargemen. We forced the bargemen toward the back of their barge, up the ladder and into the small pilothouse.

"John," I said, "you stand right here. Don't let any of the crew down that ladder, and keep our men away."

I sent those who needed it to the hospital, and I sent a message for our station leaders to come down to the docks. Whenever possible, the station leaders should see and hear for themselves what actually happened in events that could have repercussions for the whole mission.

I thought I was gaining control of the situation when another fight broke out. Two of the crew had hidden below. When it was quiet on deck, they assumed the fight was over and they could safely show themselves. They were wrong. Our men saw them and began beating on them. I walked into the middle again and got them separated, but not before the bargemen had been soundly beaten. I escorted the two victims back to the relative safety of their crew.

It is always hard to accept the savagery that lurks below the surface in Africa, ready to erupt at a moment's notice. Yet, in all this fighting not one man from either side ever hit or even shoved me.

Sweat poured down my face as I told John, "We've got to have this cement. That's more important than anything." John agreed.

Then I turned to my men. "If I hear one more word..." I left that sentence unfinished for their imagination to supply its ending. "We'll sort this out later. The important thing now is to get our twelve hundred sacks of cement off this barge."

Some of our men returned to the hold and began passing the bags of cement up from hand to hand. Men on the deck took the bags and stacked them for others, who helped the carriers put them on their heads and take them to the truck. At the truck other men stacked and loaded the cement for transport.

Dr. Dan Fountain, Musiti Paul, Pastor Nelson Pambi and Tata Ngunza arrived in response to my call. I told them what I knew up to that point. Then I called the workmen who had been most involved and questioned them one by one within hearing of the station leaders.

What had started the fight was easily understood by anyone who knew the Congo.

The barge was carrying a load of beer for Kikwit in the same hold with our cement. It had been a long, hot trip. The captain sent a few of his men down into the hold to break into the beer shipment and bring some of it up. These men served themselves first, lounging around the hold and consuming several bottles before taking the rest up on deck. Before long they were pretty well soused.

They started taunting our sweating laborers. Translated into English, it went something like this: "We sit here and drink beer and have fun and you guys have to unload cement. You're nothing but a bunch of bloody scum." That established a mood that was not conducive to peaceful coexistence in the Congo.

Heavy steel beams hold the hatch cover down when the barge is moving, and as the bargemen crawled out of the hold with the beer, one of the beams dropped on our men who were working down below. The beam hit one man on the arm, breaking the bone. This was the man I first saw with bone sticking out of his arm. The beam hit another man in the head, cutting a deep gash from his forehead to behind his right ear. There was a lot of blood from both injuries, and when blood flows that's sure to arouse emotions. Anyway, it was a hot day with boring work, and fighting is much more exciting than unloading cement. So that's how it started.

When the work was finished my workmen said to me, "Tata Scott, please let us kill those bastards. Just let us throw them off the barge and let them float down the river."

"No!" I told them. "Absolutely not!" I made my workmen get high up on the river bank, but I couldn't make them leave. They stood menacingly in the lengthening shadows, muttering threats to the bargemen who cowered around the pilothouse of the tug.

Only after the last sack of cement was safely off the barge did we allow the captain to come down. We told him, "You're responsible for this. Your crew started it. Some of our men had to go to the hospital, and you must pay their hospital bill. If any of your men require treatment they'll be taken care of, but you have to pay their hospital bills, too."

He said, "No. I won't send my men to your hospital. All I want is to get out of here. I will pay the hospital bills, but I'll never come back to Vanga again!"

I said, "OK. That's up to you. But you know your men were responsible for this."

Dr. Dan estimated the cost of treating the broken arm and the busted head. The captain paid him and got ready to leave, his ebony face a combination of fear, relief and hatred.

The captain ordered his men to cast off the heavy cables used to tie up to the dock. However, his crew were afraid to get off the barge to do it. He even pleaded with them, which was probably a first for a barge captain, but they still refused. I wanted them out of there as much as the captain wanted to be gone, so I told my workmen to cast off the cables. They obeyed, but they refused to do it right. The cable should have been fed back slowly to the men on the barge; instead they released it from the dock and dropped it, coiled, into the river.

Suddenly freed from the dock, the tug and barges were caught by the current and carried out into the river. They were crosswise in the current and floating toward an island before the captain could start his engine. By this time, the loose cable was entangled in the propeller.

Mad as I was at the captain, I couldn't help but sympathize at least a little. Here he was, crosswise in the current, his propeller hung up with his own cable, drifting toward an island as darkness fell, and with a drunken crew to top it off.

As the setting sun brought a close to that day, I thought, "Perhaps this really wasn't a new day in Africa, after all."

Sometime later I got a convocation (a summons to appear in court) for commandeering a barge. I went to the officer in charge and told him exactly what had happened. Then I said, "You should be thankful we acted as we did or you would have had a worse problem on your hands. If I had not commandeered that barge, the men of Songo would have floated corpses down the river." That's the last I heard from the court.

The captain did bring his barge back eventually. When he came he brought gifts, and his men walked a fine line all the time they were docked at Vanga.

CHAPTER 15

Vanga—1962-1963

Our daughter, Sharan, met and fell in love with a fine young man while attending college in Kansas. Jerry Wheaton was the product of a long line of Christians and leaders in our denomination. He and Sharry planned their wedding for June of 1962, and that presented a dilemma for us. We could not leave our work without great loss of momentum, and certainly we would miss the deadline for completion of the Ag School. On the other hand, Sharry was "the apple of our eye" and we did not want to miss her wedding.

Dolores and I agonized over this and finally proposed an alternative. It would cost no more to fly them to Congo for their honeymoon than for us to fly back to the States for the wedding. This plan would give them a memorable trip and allow us to have more time together. We wrote to them with this suggestion and anxiously awaited their response. With that settled, in our own minds at least, we turned our attention back to the work.

One day Dolores punctured her ankle with a stick while visiting at the Ag School site, and the wound became badly infected. Tata Mbidika saw her soaking her foot in hot water.

"Mama," he said, "you need the fat of a *boma* for your ankle. The *boma* does not bite, so his fat will heal you."

Before she could protest that she didn't care all that much for snakes and having a part of a boa constrictor, even a dead one, wrapped around her leg was not an appealing idea, he was gone. He found one of the native teachers who had the desired material "in stock" and returned just moments later, handed me the messy glob with instructions on how it should be applied, and assured us that by morning the ankle would be fine. I remembered that in my Kansas childhood we used a poultice of bacon fat to "draw out the poison," and decided it could do no harm. Sure enough, by morning the swelling was gone and the ankle was well on its way to healing. It was just one of several times we came to appreciate that many of the native cures had more than superstitious effect.

While the airplane saved far more time than anyone could imagine and made it possible for me to accomplish more than ever before, it also had a way of encroaching on the daily agenda. Just as a medical emergency cannot be put on hold, neither can a fellow pilot who needs help.

John Strash, the MAF pilot, landed at Vanga with two passengers. "I'm flying in from Lubondai, Scotty, and I stopped to see if I can gas up here," he said.

"Sure, John," I answered, and instructed one of my men to roll out a fuel barrel and fill his tank. It's second nature for a pilot to look over a plane when he's around one, and I noticed a problem.

"John, I don't know if you know it or not, but you've got a notch in your propeller that's pretty big. Why don't you take the time to let me file it out for you before you take off?"

John gave the prop a quick examination. "I think it'll be all right, Scotty. I'm already late getting back to Leopoldville, and I don't want to be even later. I'll get it taken care of after I'm home." A few pleasantries were exchanged, and John was soon airborne.

He had crossed the Inzia River when three inches of the prop flew off, setting up such a vibration that it threatened to shake the plane to pieces. He cut the engine and was fortunate to see a road on which he could make a dead-stick landing. Once safely on the ground, he restarted the engine and taxied slowly down the road toward a small stream he had spotted from the air and thought offered a good place to camp out for the night. A native was walking along the road in the opposite direction, and as he passed the plane he smiled, waved and said, "*Mbote* Tata," as though it was the most natural thing in the world to see an airplane taxying down a dirt road in the interior of Africa.

John called Leopoldville MAF on his radio and explained the situation to Wes Eisemann. Wes then called me by radio and asked if they could use my plane to fly out the two passengers who were with John. My Supercub could handle short takeoffs and landings, whereas MAF didn't have another plane that could get in and out of there. Of course I readily agreed. When the "rescue" arrived, four inches were cut off the good end of the prop and the damaged end was filed down to create a reasonable semblance of balance. The seats were removed from the MAF plane and transferred to my Supercub, along with everything else that could reduce its weight. The two passengers were flown out in my plane, and John managed to limp back to safety with the makeshift repairs.

Inflation was fierce in the Congo, and it had its effect on my men as well as on my budget. The government attempted to control inflation by regulation, but that was even less effective in the Congo than in America. I was sympathetic to the problems it created for my workmen. At the same time, I was limited both by the funding allowed for the job and by government regulations. Most of my men could neither read nor write, and they were not sophisticated enough to understand the complexities involved. They knew only that it was getting harder and harder for them to manage. The economic squeeze they were in prompted two episodes of "labor trouble."

The first incident came when my rock crew staged a minor strike because they felt I wasn't paying them enough. I told them I was paying what we had agreed on, which was all the job could afford. If they didn't want to provide rock for the foundations, we would substitute concrete block, and they would have no job at all. This did not set well with the men, so they reported me to the government.

The government sent an investigator immediately to clarify the situation. Many meetings and many discussions later, the government man determined that I had been paying ninety francs too much and would have to reduce my payment or face grave consequences. This sat even more unhappily with the men, but there was nothing either side could do about it.

One day shortly after that, I was suddenly surrounded by all my workmen at the site of the Ag School—some two hundred angry black men encircling the only white man within miles. Our relations had always been good, but the ties of loyalty are fragile when emotions get out of hand. The increasing number of incidents throughout the Congo in which white men and women had been harassed, beaten and even killed was a reminder that we lived in a foreign country with a different culture. The fact that we were there to help the Congolese was no insurance that our motivation would protect us.

"What's this all about?" I asked, trying as best I could to show neither my anger nor my fear.

"You are cheating us! You have been cheating us all along! You have been taking our wages and using them for yourself!" The words cascaded from the angry black face of a recently hired mason. "You say you want to build this school for our people, but you are doing it only so that you can rob us and have our wages for yourself!" The muscular body that had prompted me to give this man a job in the first place was glistening with sweat and trembling with an inner rage. A chorus of grunts indicated the other workmen were responding to the intensity of his emotion. Clearly it was no time for logic.

Two steps brought me face-to-face with the spokesman, and I grabbed his shirt with my left hand, pulling him even closer. "You have been a troublemaker ever since you came to work here," I challenged, and realized only then how true my words were. He had been at the center of every *mambu* that occurred since he came to work. It couldn't be accidental that the trouble with my workmen came after his employment.

"You did not come here to work," I was shouting in his face. "You came here to cause trouble. These other men are here because they want to work. They want to feed their families. But you only want to disrupt this job." I paused, both to catch my breath and to shift my weight slightly so that I would be better positioned if he decided to take a swing at me.

"You are fired," I said. "You leave right this minute and I don't ever want to see you here again. If you ever come back I'll beat you within an inch of your life." I gave him a shove that sent him stumbling backward into the arms of a burly carpenter. He regained his feet and I could see indecision in his eyes as he glared at me. He was sizing me up, not sure that he wanted to mix with me further.

"Get out of here or I'll take you on right now," I threatened. Our eyes locked for long moments like two male lions challenging for supremacy. And as with the confrontation between lions, the weaker wisely decided to give way to the stronger. He turned and left the circle of men.

"Now the rest of you men, get back to work," I ordered. "If I have to put up with any more of this foolishness I will close down this job. You will all be out of work, and there will be no wages for any of you. There will be no school, and there will be no jobs. It will always be just like it was before we came." I knew I couldn't, or wouldn't, halt the work on the school, but I prayed they couldn't read my mind. The men stood motionless, perhaps awed by my confrontation with the loud-mouthed troublemaker and his retreat, but also contemplating the possibility of total unemployment.

"You heard Tata Scott." The voice belonged to a withered old man who was one of the senior carpenters. "You have known him for a long time and he has always been fair. What do we know of the one who just left? He talks of Lumumba and the power of the people, but he does not work well himself and he does not show any power when he is confronted. His ideas are as weak as he is. Let us go back to work."

And to a man, they did. The agitator was not heard from again, though I learned that he had obviously been a "plant" by those elements in the Congo who wanted every vestige of white presence eliminated. The work on the school resumed with enthusiasm, and we had no more labor trouble.

Another day I missed Kingoi, one of my workmen from the job. "Where's Kingoi?" I asked.

The others snickered. "He's in the hospital," one of them finally answered.

"Oh, really? What happened?" He had no physical problems that I was aware of.

"Why don't you ask him?" That was the most I could learn from any of the men, so I went to the hospital and found Kingoi on his bed, a bulky bandage at the stump of his arm where a hand had been the day before.

"What happened?" I asked.

"I was cutting palm nuts and fell out of the tree. I landed on my machete and cut off my hand."

Kingoi was not the first man to fall from a palm tree with a machete. I felt sorry for him. "The people here at the hospital will take good care of you," I assured him. "You get well, and as soon as you are able to come back to work we'll find something you can do."

Of course, the subject came up again with my men later in the day. "It's really a shame Kingoi fell out of the palm tree," I said. The men began to laugh. "What's so funny about that?" I asked, then remembered that Congolese often laugh from embarrassment as well as humor.

"Tata Scott," one of the men confided, "Kingoi didn't fall out of a palm tree. He was stealing fish from his neighbor's pond last night, and the neighbor caught him. He said, 'Kingoi, do you want me to kill you or do you want to cut off your hand?' Kingoi said he wanted to live, so he laid his arm on a tree stump, and the neighbor cut off his hand with his machete."

"But a lot of people steal," I protested. I stared at the man incredulously. Stealing is almost a way of life for many of the Africans, and while I certainly did not question the accuracy of what was reported, it just didn't fit with what I knew to be common practice.

"Oh, there's nothing wrong with stealing," the man said. "The mistake is in getting caught."

"You know people who have stolen things. Why don't you cut off their hands?" I asked.

He looked at me as though I had asked the most stupid question imaginable. "I would have no right to do that unless I caught him stealing from me. Then I could do whatever I wanted. Or I could have someone else cut off his hand for me, and that would be all right because I had ordered it. But no one else could punish him unless I asked them to."

Sharan and Jerry were married on June 8 and arrived in Leopoldville five days later. The trip was a homecoming for Sharan but a totally new experience for Jerry. We had evaluated the political and military situation in the Congo, and while there were dangerous areas, we felt there was no serious risk if we avoided the "hot spots."

We took time away from work to show off the newlyweds at most of the stations, but made up for it by putting Jerry to work when we were at Vanga. The Ag School was just over half-finished, and we had the roofs on twenty-three buildings. Jerry proved to be both willing and capable, doing anything that was suggested and doing it well. Dolores and I immediately approved of Sharan's choice of a husband, and we thoroughly enjoyed the month they spent with us. But time sped by quickly, and we were putting them on the plane for home much too soon.

Our assessment of the minimal danger to Sharan and Jerry proved to be correct, but things were deteriorating rapidly.

Wes Eisemann flew the MAF plane into Nioki. Soldiers surrounded the plane as soon as it landed. They marched Wes and his passengers into town at gunpoint, threw them into a cell in midafternoon, and did not release them until twenty-four hours later, having given them nothing to eat or drink for the entire time. They were roughed up some but not seriously injured. No formal charges were ever filed and no explanation was given as to why they were detained or released. We didn't expect this sort of thing to happen so close to us, though it was mild compared to what was happening in some other parts of the country.

The South Kasai declared its independence from Congo, led by Kalonji, king of the Baluba, and of course the military responded. King Kalonji became wanted by the central government for the crime of treason, as serious a charge as they could think of for one who led his territory to secede. Only after concerted military action, and perhaps an element of betrayal, was King Kalonji arrested and brought to Leopoldville to await trial. It was becoming all too evident that the Congo as a nation was still far more of a hope for the future than a reality of the present.

In spite of the distractions, we had the Ag School ready for the first classes on September 4. Much remained to be done before we could consider the facility completed, but the classrooms, dormitories, houses, shops, barns and all the essentials were in place and ready for use. As we watched the staff and the first forty students, half of them with their wives, move into the facilities, we could hardly believe that just over a year had passed since John and I began dreaming our dream.

King Kalonji escaped from prison in November and was flown out of Leopoldville to some unknown destination by an Air Brousse pilot. Since an airplane was involved, an unofficial but general suspicion fell on everyone who had anything to do with aircraft. We were particularly concerned about the effect this might have on mission aviation. We had been extremely cautious not to get involved in politics in any way and to avoid even the appearance of such involvement.

On the night of December 9, I badly needed rest, because malaria symptoms had plagued me for the last four days. Dolores and I had just gone to sleep when the sound of military vehicles driving into the station awakened us. There was a pounding at the door. I opened it to see an officer in full dress, attended by two armed men.

"You are Tata Scott?" He was a no-nonsense man who made it obvious that he could not waste time on pleasantries.

"I am." Many whites had been roused out of bed and whisked away in the night, some never again to be seen alive. "Would you like to come in?" My mind raced through possibilities I had not previously considered.

"Thank you, no." There was the faintest hint of a smile on his face. "I have a message for you from a very important man in Kikwit." He handed me a crisp envelope with my name handwritten on the front. "I shall wait here on the veranda for your reply."

I stared into the darkness over his shoulder, trying to collect my thoughts, and saw Maurice Entwisle approaching.

"Thank God you're all right, Scotty," Maurice said after he entered the house. "They came to our house first because they didn't know where you lived. I followed them over here because...well, you never know anymore."

The envelope in my hand trembled as though it had a life of its own. Finally I got it open and read its contents:

Dear Mr. Scott,

I am writing to you in an emergency. The president of the assembly of Kwilu Province has a number of appointments in Leopoldville tomorrow morning, December 10th. These appointments are of such a nature that they must be met. The Air Congo has failed us today. The only possibility we see is if you could come with your plane and take the president.

May I ask a personal favor of you in doing this as an exception in this very urgent case. Your charges will be taken care of by the provincial government since it is in behalf of urgent government matters that this trip is to be made. Would it be possible for you to be at Kikwit at 7:00 a.m.?

Thanking you in advance for this exceptional service, I am, sincerely yours,

Rostand J. Munungu

Tata Munungu was a dear friend who served as Secretary of Health and Sanitation for the province. Such a request could hardly be ignored, but the recent events, and the suspicion associated with anyone who flew, raised red flags all over the place. "Why me?" I thought. I was glad Maurice was with us, and I asked his advice.

"Scotty, I can't give you any light on this whatsoever," he said. "If you don't go, you're dead meat. You know that refusing the request of a Congolese official can lead to all sorts of trouble. But if you do go you're in equally deep trouble. Any time we get drawn into the crazy politics of this country in any way it will make some faction see us as the enemy. Lumumba's followers around here will see complying with such a request as siding against them. It looks like, no matter what you do, you're really bad off."

Dolores and I continued to discuss the pros and cons and prayed for guidance. Dolores clearly thought I should not go.

"Dolores, I think I have the answer," I said at last. "If I feel all right tomorrow and if the weather is OK, then I think I have to do it. Get me some paper and help me draft my reply." We worked out the wording together:

Dear Tata Munungu,

I have received your message. I have been sick for four days, but since this is an emergency I will go and expect to fly, the weather permitting. The plane should be there by 9:00 am. If the plane is not there by that time it will mean that Mr. Scott was prevented

from arriving due to another attack or due to the weather.
Sincerely,
C. Scott

The officer on the veranda had lost none of his military bearing as I handed him the reply.

Unfortunately, when I woke up the next morning I felt better than I had for days, and the weather was perfect for flying. As a final check I talked to Dan Fountain. He also was concerned about the impropriety of our involvement and the possible recriminations from the military, the Lumumbaists, the separatists or any of the other factions that made up the chaotic political mosaic.

"If you are going, then I'll make this suggestion," Dan said. "Take off like you're going to Leopoldville and then when you're out of sight of Vanga, drop down and circle around to Kikwit. Don't let anyone else here know you're going to Kikwit."

We gassed the plane and I took off, headed due west toward Leopoldville and gained altitude for several miles, until Vanga was far behind. Then I dropped altitude and banked left on a heading for Kikwit. I had flown into Kikwit before and was not looking forward to the landing, since the airport manager was a genuine pain. His job was not particularly important to anyone except himself, but he used every opportunity to demonstrate his authority, usually in totally inappropriate ways. On seeing me land he was even worse than usual. He had me escorted straight into his office.

"You have no business coming into this airport without advance permission! Why didn't you send a telegram?" His tone indicated that he was both angry and scared in addition to being his usual officious, obnoxious self.

"You know I can't send a telegram from Vanga."

"You have no business coming in here like this! You could get me fired."

"I got a letter from the Minister of Health and Sanitation and he asked me to be here this morning," I said.

"The Minister of Health and Sanitation has nothing to do with Kikwit," he fumed. "You're in really big trouble because..."

There's no telling where that conversation would have gone had it not been interrupted at that point by the appearance of a caravan of four long, black limousines.

"Who did you say called you to come here?" The airport manager could barely get the words out.

"I don't know any more than what I have already told you," I said.

"Munungu Rostand is a very dear friend and he sent the military last night asking me to be here this morning."

"Oh, Tata Scott, please forgive me" he said, alternating anxious glances between me and the limousines. "I didn't mean to jump all over you." There were actually tears in his eyes as he begged for my pardon. "Now please leave here and go to your plane, and please forgive me."

As I stepped outside, I saw that the four limousines had discharged their occupants. The passengers, all dressed in elegant black suits with stylish shirts and ties, formed a double line from the cars to my plane. I would have to walk down that human corridor and felt most conspicuous in my baseball cap and shorts.

"Mr. Scott?" The man who stepped forward to address me bowed slightly.

"Yes."

"I am the protocol officer and I'd like to introduce you to His Excellency, Kalonji."

Now it was my turn to be frightened. We all knew of King Kalonji's escape and the government's search for him. Munungu Rostand, knowing that I would never agree to fly King Kalonji anywhere, had taken advantage of our friendship by making me think this was a legitimate politician. I had two pictures in my mind. Neither of them had a happy ending. One picture was of me refusing to make the flight and being shot here on the Tarmac; the other was of me being shot after we landed in Leopoldville. I shook Kalonji's extended hand and then was introduced, one by one, to the other high muckety-mucks in the party.

"I am most grateful you could come." Kalonji was younger than I had expected and most personable. "It is appreciated that you will take me and my secretary to Leopoldville."

"I can only take one person," I said. "The plane is not large enough for more. There are only two seats. But I will take you." A glance down the aisle of men standing at attention removed any hesitation.

"But my secretary is important to me," Kalonji said. "I really need this man with me."

"Sir, it is the weight that makes it impossible," I said. Kalonji was huge for a Congolese, a good six feet tall and a well-muscled 200 pounds. His secretary, though smaller, was still at least 135 pounds. "My plane will not fly with that much weight."

"Very well," Kalonji said. "Let's be on our way."

"I hate to say this," I told him, "but everyone is going to have to wait until I put some gasoline in the plane." I had enough gas in the tanks for a flight to Leopoldville, but I didn't have any reserve if we

151

should run into trouble. I had brought a couple of jerrycans of gas from Vanga to top off the fuel before takeoff at Kikwit. I got my gas cans out of the plane, found a stepladder and climbed up to the wing tanks. How silly can a man feel? Here was a white man dressed for a Saturday afternoon softball game climbing around his little plane while immaculately groomed Congolese dignitaries stood at attention watching his every move. Kalonji came to the foot of the ladder.

"You have a luggage compartment. I have only a briefcase," he said. "I can hold the briefcase on my lap and my secretary can crawl in the luggage compartment." I could not keep from smiling at the picture this brought to mind.

"No sir," I said as emphatically as possible. *"N'est pas possible."*

When we were airborne I set a course for the first emergency landing area I knew of. When we were over that, I altered our course to take us over the next closest bailout place I remembered, zigzagging in this way all the way to Leopoldville. It lengthened our flying time considerably, but a healthy fear was motivating me. If anything happened to us and he was killed or injured, I would be in prison for the rest of my life—unless they executed me on the spot.

The Supercub does not lend itself well to conversation, and I really didn't want to know any more about this man than was absolutely necessary, so few words were exchanged on the flight. Anyway, my attention was divided between visually navigating from one safe landing area to the next and trying to devise a plan of escape from the Leopoldville airport if it proved necessary.

The limousines at Kikwit were nothing compared to the caravan awaiting us at the airport. Motorcycle escorts, an armed honor guard and assorted dignitaries formed to receive my passenger as I taxied the small plane. To my surprise, Kalonji let the assemblage wait while he talked with me. "Mr. Scott, you have been of greater service to the Congo than you can realize. I am deeply indebted to you and would like you to come to the capitol and have lunch with me now."

"Thank you very much," I said. My stomach was still churning so much that lunch was the last thing I wanted to think about. "I understand how pressed you are for time, and I must go immediately to our mission station and meet with our secretary." Reporting to a superior was a duty that any Congolese would graciously accept as a priority.

"Then you must make it another time," Kalonji said. "I want to give you something." He opened his briefcase and took out an eight-by-ten inch portrait of himself, which he autographed and handed to me along with a biographical sketch. He must have kept his escorts waiting a good five minutes while he expressed over and over his appreciation for my service and reiterated his invitation to call, to visit, and to have lunch with him.

Later, as I read the biographical sketch, I realized that this man, president of the National Assembly of the Democratic Republic of Congo, was a nephew of King Kalonji, not the wanted man himself. He proved to be a good friend over the coming years, hosting parties for us, inviting our young people to his palatial home to enjoy the swimming pool, and on several occasions cutting through bureaucratic mine fields to make our lives and work much easier.

CHAPTER 16

Vanga—1963

Many people assume that ministers and missionaries have all the elements of their spiritual experience permanently in place and never have to deal with the questions and problems faced by laymen. Nothing could be further from the truth. We do deal with spiritual and moral issues of life and work, and we seek to apply the teachings of Christ to all we do. Perhaps this causes us to have unreasonably high expectations of ourselves and of those with whom we interact.

Our construction schedule was onerous, particularly in the face of so many distractions. We broke ground for a Medical School at Vanga before we finished the last of our work at the Ag School. The Medical School required the usual classrooms and laboratories, as well as additional housing for the students. While not on the scale of the Ag School, it was an important and significant project. We also began to plan for a secondary school in the area. We also had six other projects under way at various stations.

The other missionaries were as deeply involved with their many responsibilities. This was what all of us had come to the Congo for, yet the strain was beginning to show in our interpersonal relationships. The tumultuous political and military environment with its constant uncertainty only exacerbated the stress.

It was truly a godsend that the Reverend Fred Judson came from California to lead us in a spiritual retreat in the spring of 1963. The time he spent with us and the depths of faith to which he led us came like the end of a spiritual dry season. Love, understanding, patience, renewed commitment, and inner strength all sent up tender shoots through the hard crust of frustration and grew daily. Above all else, however, he brought us back to the reality of God's constant presence and His unchanging love for us. In the next year we would each face dangers and crises with renewed confidence in divine leadership, crises that could not have been resolved as they were without the preparation during this time. Perhaps equally important was the fact that while the problems we faced multiplied, frustration was replaced with genuine joy. We were on a constant spiritual high that carried us on its crest even into the valleys of deepest darkness.

We had identified what we thought to be the perfect location for the secondary school, just a few kilometers from both Vanga and the Ag School. The three installations would form a triangle, each able to maintain its own identity and yet situated so that communication and support services would be maximized. Now all that remained was to get proper title to the land.

The chief of the village of Bilili greeted us with all the formalities due visiting dignitaries, even to the point of wearing an old suit coat over his tattered shirt and ragged shorts. Certainly the temperature did not warrant clothing, but a coat of any sort is a mark of distinction and is worn on any occasion when one wants to show his status.

"My friends, the land you request has belonged to our people for many generations and we would be filled with joy to give it to you. We want our children to have education and will be happy to have the school on this land. But we do not wish you to have further trouble, so you must know that the people of the village of Milundu also claim the land. Of course, their claim is groundless, but for your sake you should let them know that we want to give the land to you."

So we visited the chief at Milundu and received an equally cordial reception.

"Of course, we will give you the land," he said. "The claim of the people of Bilili is foolish. The land belongs to us. It has been our land for generations, even though the people of Lusekele also lay claim to it."

We thought it prudent to visit the third village, where the same reception, the same offer and the same claim of ownership greeted us.

"What do we do now?" I asked Maurice Entwistle.

"Let's see if we can get a government ruling," he answered.

The government sent an official who called the three chiefs together for a palaver to settle the issue.

On the appointed day we arrived early along with the official and waited under the *mambu* tree for the three chiefs. But when they came they did not come alone. Each chief brought with him all the elders of his village and many of the younger men. By the time we were all assembled, it was a sizable gathering. The government official opened the proceedings. He paid proper respect to each of the dignitaries present, the solemnity of the occasion, and the importance of the ensuing deliberations. Then he made a brief statement.

"This land has seen much bloodshed and conflict for many generations. Now it has an opportunity to be the site of a school where our children can learn. These people from the mission will build classrooms, dormitories, houses for teachers, all the things necessary for such a school. But you must settle the claims to the land among yourselves so that when the school is built there will be no further conflict."

The chief from Bilili rose to his feet, again wearing his suit coat in the tropical heat. "Let me tell you of the battle which took place on this land many, many years ago when Ndobe was our chief," he began. Then he recounted the details of the battle as though it had occurred less than a week ago, often assisted by the men of his village, who pantomimed dramatic events by swinging make-believe machetes and war clubs or shooting imaginary arrows. He told of the bloodshed, the men who were lost in the battle, and how the people from the village of Milundu were routed. The sun had moved from its morning position to well overhead by the time he brought the battle to its victorious conclusion. "There was no question as to who owned the land at the end of that day," he said.

Then the chief of the village of Milundu stood. He wore an overcoat that hung too loosely over his shoulders and came almost to the ground. His ebony face was covered with sweat, though whether from the unnecessary clothing or his agitation over the preceding recitation I could not tell.

"What you have heard did indeed happen many years ago," he began. "But after that..." and he gave an equally long and dramatic account of a subsequent battle from which his village emerged the victor. He also concluded his remarks by saying, "There was no question at the end of that day whose land this was."

The chief of Lusekele had no coat, but a leopard skin hung over his shoulders.

"It is good to hear the history of long, long ago," he said. "But after the events that have been recalled here this morning there was a real battle." He paused for dramatic effect. "And I will tell you of it after we have eaten lunch and rested a bit."

"Maurice," I said, "at the rate this thing is moving we're not going to have it settled until dark."

But it was not settled that day, nor the day after, as the palaver continued along the same lines. At times I felt the intensity of the drama would lead to a free-for-all among the men, but they kept their peace and seemed to enjoy the prolonged discussion.

On the morning of the third day the leopard-skin-clad chief rose to again address the gathering.

"My people and I have shelled peanuts and have come to a decision. Nothing any of you has said convinced us that you have any claim whatsoever to our land." I sensed disaster on the way, but was delighted when he continued. "Nevertheless, it is important to us that the school be built, so we are leaving it in your hands. Whatever you decide, so long as it provides for the school, will be accepted by us. I and my people now leave this place and this decision with you." As one, the men from Lusekele rose and left the meeting. Now it was a decision between only two villages, but reducing the number of claimants only intensified each side's belief in its rightful ownership.

Through the rest of the morning, past lunch and on into the afternoon the discussion continued. Then in midafternoon the chief from Bilili rose and gestured to his men. They stood and formed a wedge with the chief at its point. Instantly the men of Milundu formed a line against them.

"Now comes the battle," I thought to myself.

Instead, the chief of Bilili reached into an inside pocket of his coat and withdrew what I first thought to be a knife, but which proved to be a piece of cast iron about ten inches long. It was shaped into a heavy ball at one end and tapered to a point on the other.

"Many times in these three days we have referred to the symbol of ownership of this land. This is it," he said, raising the tool as though it were a royal mace.

"Long, long ago our people learned how to make iron on this land. They took the rock from the ground and melted out the iron. They used this tool to shape the iron. With the round end they pounded out the iron to its proper shape, just as we have pounded out our claim to this land. Around the other end they shaped the iron into rings or bracelets or whatever form the iron should take, just as our claim to this land has been shaped by battle." Sweat was pouring from his face and his hands trembled with the intensity of his emotion.

"This is the symbol of ownership of this land and it belongs to our people. We know this because we hold this symbol and handle it with confidence. If anyone who does not own this land were to so much as touch this iron he would die immediately." The men on both sides were awed by the introduction of this totem.

157

"Now let this matter be settled for all time," the chief continued. "Is there any man of Milundu who would dare to touch this iron? Is there any man of Milundu willing to die in order to prove our claim? Is there any man of Milundu so foolish as to test the power of this totem?"

From the line of men facing this magic object one man came forward. Tall and lean, the speckled sunlight dancing off beads of sweat on his forehead, he stepped up to the chief.

"You bet there is," he said matter-of-factly, and with a hand that showed not the slightest tremor he took the iron from the chief's hand.

Both sides stood frozen in awe.

He turned and walked straight to me, handed me the iron, and said, "Tata Scott, this is your land. Let us have a school."

Without a word the men from Bilili turned and left the meeting.

The matter was settled from that moment. We filed the land survey with the government and I never heard another word about contested ownership of the land.

Dickens might as well have been writing about the Democratic Republic of the Congo in 1963 when he referred to the best of times and the worst of times.

The military was as inefficient as it was unpredictable. Soldiers came without notice or explanation and made camp on our airstrip, denying us use of the landing strip for more than two weeks. They stopped at the station and demanded gasoline for their vehicles and sometimes the use of our vehicles as well. Reports of violence throughout the land continued to reach us, accompanied by gruesome details of brutality. The government was all but immobilized by constant power struggles. Martial law was declared in Leopoldville again.

Bands of young men, called *Jeunesse*, were active in the province, destroying anything and everything Western. Their leaders, trained and financed by Communist China, convinced them that magic would protect them from harm as long as they obeyed the leaders. They terrified the populace, wreaking as much savagery on Africans who displayed any evidence of Western influence as they did on whites. The leaders had learned how to organize an insurrection, but they had no idea of how to control it. Building supplies were increasingly difficult to locate. We thought it the worst of times.

But at the same time, we continued in the joy of spiritual renewal. No matter how difficult it was to procure needed supplies, they always materialized in time to keep the work flowing. We experienced a special burst of parental pride when Johnny rescued a visiting doctor from drowning in the river and revived him with the technique he remembered from reading an article in *Boy's Life*. The Ag School was completed, and final payment on that job eased our cash-flow problems. The nursing school was nearing completion and the secondary school at Milundu was coming along. Other projects were on schedule. In many ways it was the best of times.

Dick Knarr was the pilot for IPOC and an especially close friend. He and I arranged to fly his plane to Salisbury, Rhodesia, to get supplies needed for our work. Johnny had been home for the Christmas break and had to be back at school. Dick and I planned to drop him off at Leopoldville on our way to Rhodesia. I persuaded Dolores to fly into the capital with us and stay there for the short time Dick and I would be gone. She packed the few things she would need in an overnight bag, not suspecting that it would be months before she could return to Vanga.

CHAPTER 17

Vanga—1964

Dick Knarr dropped me off at Vanga on our return from Salisbury. I intended to get the Supercub and fly it to Leopoldville to pick up Dolores. I expected a warmer reception from my colleagues at Vanga than the abrupt greeting I received.

"Scotty, they've been calling for you on the radio. They need you at Kikwit immediately."

"Hey, I just got back. I've got to pick up Dolores and bring her back," I answered.

His brow furrowed with dismay. "Don't you know what's been going on since you left?"

"I know we've had a long trip and I'm tired," I said.

"The *jeunesse* have struck in force here in the province. Independent missionaries at Mukedi heard of a raid on the Roman Catholic station near them last Thursday. They found the three priests there had been dismembered and murdered. There were also seven nuns who had been abused and violated. MAF flew in the next day and evacuated the nuns, but it was a hairy business. MAF couldn't have landed if the local chief had not taken his shotgun out on the landing strip and driven the *jeunesse* off the field. They got the nuns out, but the chief was killed shortly after the plane took off." He paused for breath, acknowledging the heroism and support of this African leader.

"We've been getting reports of other action all day. Government posts have been attacked and burned. Commercial centers overrun and sacked. Mission stations have gone off the air." For a mission station to "go off the air" needed no further explanation. It meant that the station had been overrun and the missionaries had been killed or had

160

fled into the jungle.

I slumped a bit. "Sounds like '60 all over again," I said.

"Maybe even worse," he said. "It was just craziness and frustration in '60. These gangs are organized, and they have recruited thousands and thousands of young people. They are dedicated to overthrowing the government and destroying every vestige of Western influence."

Within two hours I was landing my Supercub at Kikwit.

Kikwit is located up-river from Vanga, a major center for that area and capital of the district. A number of independent missions operated in the area, coordinated by a loosely knit organization headquartered in Kikwit even though most of its stations were across the river, directly in the path of the *jeunesse*. I contacted an official of that organization.

"What's the situation?" I asked.

"We really don't know," he said. "What few bridges there are have been destroyed. All the *bacs* have been either sunk or cut adrift. Large trees have been cut and dropped across the roads. There is no way for us to get in or for them to get out. We received some radio transmissions that rebels were burning the station, and then their radio went dead. Of course, the first thing the *jeunesse* do is smash the radios.

"What we need right now is to find out for sure what the situation is with our stations," he told me. "Will you do the aerial survey for us? Of course you can't land at these places, but the UN has promised to bring in a helicopter to evacuate anyone in immediate danger. Their helicopters can fly to a specific place and back if we tell them where they're needed, but they don't have enough hours left on the engines to do surveillance." As a pilot I understood the great risk to plane, pilot and passengers if an engine was operated beyond a given limit.

"Of course," I answered. "But you'll have to show me where your stations are located."

"Our most immediate concern is for Irene Farrell and Ruth Hagie. We have a report that Irene has been killed and Ruth's hands have been cut off."

"How did you get that report?" I asked.

"A runner brought us a note from Ruth saying Irene had died with an arrow in her neck. Then the messenger told us that Ruth's hands had been cut off."

"Show me where the station is."

He took out his maps and located Mongungu for me.

Navigating in the Congo is very different from navigating in the United States. There is no system of beacons to establish electronic vectors, the basis of I.F.R. (Instrument Flight Rules). There are no real roads to follow and villages all tend to look alike from the air, depriving pilots of the sort of clues used in V.F.R. (Visual Flight Rules). So I flew by what we called I.C.R., "I Count Rivers" and I.F.R., "I Follow Rivers." Rivers are easily detectable from the air and served our navigational needs almost as well as interstate highways. Thus I was able to locate Mongungu.

When I flew over the station I saw Ruth Hagie and knew that if Irene were alive she would have been there also. Ruth's hands were both intact. I dropped a note to Ruth:

"If it is safe for me to land I will attempt a landing on the road and pick you up. Sit down on the ground if it is all right. If I should not land for any reason, stand with your hands on your hips."

When I made the next pass over the station, she was standing with hands on hips. We arranged for a helicopter to pick her up as soon as possible, though a couple of days passed before she was evacuated. She was brought immediately to Vanga for a medical checkup, and I greeted her as she came off the helicopter.

"I was the one who dropped that note. Why in the world didn't you let me try to land and pick you up?" I asked her.

"The same people who killed Irene were still there in the crowd, and they wanted me to get you to land," she told me. "I knew that if you landed they would have killed you. I cared more about you than I did about myself." (When Ruth wrote her story she didn't tell it that way, understandably. She would never want to portray herself the hero she was, but just as one who put her safety in the Lord's hands.)

We had to make a decision about our continued presence at Vanga. None of us had any desire to be martyrs, yet there were many reasons not to evacuate the station at this time. The medical work was needed now more than ever. The construction jobs I had going provided the best employment in the area. Shutting down the projects would throw hundreds of men out of work and add to the discontent on which the *jeunesse* fed. The schools were in session, and we did not want to see the students' education interrupted. But at least as important as these reasons was the psychological impact our withdrawal would have on the Africans. They would interpret our departure as admission that the *jeunesse* were indeed a powerful force, too powerful for us to confront. But there were the wives and the children...

Since Dr. Judson's time with us, prayer had become an even more potent and energizing force for all of us. Almost every day, all the missionaries would spend a half an hour praying together. We set aside one room exclusively for prayer, and when any of us felt at the very end of endurance, that room became a retreat and a wellspring of strength.

There were eight men on the station and all of the wives except Dolores; I had been too busy flying reconnaissance to bring her back from Leopoldville. We men met for prayer, each of us praying that the Lord would lead us to do the right thing. We knew all too well of people in similar situations making brave, but unwise, decisions. As we prayed, it became clear to each of us that there was only one course to follow: evacuate the women and children as soon as possible but keep the men on the station.

When the women were told of this decision, there was not a single objection or word of discord. Many of the same people who, a few years before, had been almost immobilized by the prospect of having families separated now accepted this as the Lord's will. The strength we had experienced through prayer translated itself into a certainty that we were doing what our Lord would have us to do. The families evacuated to Leopoldville, not without concern, but certainly without fear.

Having the Supercub at Vanga offered a degree of assurance we had not experienced in '60, but it did not come close to the expectations some placed on it. Soon after the women and children were settled in Leopoldville, we heard a broadcast over the Voice of America saying that the women had been evacuated and eight men remained on the station, with a light plane standing by at Vanga to evacuate the men if necessary. I called MAF in Leopoldville and asked them if they could work out the seating arrangement for getting all eight of us in the two-passenger plane.

The rioters' technique was to send word into a village that they were coming and they wanted the village to feed and take care of them in other ways. If the villagers refused because they feared retaliation by the military, the *jeunesse* considered this to be collaborating with the enemy and an excuse to kill all the men and burn the village. In most villages, the people scattered in fear and hid in the jungle. With this intimidation, as few as a dozen *jeunesse* could take over a village.

My days settled into a routine. First, organize the construction projects with as little of my time as possible. Then, check out the daily reports of *jeunesse* approaching villages in the area of our station at Vanga. I recruited Pastor Pambi, or Musiti Paul, or Norm Riddle, or

Maurice Entwistle or someone else as an observer and flew over where the *jeunesse* were reported to be. Usually we saw little or nothing, and at most a dozen men, so we would return and tell our station council it was just another big lie. But the next day similar reports would come and require checking out.

Sometimes, a runner would relay word that the *jeunesse* were massing to come in and burn Vanga. The message would say, "We've got so-many-thousand men, and we want to give you time to get out because we're going to kill everyone we see. There is not one worthy person left among the Africans, because everyone at Vanga is a tool of the West." It was their attempt to unnerve everybody.

There were also regular reconnaissance flights over outlying stations or other places where whites were reported in danger. I always flew over stations that were reported to have been hit by the rebels. One I remember most clearly was the Balaka station where Dr. and Mrs. Eiker maintained an excellent medical practice. They were Swiss, working with the Congo Inland Mission, and a really wonderful couple.

When I flew over their station, nothing was left but the charred remains of what had once been a fine ministry. The houses, school, dispensary, everything was gone. There was no sign of life. Then several days later, I got word that the Eikers were alive and hiding in the jungle. Immediately, I flew over the remains of the station again and this time saw several people in the clearing. I dropped a note to them that said, "If the missionaries are dead, sit on the ground; if the missionaries are alive, start walking toward the jungle where the missionaries are hiding." They walked toward the jungle, and I contacted Leopoldville for a UN helicopter to evacuate them.

I learned later that when the Eikers were captured by the *jeunesse* they suffered all sorts of brutality and humiliation. Among other things, they were marched from village to village to be shown off by the rebels as a prize. When they entered a village, the captives would be driven before the marchers like cattle, their hands bound and the rebels beating them from one end of the village to the other. Then when they were out of sight of the village, the bonds would be taken off and the Eikers marched to the next village, where they would again be bound and the same scene re-enacted. The Eikers managed to escape and returned to their burned-out station, where they hid in the jungle nearby.

The UN helicopters were flown by Swedes, and I will never forget one big Swede in particular. I never saw him without a submachine gun in his hand, which he carried like I would a six-shooter. As soon as the helicopter touched ground he'd step out, a big cigar in his mouth and the machine gun in his hand, and greet the people. "Hi, boys. Everybody's happy, aren't we?" Then out of the side of his mouth to those he came to evacuate, "Get the hell in the helicopter! Get the hell in there!" Then back to the local assemblage, "Everybody's gonna smile and be happy, aren't we?" In a matter of seconds the evacuees would be aboard and the helicopter airborne.

Medical emergency flights continued along with all the other demands. One such flight stands out with painful clarity.

A twelve-year-old girl at Boko was in terrible agony, and the personnel there could not determine the cause. They were convinced that if the cause was not found and corrected, her life would be at risk. They asked that a doctor be flown in to examine her. Musiti Paul was available, and we took off for Boko.

The weather posed somewhat of a question, but that was nothing unusual on such flights. We lived and flew in what we called "Thunder Boom Alley." On a single flight Dolores and I had counted as many as twenty great thunderheads with lightning, thunder and torrential downpours under them. From the plane we could see all this weather and fly around or between the storm cells. The trick was not to get caught in the wind they produce. I felt we could make the trip to Boko safely, so we taxied down the runway and took off into a fairly clear sky, heading out on our mission of mercy. We soon encountered a weather front, an ominous black curtain drawn from the heavens to the ground below. I flew parallel to the front until I came to a river and saw what looked like a tunnel through the cloud. There was no sign of disturbance in that hole in the curtain. Most such fronts are not very deep, and I reasoned that if I could get us through the tunnel, we would come out in relatively clear skies on the other side.

"Thank you, Lord. We're going to make it," I said and banked sharply to head through that narrow escape hatch. When we entered the tunnel, the winds must have been at least a hundred miles an hour, because they tumbled the plane and rolled it like a kite about to nosedive. I don't know why it didn't tear the wings off the plane or how I managed to turn tail and run, but I poured on full power and regained control somehow. I can only say a Greater Power gave me something special at that moment. When we were back to a degree of safety, I turned around to look at Musiti. He was as frightened as I had been and knew without my having to tell him that we had just survived a very close call.

I found an emergency landing strip and set the plane down. We had time to take out the heavy augers I always carried and tie down the plane and let the storm pass. We waited out the storm inside the plane, then continued our flight to Boko without further incident.

When Musiti examined the girl after our arrival, he discovered that she had started menstruation, but there was no opening for the menstrual fluids to escape. She had to be evacuated to our hospital at Vanga for the complicated surgical procedures required to correct her problem.

Musiti continued to fly with me whenever necessary, but I suspected that he was somewhat less enthusiastic after that flight. As for me, I reflected that I had made a poor and dangerous judgment: I should have known that something was causing that opening and I should have reasoned it was a wind tunnel. I thanked the Lord for delivering us from that predicament and vowed that, in the future, I would try not to put God to such a test again.

The days stretched into weeks and the weeks into months of relentless strain and struggle, and not just for us on the station but also for our wives back in Leopoldville. Dolores and June Eisemann manned the radio in Leopoldville and were on the air from early morning to dark, keeping contact with MAF, the outlying stations, and anyone else involved in or at risk during those perilous times. They and their radio became the nerve center of all our communication. They kept in touch with the American embassy because it was the avenue to get UN helicopters when needed. At the same time, the embassy depended on this information to stay as up-to-date as possible in the confusion of the rebellion.

The women kept us current on what was happening in Leopoldville. They told us who had arrived in the capital, so we knew which stations had been safely evacuated.

One of our churches across the Kwilu river from Vanga is located in the Busala area. A year or so before the *jeunesse* uprising, the people at Busala decided they wanted a landing strip of their own. I selected the best of several sites they made available and explained to them how long and level the runway must be for landings and takeoffs. They did all the work themselves, painstakingly moving dirt, basketful by basketful. The work was completed, but the strip was "off limits" because it had not yet cleared MAF specifications.

Soon after our wives were evacuated, Tata Walusai, the pastor of the church at Busala, came to Vanga. I used the need to get him home safely as an excuse to fly into Busala, both to check out the strip and to survey the *jeunesse* in the area. When we landed, hundreds of people from nearby villages flocked around the plane. They screamed, laughed, sang, danced, and really had a celebration. This was the first plane to land at their new airstrip, and their pride was unbounded. They had done an amazing bit of work, considering the lack of tools, finances, and experience they brought to the task. But they were to do an even more important and amazing job.

The *jeunesse* had spread across central Congo like a grass fire, using fear, threats, terrorism, savagery, and superstition as the mainstays of their arsenal. Village after village fled before their terror or was totally destroyed. Then they came to Busala and Pastor Walusai.

Pastor Walusai was senior pastor in the Busala area, responsible for overseeing the work of many churches in the surrounding villages. He was a meek man, his half a century making him an elder in Congolese society. He was small of stature and at times appeared almost timid. His appearance did not attract admiration, but his performance won respect.

It became obvious that the *jeunesse* were massed for an attack in Busala, with the next goal of pressing on to Leopoldville, capturing the city, deposing the government, and establishing a utopia devoid of all vestiges of Western influence. But Busala lay directly in their path.

Pastor Walusai called the men from all the villages together to discuss what they should do. Most of the men argued that flight was preferable to being slaughtered. A few believed that giving the invaders food and anything else they requested was the wiser choice. The discussion dragged on. At length the pastor addressed the gathering.

"I know for a fact that they have destroyed villages and all the mission stations in their path. They burned those stations, they destroyed the books, they killed the teachers and they killed the nurses. In villages they have killed all the men they found and scattered the women and children. There is nothing worse for a village than losing its women and children. They are going to come into Busala. They want to intimidate us, intimidate our villages, one village at a time. After they leave, the military will come behind them. Whether they find that we have fled from these rebels or that we have remained in our villages and fed them, the military will take a terrible toll on us for having cooperated with the *jeunesse*." All this was delivered as the insight of a wise but timid man. Then his manner changed abruptly, and he exhibited a fire the villagers had never seen in him.

"We have only one choice," he continued. "We must lay an ambush for them. We must kill them and chase them out. If we fall in the fray we are better off, because we will have died doing the right thing."

The discussion continued, but now with a different tone. Their spiritual leader had become their leader in fact, and they vowed to follow his direction.

Men of Busala gathered by the hundreds and set up an ambush along the road. They had little more than the most primitive weapons—knives, machetes, bows and arrows, spears—against the high powered and sophisticated weapons the *jeunesse* were reported to have. But they depended on the element of surprise. As the column of *juenesse* approached Busala, lines of men were concealed on each side of the road. At the signal, the villagers dashed out of hiding with an intensity and savagery born of fear. They slashed and hacked but heard not a single shot. When the battle was over and the band of *jeunesse* thoroughly crushed, the men of Busala inspected the grim site.

They discovered the guns were made of wood. Most of the spears and arrows had no metal points. "They are *kifanifani*," the men said. "Both the weapons and the *jeunesse* are *kifanifani*." *Kifanifani* means "phony," "counterfeit," "pretense"—not the sort of words that had been applied to these feared bands in the months before.

The westward thrust of the *jeunesse* stopped at Busala. After that encounter, they abandoned their hope of capturing Leopoldville and instead turned north toward Stanleyville. Months and months of fighting and bloodshed would follow before the reformed army of General Mobutu, reinforced by mercenaries, could claim a final victory over the *jeunesse*. But as far as our area was concerned it was the turning point in a savage and senseless war, a turnaround made possible by a little man who might have been voted least likely to be a hero.

The end of the *jeunesse* rebellion in our area allowed us to resume a near-normal schedule as the wives and children returned to the interior. "Near-normal" is the best that can be said, because there continued to be spontaneous uprisings and fighting, triggered by tribal rivalries, local power-grabs, or hooligan gangs out for excitement. The military continued their ineffective (and at times almost comic) pursuit of law and order, often creating more chaos in the district than what they had come to suppress.

During the worst months of the rebellion, my aircraft had been involved in the safe evacuation of almost fifty people who certainly would have perished without the reconnaissance we provided. I wondered what would have happened to those people if my plane had developed a major problem there in the interior, where no repair was possible. Fortunately, it had performed wonderfully, despite being flown to the limit of its time for overhaul. A way had to be found to ensure the safety and continued performance of the plane. Since little expertise could be found in the Congo, and none at all in the interior, perhaps I should acquire the needed skill myself during our upcoming furlough.

Meanwhile, the work continued: projects to be completed, accounts to be put in order, and our personal property to be taken care of either by storage or disposal. I built a two-story storage shed behind our house for tools and household goods, but painfully decided the Supercub had to be sold.

My preacher brother had come to be a speaker at our annual missionary conference, and he extended his visit for three more weeks. As I flew him back to Leopoldville for his return home, he asked me what I was going to do about the plane.

"I hate to part with it, but we've decided we will sell it," I said.

"You've got to be kidding," he said. "You've flown the engine out. You've put this plane through more in the last few months than it was ever intended to hold up under. It needs an overhaul. The Congo isn't really a thriving market for light planes at best, and you think you can find somebody to buy *this*?" His disparaging remark about my plane was tempered by his smile and the fact that he did not hesitate to fly in it.

"God wanted me to have it and made it possible for us to get it in the first place. He will help me get rid of it. Sure, I'll find someone who wants it."

He shook his head and grinned. "You probably will. But I'd never thought of enlisting God as a used-airplane salesman." We flew on in silence for a time, and then he said, "We're both Christians; we each have a deep personal faith; we're both in full-time Christian service; we both serve the same Lord. I rely on God every day of my life for strength, wisdom and guidance. You do also, but then you expect God to arrange the specific details for you. I just don't understand that theology."

"I don't understand it either," I answered. "I just know that my Lord wants things done and He does a lot of them through me. He provides whatever is needed. I don't have to understand it, just accept it."

We landed at Leopoldville and I taxied to the private plane area. While I was performing the tasks necessary to leave the plane, I noticed a middle-aged man in a business suit walking around the plane. I nodded to him and smiled.

"Beautiful plane you've got there," he said. "I've been looking for one just like it. Do you know anyone who has one for sale?"

"I'll sell this one," I said, "but not for a couple of months. I'll need it for myself until then."

"That's no problem," he answered. "I'll be out of the country for a couple of months myself, so I won't need it until I return."

There on the Tarmac we made arrangements for the sale. I told him what needed to be done to the plane and we agreed on a price that left me ecstatic. My brother stood watching and listening and just shook his head.

As I reflected on this term of service, I thought of the troubles that convulsed the country and the problems we had confronted. It appeared that this new nation was tearing itself apart and would die in its infancy. Yet symbols of hope always appeared, even at the darkest moments. In those months while we were surrounded by terror and death, we received word that Sharan and Jerry had presented us with our first grandchild: a new life had come into the world, promising continuity and survival in a way that perhaps only grandparents can fully appreciate. Always when things seemed most hopeless, God gave us the support and strength needed.

I thought of a flight Dolores and I had made from Leopoldville to Vanga in the Supercub. Thunderheads reared up menacingly all the way through "Thunder Boom Alley." I threaded our way around them, and then straight ahead a magnificent rainbow spread from horizon to horizon, its colors more vivid than any other I remembered. As we approached the rainbow, it began to bend around us until it was a complete circle, embracing the small plane and filling its occupants with a sense of God-given exhilaration. We flew through the heart of the rainbow and into the smooth, clear air ahead.

CHAPTER 18

California—1964-1965

This was the most hectic, satisfying, anxious and significant furlough during all our years of service. It was filled with a mixture of pressure, anxiety, joy, accomplishment and plain hard work for me.

The greatest joy was our granddaughter, Sandy, a beautiful baby and the perfect image of her mother. Seeing her in her crib, Dolores and I were carried back over the years to remember ourselves as young parents, looking down at infant Sharan. We thought the same thoughts grandparents have experienced at such moments since time immemorial. What lies in store for this child? What forces will shape her life and character? Will she find a world that is better or worse than the one we know? Was there ever a more beautiful baby in all the world?

The hard work for me came as a result of my decision to enroll at Northup Institute of Technology in Fullerton, California, and get the A & E certification. This certification, granted by the Federal Aviation Authority, allows a person to inspect and accept or reject the airframe and engines on any aircraft. In order to know if everything is right, one has to know what right is and how it should be made right. That was the skill I most wanted and needed. This training would allow me to do any repair necessary on my plane and ensure my own safety and that of others who flew with me.

"I count forty of you here this morning," the instructor said on our first day. "Well, take a good look at one another, because most of you won't be here all that long." If his desire was to grab our attention, he succeeded. "Even though you have been screened as advanced students, don't forget that this is a two-year course, compacted into one year. There won't be more than ten of you able to finish this course."

It proved to be an optimistic prediction: only nine of us graduated. I was one of the oldest men in the class, had never been a particularly good student, and now was up against as exacting a course of study as I could imagine. Perhaps realizing all these obstacles made me apply myself to the course with a discipline that was woefully lacking in my youth. There was little time for recreation, a minimum of speaking engagements accepted, and usually not much sleep as I studied hour after hour to meet the rigorous demands. It was a year that left me fatigued, both physically and mentally, but in the end I graduated fifth out of the nine and was awarded my certification.

It was near the end of the year at Northup Institute when I got the distressing word that my mother, back in Oklahoma, had gone to Tulsa for surgery. The doctors found such a mass of cancer around her pancreas and other organs that they simply closed her up and sent her home as a helpless case. I was torn between my deep love for mother and the constraints imposed by my studies. If I did not immediately go to Oklahoma to see her, it might well be too late after the course was over. On the other hand, if I took time away from classes, there would be no possibility of graduating.

Fortunately, other members of the family rallied to the moment and allowed me to remain in California. My younger brother and his wife insisted that mother be given every possible chance for survival and took her to the Mayo Clinic in Rochester, Minnesota. The doctors there decided they could perform the surgery. It proved even more extensive than they had thought, but after almost twelve hours of surgery, during which they removed the pancreas and numerous other parts of her anatomy, they gave her a fair chance of survival. My brothers, sisters-in-law and niece took turns staying in Rochester with mother during the weeks of her recuperation. That is the way our family has always operated: everyone and anyone doing whatever is necessary. Without this kind of family support I would never have been able to graduate.

This story has a happy ending. Within months of the surgery, mother was able to return to work. Her surgeon, whose scalpel also provided the famous appendix scar on President Johnson's abdomen, called mother his "Miracle Patient." She had to watch her diet somewhat but lived a full life for the next twenty-three years with no recurrence of cancer, dying at the age of eighty-eight from causes unrelated to the disease.

Our furlough was ending with only enough time for a stop-off in the Midwest for a final visit with the family. Our bags were packed and I was loading them in the car for the drive to the airport. The phone rang just as I was carrying the last bag out the door.

"Mr. Scott?"

"Yes."

"Mr. Chester Scott?"

"Yes."

"Mr. Scott, you don't know me, but I want you to come to Colorado so we can talk."

"I'm sorry, but that isn't possible. We're just now leaving for the airport to visit our family before going back to the Congo."

"The best flight for you leaves Los Angeles for Colorado Springs in an hour and forty-five minutes." The strange voice gave me the airline and flight number. "I've checked and they have space available, so you call and confirm with them as soon as we hang up. I'll be leaving my home right away so I can get there and meet you at the airport."

"You don't understand," I interrupted, trying to control my irritation at the arrogant presumption of this man. "Our schedule just does not allow us to..."

"No, *you* don't understand." It was his turn to interrupt. "My name is Neil Dorsch. I'm just a wheat farmer out here in eastern Colorado and I don't know much, but I know how to build water systems, and God called me to go to the Congo and build a water system on one of our mission stations."

"That's wonderful, Mr. Dorsch. And let me assure you that when you get to the Congo I will give you whatever help I can. But in the meantime..."

"In the meantime we'll have to design the system, order the supplies, get them assembled at the right place, but we can discuss all that after you get here."

There was no way to say "No" in a way that made sense to Neil Dorsch, so after repeated protestation on my part and continued insistence on his, I agreed to meet him in Colorado Springs for a brief conversation.

The man waiting for us in Colorado did not need to be identified. Both his size and his bearing conformed perfectly to the take-charge-and-don't-accept-excuses personality he projected over the phone. He was a mass of energy, not easily contained by his husky farmer's body,

173

and the bear hug he gave each of us left no doubt as to his strength or his joy that we had come.

"You ever see the new Air Force Academy?" he asked, lugging most of our baggage from the claims area. "It's right on the way home and something you don't want to miss."

"Mr. Dorsch, I thought we could just talk here at the airport and then be on our way."

"Nonsense! Now that you're here, you've got to see two of the greatest sights in Colorado: the Air Force Academy and the town of Flagler." His smile was infectious, making his face almost cherubic, and we began to warm to the sensitive and dedicated man inside that burly body.

It took somewhat longer to see the Academy than it did to see Flagler, a tiny farming center sitting like a rejected hitch-hiker on the highway that stretches endlessly across the arid plains between Denver and central Kansas. Cars whizzed past, but nobody stopped or slowed to look. Flagler's most noticeable feature was its grain elevator; but grain elevators are too common in wheat country to attract much attention—unless, of course, one takes the fragile cage of the lift to the top, an experience Neil insisted we would enjoy and which we dutifully endured.

Audrey Dorsch was as gracious as Neil was abrupt and did everything a hostess can do to make us comfortable and enjoy being in her home. And a lovely home it was. I was predisposed to expect the "two rooms and a path" type of farm home I had known as a youth, but the Dorsch's house could have been transplanted to suburbia anywhere.

"How many acres do you farm?" I asked.

"Never figured it out, but I could easily. Out here we figure in terms of sections, not acres."

"A section. You mean a square mile?" I had always thought of 360 acres as a large farm.

"Yep! Right now I'm working about twelve sections."

"So much land! How is that possible?"

"Machinery," he answered. He showed me his tractors, and they were like nothing I had ever seen before. Completely enclosed, air-conditioned cabs sat atop enormous power, the multiple wheels encircled by mammoth tires. Stereo music playing inside the cab could be turned down, allowing Neil to call Audrey or several other locations on the CB radio. This type of farming bore no resemblance to what I had known as a boy and even less to what we might hope to develop at the Ag School in the Congo. The largest and newest of the four tractors was his pride and joy. "With this baby I can prepare a fifty-foot swath.

That's why I got it. I can get all the crops in and still have time to go to the Congo and get back before harvest."

"How did you hear about the need for a water system on our station?" I asked.

"Jerry Weaver spoke here at our church and told how there is no running water there, how it has to be carried from the spring. That's when the Lord spoke to me and told me to go there and build a water system for you."

We drew up the plans for the project, determined the materials needed and set up a schedule. Then, just before we were to leave, Neil said, "There's one more sight you have to see in Flagler: the Flagler International Airport." The airport turned out to be a closely mowed strip running along the edge of a wheat field. At the end of the strip stood a hangar large enough for only one plane. "It's the only plane here, but it's a beauty." And indeed it was: a Cessna 172 Skyhawk, fully equipped and in almost mint condition. "Too bad about it," Neil continued. "Belongs to a good friend of mine who overextended. The bank's going to take it back tomorrow because he's behind in his payments and there's no way he can hold onto it."

"How much does he owe on it?" I asked. Neil named a figure that was just a thousand dollars more than we had in our checking account. Half to myself, I said, "Exactly the plane I'd like to have."

"Do you fly? You never said anything about your being a pilot."

I told him a little about the Supercub and noted that I had just earned my A & E license.

"Scotty, if you could buy this plane it would save my friend's credit rating, and without good credit a farmer is dead these days. I'll tell you what. If you'll buy the plane, I'll give you a thousand dollars toward the price of it." I looked at Neil to see if he was serious. He was. Here was another example of how this wheat farmer interjected himself into the lives of other people to accomplish what he felt needed to be done. Before the day was over, Dolores and I were the proud owners of the Skyhawk.

Johnny and I flew the plane to New Orleans, where it was dismantled and crated to be loaded on a ship. As had happened so many other times in our life, a totally unexpected, and in many ways illogical, series of events proved to be the way God worked things out.

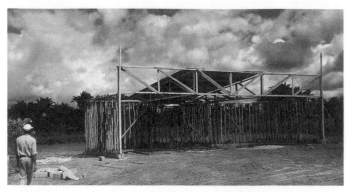

I built the hangar with no idea of what plane might occupy it.

The Supercub arrived on the day I finished the hangar.

Later, we built landing strips at all the stations, such as this one at Boko.

Many of our workmen commuted from villages across the
river.

Only one species of tree will endure in a bridge, and
many of them had to be dragged through the jungle
for miles.

The manioc being carried here
was all these women knew to
grow in their gardens.

Women graduates of the Ag School
learned to sew as well as how to
grow a variety of vegetables.

Charlie Sierra Sierra was shipped in a crate. I reassembled it myself.

Virginia Nickerson went home for six weeks. I built this house for her while she was gone.

Building the pediatrics hospital at Kimpese, a 'Class A, reinforced concrete frame, partial three floor' structure.

The pediatrics hospital at Kimpese completed.

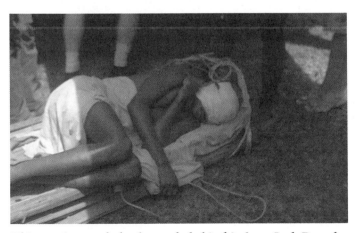

This man's muzzle loader exploded in his face. Jack Rumohr
and I evacuated him safely.

The School of Theology in Kinshasa
was completed during our fourth term.

Gassing up at a roadside filling station

Even before they are finished, some bridges must be
crossed.

As many as 400 persons might be baptized in a single ceremony.

Relaxing at the end of a perfect day.

This capitaine from the mouth of the Congo River fed us well.

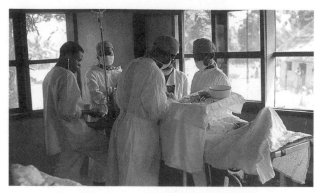

Zairian doctor and nurses performing surgery at Busala.

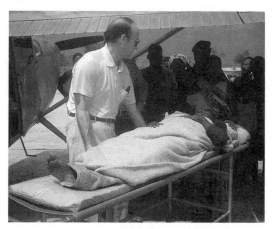

Medical evacuation to Kimpese became almost a daily routine.

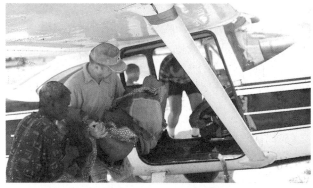

Each patient required and received personal attention.

**Over a century of mission-
ary effort has not eradicated
superstition and fear.**

We replaced the engine in this truck in our open-air garage.

The engine was flown in from South Africa.

Putting up the trusses at Nselo.

Dolores made life more beautiful for everyone wherever she was.

Charlie Papa Echo took us to every station in a single day.

Aerial view of the medical complex at Kimpese.

Our family as retirement neared.

CHAPTER 19

Vanga—1965

Things were bad in Congo before we left, and they had deteriorated in our absence. The economy was in shambles, inflation grew daily, supplies varied from scarce to non-existent. Social structures showed equal devastation.

Rebels and frightened citizens were coming out of hiding and seeking help, particularly medical help, which overtaxed the limited resources. Even such basic supplies as powdered milk could not be found anywhere. No alcohol was available for medical needs, even though a new brewery had opened in Leopoldville and beer was plentiful.

Still, we were able to scrounge the materials Neil Dorsch and I had listed back in Colorado, and by the time he arrived in January, everything was in readiness for him. For weeks he and his crew worked feverishly and completed the first water system Vanga station had known in its fifty-four-year history. Huge concrete reservoirs collected and held the water pumped up from the spring. Pipes carried it to the hospital, the school, the houses. The running water did not transform our lives by any means, but there is no way to express what an improvement it meant for us. Nor are there adequate words to convey our appreciation for Neil, both for his work and his person. His faith was as obvious as his enthusiasm, and both had a lasting impact on our workmen and on us.

The dearth of material was temporarily forgotten when the Cessna Skyhawk, designated 9Q-CSS, "*Charlie, Sierra, Sierra*", arrived, securely packed in its crates, waiting to be reassembled. My training at Northup Institute gave me absolute confidence that, once I had put the plane together myself, it was in perfect condition. Larger, faster, and more stable than the Supercub, it was to play a vital part in our lives and the lives of many others in the coming years.

Even manioc, the staple of the Congolese diet, was in short supply. Because of the shortage, the government decreed that no one could ship more than five sacks of manioc out of the Vanga area. This led to what we came to call wistfully "The Great Manioc Crisis," though it was not funny at the time.

Kidieke, our headman, greeted the police who came to our house during our absence.

"Tata Kidieke, we must use the storage shed Tata Scott built."

"Why?" Kidieke asked.

"We arrested two men just outside this station with 120 sacks of manioc. They were taking them out of the province to sell elsewhere."

"Put them in your jail. You don't need to lock them up in the shed."

"Of course we will put them in jail, but we need a place to store the manioc."

"Well, use your own storage facilities," Kidieke protested.

"The government doesn't have any secure building in this area. Tata Scott has let us use his shed before and would want you to cooperate with us now." Kidieke didn't miss the implied threat. He gave the keys to Mbidika with instructions to help the police transfer the sacks of manioc. But handling 120 sacks of manioc was a hard, hot job that was below the dignity of policemen. They instructed Mbidika to take the two culprits and make them transfer the contraband while the policemen refreshed themselves on our veranda.

Three days after this incident, we returned from our trip to see police surrounding our house. An air of tension swept over us even before we were out of our car.

"What's the problem?" I asked the uniformed policeman in charge.

"Our manioc is gone. We came back to get the evidence and it is gone! Someone stole our manioc!" His outrage was seeking a target on which to focus. "I'll not have people stealing things I'm responsible for. This could cause me great trouble."

Gradually, details filled in enough to give me the gist of what had happened. "None of my people would have taken your manioc," I assured the policeman.

"How do you know? You weren't even here. You are the big *mundele* here and you were gone. You weren't here to oversee your responsibilities." His ominous glare told me what was coming next.

"Since you are the biggest authority here, this is all your fault. I shall arrest you and take you to Bulungu."

"That would not be a good idea," Kidieke warned. "Tata Scott and your *commissar de police* are very good friends. Your *commissar* would not be happy with you if you inconvenienced his friend."

"I have to arrest somebody," the policeman said.

"Well, you're not going to arrest any of my men just to cover your own tail," I said. "If we find who is responsible, you can arrest him and take him to Bulungu. But you're not taking anyone off this station until there is some proof of guilt." Suddenly he was all smiles as an idea dawned on him.

"Of course! We shall have a trial." He looked back at our house with its shaded veranda. "I shall use your veranda and we will question everyone involved."

Thus began three days of prolonged, rambling proceedings during which practically every workman on the station was interrogated. The trial was doubtless extended because Dolores brought rolls and coffee or tea to the policemen regularly, and because they found the drama of conducting their own trial much more satisfying than any other duty they could think of at the moment. When the police had used up all the time they thought they could get away with, they had learned nothing more than they knew in the beginning.

Still, the policeman could not return to Bulungu with neither the manioc nor suspects. He arrested Kidieke, Mbidika, and three other of my workmen and took them, over my strongest protestations, to the government center in Bulungu.

I made the trip to Bulungu to see if my friend, the *commissar*, would intervene.

"With the shortage of manioc this becomes a grave offense." The heat in the tiny office was stifling, but there was something else contributing to the sweat beading my friend's face, something I could not fathom and which he was not disposed to reveal.

"You know that none of my men would steal the manioc," I protested.

"I know many things, my friend," he said. "Sometimes, things we know get in the way of other things we know." It was clear these words were prompted by events and conditions of which I was, and would remain, unaware.

"Kidieke is my headman and I need him very much." If I could not penetrate the complexity of the situation, at least I could press for the release of my men.

"Tata Scott, as much as I want to be of help to you, this is a situation in which you can have no part. This must be resolved without any *mundele* having his hand in it. *Ka diambu ko.*" This is a very useful phrase meaning "there are no more words." It can signal agreement, dismissal, a final word of farewell, or a host of other things, such as "there's no way to explain it," depending on the inflection and tone of voice. His tone made it mean dismissal.

"I trust you," I said. "I'm sure you will do the right thing."

Back at Vanga, I recounted this conversation to Pastor Pambi.

"We shall have the committee of African leaders of the station look into it," he said.

The committee made several trips to Bulungu, and within a week all my men were released. I was never told who the committee met with, what transpired in those meetings, or whether the manioc was ever recovered. Content to have my men back on the job, I was happy to let the whole thing drop.

But justice in the Congo often worked in ways that left us with a host of unanswered questions. Tribal wisdom usually worked through the system to achieve justice in ways that amazed us, even when it left us confused; but on occasion judgment and punishment were arbitrary and often, by Western standards, brutal.

Someone stole the money-box from the hospital, and the officials made the man who had the key to the box and the *sentinel* (watchman) each pay a fine equivalent to one-half the loss. Search for the actual thief ended as soon as the loss was covered.

It was also about this time that the soldiers arrested twenty boys and fined them five hundred francs each for "indecent exposure." Their crime was bathing in the river. Of course, everyone regularly bathed in the river, men and women equally lacking any thought of shame or modesty in their nudity. But on that day the soldiers had the authority and needed money. *Ka diambu ko.*

Not all the justice is handled by government authorities; much of it rests with the village and the family. One of the firmly held traditions is that the head of the family is responsible for the well-being of the family. If something bad happens to a family member, it is assumed the head man did not do his job, and so he has to pay.

Kalengi was one of my best carpenters and a good friend. His father was head of the family and Kalengi was next in line. Something bad happened to a member of the family (I never did learn what; perhaps a child was struck by lightning or a woman killed in her manioc field by a wild animal) and the family council decided that the father had not protected his family properly. They decreed that this omission called for the father to be killed.

"Kalengi is next in line, so it is up to him to kill his father," they told him. "Since Kalengi is a carpenter, he should kill his father with a hammer."

Kalengi was not the sort of man who could do this, no matter how firmly entrenched the tradition, yet he knew that if he failed to carry out the will of the council, he also would be killed. The night he was supposed to dispose of his father, Kalengi ran away, and other family members handled the gruesome task themselves.

Kalengi eventually returned, but for years following that incident he could not speak in a normal voice, uttering instead a squeaky semblance of words.

Another incident of this sort began with a call for me to go to the school and pick up a student who had gone crazy and take him back to his village. His village was far across the river from the station, and Ruth Engwall happened to be there at the time on a research project of some sort.

"What happened to this boy?" I asked at the school.

"There is a medical practitioner in Leopoldville who sells drugs which supposedly enhance the mind so that students can pass their tests," the teacher told me. "Unbeknown to the missionaries, the students send him money and he sends them the drug. However, the drug usually either kills them or drives them crazy."

We drove the boy to his village where I explained what had happened to him. "He made a bad decision," I told them. "He sent off for this drug and it has made him completely *kilaukidi*." We left the boy there and returned to the station. But the issue was not settled.

The men of the village gathered under the *mambu* tree, the traditional site where men-only decisions are made. They determined that the head of the family was responsible for this tragedy and would have to pay with his life. However, the victim-designate was a senior statesman and the government would never stand still for his murder if committed by an individual. The answer for them was that all the men of the village would share in the act.

Word of their intention reached the statesman, and he made a mad dash for the only place of sanctuary he could think of, Ruth Engwall's house. He almost made it. They caught him on her veranda and, with Ruth screaming at the top of her voice for them to stop, they killed him while she watched helplessly.

To the Western mind, the arrangement of marriage in the interior Congo approaches a crime, though it is a custom that has endured for centuries. Boys and girls do not choose one another as life partners; their marriage is arranged by the parents. Always there is a "bride price" ranging from five dollars to as much as seventy-five dollars. If the girl is a bit on the chunky side, the price is higher, but if she verges on the slender, she may be had for as little as a goat. It is not at all unusual for a man needing money to arrange the marriage of his twelve-year-old daughter, frequently to an older man.

The girl is required to have a child within two years, and if she doesn't her husband can return her and demand his money back. If the girl remains childless, she may become common property of the village. We have found that in some cases the sterility is the husband's, but that is of no relevance and does not change the consequences for the wife. But if the young bride does have a child, she will be expected to have another child every two years. She not only has the children but has sole responsibility of raising them. She also maintains the home and does the gardening, providing the living for the family.

The husband is required only to provide a house for his family, though that is not as simple as it sounds. It will take him two years to build his house from trees he cuts, interlace the timbers with vines and then plaster it all with mud. When that house is finished he immediately begins to build another, because by the time he finishes the second house, the first will have been destroyed by termites. Nevertheless, he finds time to hunt and fish a bit, sit in the shade with other men of the village, and discuss weighty matters that are beyond a woman's comprehension, and not infrequently indulge himself with a bit of palm wine.

Some American customs must seem as strange to others as theirs do to us. The custom of the Spring Break for students, with its mandatory trip to the beach, was introduced by Johnny and three of his friends in their sophomore year of high school. Since Florida was too far away, the boys planned a trip to Moanda, a lovely stretch of beach on the Atlantic coast, near the mouth of the Congo River, where we have enjoyed many vacations.

One of the boys in this group was Sandy Close, the son of Dr. Bill Close, who was the personal physician to President Mobutu. President Mobutu had given Dr. Close a white jeep, which he in turn made available for the boys to use on their outing. But this was no ordinary jeep: it was an Austin, made during World War II with a Rolls Royce engine, completely armor-plated even to a one-inch steel plate across the whole bottom, with specially designed tires, and still retaining the gun mount from its warrior days.

Dr. Close gave the boys a letter signed by President Mobutu, a *laissez passer* assuring them of safe conduct anywhere in the country, but the boys wanted to test their independence and resolved not to use the letter. They also extracted a promise from the parents that there would be no "air cover," either from me or Dr. Close, who, as a military pilot, had access to a plane.

They left very early on a drizzly Friday morning, and the first thing they learned was that the windshield wipers didn't work. But it was still dark and with the headlights on they could see reasonably well, so they kept going.

They got as far as Mbanza Ngungu when they came to a roadblock set up by the military. The soldiers had placed fifty-five-gallon barrels in the road with pieces of bamboo across the barrels. The problem was, they had set up the roadblock just around a sharp curve in the road. The jeep's speed, combined with the poor visibility, allowed them no time to stop. Bamboo splinters and barrels flew in all directions, as did the soldiers diving for the trees at the side of the road. The boys stopped, backed up, got out and replaced the barrels and as much of the bamboo as they could retrieve, then got back in the jeep and waited as though nothing unusual had happened. By this time the soldiers had recovered their composure and ran out from the trees, machine guns trained on these dangerous teen-age adventurers. They ordered the boys from the jeep, threw them to the ground, and with the machine guns in the boys' faces, decided these were mercenaries who were invading their country.

Johnny told me later that the *laissez passer* from the president was their "Plan C," to be used only as an absolute last resort; they were determined to make it on their own. For two hours they argued, laughed, joked and finally bribed the soldiers before they could continue on down the road for their great adventure.

I remained true to my word not to overfly them to relieve my parental anxiety about their welfare, a resolve made much easier by Bill Close's reassuring reports from the flights *he* made.

Thus began the introduction of what became almost a "Fort Lauderdale" in the Congo. The second year, the boys drove a pickup, which could handle more bodies, and were joined by a few of the teachers from the school. By their senior year, the beach was a two-week home for most of the students at the American School, though with a difference. While the parents were not prepared to allow their daughters to camp out with the boys, they were reluctant to be such spoilsports as to totally deprive the girls of any participation. The compromise most of them reached was for the family to move into the Mangrove Hotel, where they could keep their daughters under surveillance, if not under lock and key.

The nation continued its uncertain and unsteady path toward stability. Joseph Mobutu had taken complete control of the government in a bloodless coup, sending President Kasavubu back to Bas Zaire, where he lived out his "retirement" in quiet. Uprisings in Kivu Province prompted Mobutu to hire white mercenaries to augment his army, a decision that would later have grave consequences. The hired guns were excellent soldiers and fighters, but as far as character was concerned, they were a bunch of rabble. There were numerous clashes, usually with the same predictable results—the mercenaries would engage the Congolese, who, in hasty retreat, would abandon whatever arms and supplies they had.

This crisis brought on another prolonged stretch of organized and disorganized military confrontation. In addition to the tragic Congolese fatalities, many Europeans were killed, raped, and/or mutilated, continuing the bloody and brutal transition from colony to nation. The level of tension was heightened for all of us. Even the military seemed generally unsure of its role. The Reverend Marvin Hall, a minister from Kansas, visited Zaire during this period and was arrested for taking a picture of the national flag flying at the Stanley Monument. The soldiers spent two hours searching for an officer who could define their next step, but, unable to find one, confiscated the Reverend Hall's film and let him go.

Mobutu issued an order to implement his policy of "*Authenticity*", which he hoped would create more of a national identity. Western names were no longer to be used. Leopoldville, named by the Belgians for King Leopold, was officially changed to Kinshasa, restoring the native name for the original village that had stood on the site. New money was issued, as *Kutas* and bills called *Zaires* (usually referred to simply as "Z's") replaced the francs. Citizens who had Western names were to forsake them for "authentic" names. The president no longer called himself Joseph Mobutu, instead taking the name of Mobutu Sese Seko Kuku Gbendu Wa Za Banga.

Earlier, we had begun a school for younger children on the mission compound in the city. I had enclosed a carport and made it into a classroom. One of the earliest structures built on the compound was also converted into a classroom. When more room was needed, missionaries' living rooms were taken over as temporary classrooms. That first year we had seven little boys.

The hostilities following Independence made it unsafe for us to send our older children to a boarding school in the interior, so we expanded the school to accommodate the children through high school. News of this new American school spread throughout the foreign communities in the Congo, and we were inundated with students. We expanded as best we could, adding new courses each year, but every year the enrollment grew faster than our facilities. By the spring of 1966 there were hundreds of students. There were many conversations among the Presbyterians, Methodists, Disciples of Christ, Christian Missionary Alliance, the American Embassy and ourselves about having an independent American School that would adequately serve the need and that all of us could support. The entering class in the fall of 1966 made it imperative that action be undertaken immediately.

An architect was selected to draw up plans for such a school, but his knowledge of the climate, customs and conditions in the Congo proved as inadequate as his idea of the resources missionaries had at their disposal. Orville Weibe, the principal, had been buying construction material all spring, even though we had no place to build. I reworked the architect's plans, making them more realistic both in terms of cost and utility. We had also located the land we wanted. Situated just across the road from a big military camp, it promised to offer as much security for our children as any place we could find.

"We have $25,000 to help build the school," I was told at the American Embassy, "but we haven't been able to make any progress on getting the land."

"You guys know where all the buttons are," I said. "If you can't push them, who can?"

"We're doing everything that can be done." Though it was never said, I took this to mean that all the necessary palms had been greased; but still there was no signature from President Mobutu, the only one who could authorize our use of the land.

Since nothing else had done any good, I decided to talk to my friend, Bill Close. Dr. Close, the president's personal physician, was the first person Mobutu saw in the morning and the last one to see him at night. The fact that Dr. Close had his own children in the school encouraged me to approach him.

"I don't think there is anything I can do to help you, but I'll see if there is." Bill never made any pretense of influencing the president's decisions. "I sure don't know of anything I could do."

But two days later, on July 25, Bill brought us the necessary document signed by the president. "You can start working," he said.

"Thanks," Orville said. "But there's no way we can do much for the next term."

"Sure we can. We'll have classes there this fall," I assured him. "When do classes begin?"

"September 6," the principal answered. "That's just six weeks away."

"Piece of cake," I smiled. "But just in case, could you move the opening of school back to the first of October?"

Ten weeks didn't leave time for idle conversation. By that afternoon I had recruited about a hundred workmen "off the street" and was laying out the foundations even as my workmen began clearing trees. The next day the first foundation was dug and poured. Day followed day: working days, singing days, praying days, amazing days. Every day I witnessed the workmen pull the school a little higher out of the ground that had so recently been jungle, and I could only raise my eyes to heaven and say, "Isn't God great?"

The buildings rose day by day from foundations to walls to rafters to roofs: the administration building, classroom buildings, apartment houses for the teachers. Doors and windows were made and fitted into place. Interiors were finished so that equipment, much of it built by the crew, could be installed. There was no time to beautify the grounds; just get those buildings up and ready for our students!

The first classes were held on schedule, exactly fifty-one days after the first foundation was poured. Students from seventeen different countries exulted in their new facilities, but I drew on a far greater source of joy.

There were Zairians in Kinshasa who helped me put together my crew with such haste, but this crew had never worked together, certainly had never worked for me, and few had the skills needed for this job. Yet, those fifty-one days saw the development of such fellowship among the men and such commitment to the project that all of them asked, "Where is our next job, Tata Scott?" And one after another came to ask about the Christ who made our little miracle possible.

The pace of building had been frantic; workmen, trucks and equipment swarmed over the site, raising a constant cloud of dust in that dry season. Smoke from the annual burning of the grasslands clouded the air, a perpetual haze of gloom to counteract the euphoria we felt in seeing the progress of the building program. Then, just as we finished the school, the rains came. The thick layer of black dust washed away, the air lost its smoke and soot. The whole world seemed cleansed and renewed. I felt that a new page was opened in a book of promise. We could now return to Vanga and slow the pace of activity from chaotic to merely hectic.

Pangs of homesickness and joy struggled together in our minds as a letter from Sharan announced the arrival of their second daughter, Kathy.

CHAPTER 20

Vanga/Kinshasa—1966-1969

I nosed the plane up through the clouds, climbing to fifty-five hundred feet before leveling off in clear smooth air. Below, the world was wrapped from horizon to horizon in its fleecy white blanket, shutting out the intruding view of anyone who ventured beyond the confines of earthbound man. I was struck by the awesome beauty of a world topped with an even layer of whipped cream, but I was also aware that the usual landmarks I relied on were no longer visible. Caught between feeling frustration at not being able to see details on the one hand and enjoying the sense of freedom from the turmoil below on the other, I resolved that there was nothing for me to do but relish the moment and depend on my compass to guide us to our proper destination.

How like our life and work in Zaire! The daily details furnish necessary information for making decisions: a nearby village was burned by rebels last night; a report came in that 80 percent of the men in Stanleyville had been killed; we are down to our last two sacks of cement and no more seems to be available; a soldier is brought in to the hospital with an arrow protruding from his back; Dolores gets a stalk of celery and tells the cook to put it in water—he did, in a lovely vase in the living room; Andre Kidiela is arrested at Nsona Mpangu for "illegal lumber operations," whatever that means.

Yet, there are moments of prayerful retreat and quiet when all the turmoil is covered from sight by God's grace, and I am reminded that He is the one and only dependable compass for my life. I relish those moments and reconfirm my direction without ignoring the realities with which we live.

But the realities must be dealt with.

The plane opened up great opportunities in the work. We had projects under way at Busala, Vanga, Kilundu, Kikongo, Kinshasa and Nsona Mpangu. The plane made it possible for me to supervise many such jobs simultaneously, though it certainly didn't make it easy, particularly with the scarcity of materials. Still, the work was progressing nicely at what I felt to be the maximum pace we could handle. Then Wes Brown handed us an even bigger task.

Wes secured a beautiful site of forty-three acres on top of a hill overlooking Kinshasa on which to build a school of theology. Our present school at Kimpese and those of nine other cooperating missions would be merged at this new location, forming E.T.E.K. *(L'Ecole de Théologie Evangélique de Kinshasa).* It required many buildings, including classrooms and housing for students and staff, as well as the usual ancillary buildings. My responsibility was simply to design the campus and then get it built without letting up on any of the other projects going on. I was relieved to learn that John Marshall would be returning to the Congo to be coordinator of the actual construction. But design work was always exciting to me, so I threw myself into this project wholeheartedly.

Johnny was home on summer vacation and wanted to go to Kinshasa for a Fourth of July party held at the American Embassy. I had finished the plans for the new two-story addition for our hostel on the station in Kinshasa and also had to make a trip to Banza Manteke, where we were building a hospital, two residences and a duplex. I wanted Dolores to fly in with us, but she was working on end-of-the-month reports and didn't feel she could leave them for the three or four days we would be gone. At the very last minute she changed her mind, threw a few things in a small case and joined us.

Usually at this time of the year, the sky is filled with smoke from the annual burning of the grass, but on this day the air was as clear and smooth as polished crystal. We climbed to seven thousand feet, leveled off and I turned the controls over to Johnny. It was one of our most beautiful, uneventful flights ever.

As we neared Kinshasa, I radioed the tower. "Kinshasa, this is Nine Quebec Charlie Sierra Sierra. I'm inbound from Vanga. The pilot's name is Scott and my ETA is 9:45."

"Charlie Sierra Sierra, this is Kinshasa. Set your course at two-seven-zero degrees and call me on your final approach to Ndolo." The same routine had been repeated hundreds of times.

198

We landed at Ndolo airport, hangared the plane and took off for the embassy party. The following day Johnny flew to Banza Manteke with me. I took care of the work there and by late morning of the next day was ready to return to Kinshasa. I radioed Dolores for a weather report and told her that we would be landing at Ndolo airport at about three-thirty.

When we were over Banza Manteke I radioed the tower. "Kinshasa, this is Nine Quebec Charlie Sierra Sierra. I'm inbound from Nsona Mpangu. The pilot's name is Scott and my ETA is 3:30."

I was not prepared for the reply. "I don't know what the hell to tell you except 'Good luck, buddy.'"

"What's that supposed to mean?" Not really professional dialogue, but sometimes you just say whatever comes out.

"That's all I can say. Call me when you're down."

I didn't know what to do. I'd already called Dolores and she said she would meet us at the airport at 3:30. We flew on in to Ndolo. I called the tower two or three more times but received no response. As I came down the strip on final approach I saw soldiers on each side of the runway in machine gun nests with their guns trained on us and following us down the strip. Gasoline drums were being hauled out on the strip behind me. When I rolled out and taxied to the hangar, more soldiers were there, waiting with rifles and fixed bayonets. I reflected that the voice from the control tower had probably wanted to say, "Call me *if* you get down."

"Park your plane and then get out of here," a burly soldier ordered.

We had picked up some orchids for Dolores at Nsona Mpangu, so Johnny and I, each with an armload of orchids, wasted no time in evacuating the premises. At the gate, armed soldiers looked us over before opening the heavy security lock, but made no effort to harass us. Dolores and Phil Uhlinger were just outside the gate.

"What's going on?" I asked.

"Fighting broke out at Kisangani airport," Dolores said. "I heard about it just after our radio conversation. Apparently the government is closing all the airports for awhile." And indeed they did. Not only was Ndolo, the small airport, closed, but they also refused permission for incoming airline flights to land at Ndjili, the major field. A six o'clock curfew was imposed on all foreigners. Driving to the mission compound, we saw armed guards at all major intersections and particularly heavy guards at the bridges. The next day our radio transmitter was confiscated, cutting off all communication with the inland stations. The local radio station was broadcasting inflammatory messages, hinting that the unrest in the country had been fostered by foreigners.

Our sense of impending danger deepened even further when President Mobutu declared a national holiday for the entire country so the citizens could come to the public execution of four men who had tried to overthrow the government. It was obvious we were going to be in Kinshasa for a while.

Our plane, along with all other private planes in Zaire, was confiscated, and we were told it was now the property of Air Congo. We went to the airport to check on it, but were not allowed access. Of course, I protested through our embassy and the Ministry of Transportation, but there was nothing more I could do.

Fighting continued throughout the country as insurrection spread like a disease. The military responded with as much force as it could muster, usually resulting in indiscriminate suffering and death. Citizens everywhere were caught between the terror of the military and the terror of the rebels.

We received an urgent message from our friends, the Deckers, for whom we had "house sat" briefly the summer before, asking us to come by their house. Once inside, they informed us that they were instructed to leave for the States that night and asked if we would occupy the house again until the Ford Foundation named their replacements.

"Isn't this rather sudden?" I asked Jim.

"Sudden is the way things sometimes happens," was all the explanation Jim offered.

Jim seemed to be in a much more sensitive situation than merely serving as head of the Ford Foundation, but I thought it the better part of wisdom and friendship not to press the matter further.

"We'll be delighted to live here," we assured them. And indeed we were. In the midst of another Zairian bloodbath we were living again in the relative lap of luxury. Since it was impossible for us to travel outside Kinshasa to any of the job sites, Dolores and I took advantage of the interruption by enrolling at the Language Institute for a two-month course to sharpen our skills with the native languages.

John had parties at the house for his many friends, and the swimming pool resounded with the shouts and shrieks of young people almost every evening. John spent his days at the American School, landscaping the grounds and building a covered walkway connecting the buildings. I gave him a crew of men, which he ran with a professionalism belying his age.

By late September, all the other embassies had evacuated their women and children. Our embassy briefed us that negotiations were under way to settle the major issues, provided the United States could and would provide the money necessary to pay off the white mercenaries who were now the focus of trouble. A glimmer of hope rose on the horizon, but my plane still "belonged" to Air Congo. The Ministry of Transportation finally responded to my pleading, thanks again to my friend, Dr. Bill Close, and Charlie Seirra Seirra was again back in the Lord's service. We flew to Vanga with the little plane loaded with all the food and fresh meat we could get our hands on. Our missionaries who had been stranded there had not had any supplies since July, and they greeted us and our bounty joyfully. We were equally happy to pack some of our belongings and send them to Kinshasa by truck; we had been living out of our suitcases for more than two months.

The violence gradually subsided over the months, but we all knew it lurked just below the surface, ready to erupt again at any time. Violence was like a viral infection in this new nation: the symptoms flare up and the victim suffers until there is some remission, but the virus doesn't go away, it only lies dormant for awhile. Still, one should make the most of those times when the pain ceases and the days look bright again. As supplies became available, we resumed our work on the hostel, on ETEK, on putting the finishing touches on the American School, and on the other projects throughout the country, so that by the end of the year Dolores was recording more than two million zaires a month in transactions. Life settled into the familiar routines, interrupted briefly by a much-needed vacation to South Africa and highlighted by the arrival of our third grandchild, Larry Wheaton, born to Sharan and Jerry back in the States.

As much as I love to fly, I have never forgotten the dangers involved, and those dangers are compounded when flying a light plane in Congo. Tragedy is never more than one mistake or one miscalculation away.

Max Meyers was a missionary pilot for the Disciples of Christ and a good friend. An excellent and experienced flier, he was instrument-rated, held a commercial license and had logged more than three thousand hours. On a Sunday morning, he loaded his Cessna 185 with freight and two missionary wives who had come to shop at Mbandaka, then headed east along the equator for Boende, an hour and a half away.

Mary Johnson had been in the Congo for only two weeks. Her husband, a dentist, had come to work at the mission for one year and was reluctant to have Mary join him and even more reluctant for her to take this particular trip. The other passenger, Eunice Goodall, had served for years, and most of her five children had been born in the Congo.

Max was happy as he kissed his pretty wife, Carol, goodbye and waved farewell to their three children. Thirty minutes after takeoff he radioed his wife that he was running into a rainstorm. Five minutes later, Carol tried to reach him but got no response. She radioed Dr. Johnson at Boende, who took off in his Supercub to try to locate them. Unable to make radio contact, Dr. Johnson checked out all the strips where they might have landed but was unable to find them.

On Monday morning, nine planes flew north to the equator to begin a search: three planes from the American embassy, three MAF planes and three missionary planes. The rain forest along the equator is one of the largest and densest in the world. From high in the air, one can see the trees growing as close together as blades of grass on a lawn. Down close, one sees how impossible landing a plane there is and how improbable locating a downed plane would be. Nevertheless, we continued the search over an area a hundred miles wide and two hundred miles long. Meanwhile, a ground search was under way and every rumor and possible clue was thoroughly checked out. I flew for a week in the search before reluctantly returning to Kinshasa.

Seven weeks passed before ground searchers finally discovered the remains of the plane. The passengers had died on impact, and the canopy of the jungle had simply closed up to conceal the site of the tragedy.

It is hard to pick up the pieces and put them together again in a way that allows you to return to the routine and mundane, but life goes on and the work piles up and you stumble ahead until finally you are able to put the loss aside. Nonetheless, from that time on my thoughts focused more and more on the end of term and our upcoming furlough.

Before that term came to an end, however, I was in store for a truly bizarre experience.

When a missionary comes into Kinshasa from the interior, access to an automobile is a necessity. Since the mission does not provide such a vehicle, the best solution we have found is for one missionary to purchase a car to be left in Kinshasa for all to use. Of course, careful records of use are kept, and the owner is reimbursed accordingly. Dr. Dan Fountain had just purchased a new Volkswagen for this purpose, its gleaming dark-blue finish setting it somewhat apart from the more commonly seen red and light-blue and battered rusty "bugs" that formed the core of Kinshasa's traffic.

One reason the telephone seldom rings before six o'clock in the morning in Kinshasa is that few people begin conversations outside their home that early. Even more importantly, the phone system is so maddeningly undependable that even fewer want to begin their day with unnecessary frustration. But our phone was ringing.

"Hi, Scotty. Are you up?" I recognized the voice immediately as belonging to one of the MAF missionaries stationed in the capital.

"Of course," I answered. "I've been up for over an hour."

"You know I'm staying here at the Union Mission House?"

"Yeah," I replied. "I heard you mention it when you were talking to Dr. Dan on the radio yesterday and you asked to use his Volkswagen."

"That's what I'm calling about. He said I could use it, but he didn't say I could lose it."

"What do you mean?" I asked.

"I had it parked out front and somebody stole it last night." Guilt and anxiety were evident in his voice if not his words.

"I'll see what I can do," I reassured him. I knew Dr. Dan's car well because it was almost a twin to my own new VW.

As I shared breakfast with Dolores and thought about possible courses of action, I rejected them one by one. Depending on the police to find and return the car was the first thought I had and the first I rejected. Trying to locate a witness was equally futile. The only other possibility was driving around the city on the remote chance the car might be spotted. That did not offer great promise of success in a city of more than two million people, but it was the best alternative I could come up with. So as soon as the American School opened, I was there waiting for the principal, Paul Pretty.

Paul was not only a good friend but also a man who would be willing to share what promised to be a wild-goose chase.

"Someone stole Dr. Dan's car from in front of the Union Mission House last night and I'm going to go out and look for it," I told him. "Is there any chance you could join me?"

"Sure," he said. "I'd like to. The only thing I have to do is to stop at the bank and pick up some money."

I said, "That's fine. We're as likely to spot the car there as any place. I just want to keep cruising around the city until I see it."

We left the school about seven thirty and spent the morning driving randomly. The only location we specifically headed for was the bank, where at midmorning Paul filled his briefcase with enough currency to meet the expenses and payroll of the school. He tossed the case on the back seat and we resumed our search.

From time to time, Paul expressed his anger at thieves in general and car thieves in particular. "If we find them, I'm going to give somebody a knuckle sandwich," he said. I had never heard that expression before, but as noon approached I was very familiar with it.

"We'd better go back to the station and report in to our wives," I said. "Anyway, it's time for lunch." So I turned the car away from downtown and started for home. We had crossed the *Petit Pont* and come to the Dag Hammarskjold Bridge, near our station, when I saw the stolen car heading across the bridge in the opposite direction.

"There they are," I said. "Let's not let them know we're after them. I'm going to make a U-turn and then get in ahead of them." I made the U-turn in traffic and got just far enough ahead that we could easily keep them in view. I turned on to *Trente Juin*, the main boulevard in Kinshasa, and headed back for downtown. They made the same turn behind us, as I was sure they would.

In the center of Kinshasa is a large traffic circle and, since policemen are always around there, I thought it the best place to stop the car thieves. I slowed down enough to leave us almost even, then turned my wheels sharply into the other VW and ran it into the curb. There were six people in that small car. I jumped out and ran around to the driver's side, reaching my hand in through the window to grab the keys and turn off the motor. But there were no keys. The thieves had hot-wired the car.

The driver realized it was time for him to get out of there, so he gunned the motor, jumped the curb and took off. I yelled to the nearest policeman, *"Voleur de voiture!"* ("He stole that car!") The policeman jumped in the back seat of our VW and we raced off in hot pursuit. This was about ten minutes after noon, the busiest time of day for traffic in downtown Kinshasa, and we were weaving through traffic, crossing in front of oncoming cars, doing everything that makes for a good Hollywood car chase scene. All the time the policeman was leaning forward, trying to get his head out the window beside me and blowing his police whistle constantly.

When the driver saw I wasn't going to give up the chase, he turned off *Trente Juin*, into what we call the *cité*, the native section of town where millions of people live along the unkept and rutted streets. We raced through the *cité* as fast as a hundred kilometers an hour for at least thirty minutes. The other driver was jumping curbs, cutting across parkings, anything he thought might give him any advantage, but as he jumped one curb too many he blew a tire. I thought this would stop him, but he kept going. Every time I tried to get in front of him, he would cut his wheels sharply, trying to hit me. Finally, he tried to jump a curb again, and the flat tire and the weight of six people left the car without enough clearance. The impact scraped off the drain screw from the oil pan. All the oil came spilling out, and it was only a matter of minutes before the engine froze up and the car stopped.

I pulled up and stopped by the passenger side of the stolen car just as the door opened and a big guy jumped out. I swung my door open as hard as I could and slammed him back onto the other car, almost knocking him crazy.

The driver jumped out of the other side and started running. I took off after him. He was fast, but so was I. After chasing him for about a block, I was in position to give him my best high school football tackle. I brought him down and had him in a half nelson, but I immediately realized I was out of my class and had made a terrible mistake. His body felt like it was carved out of granite, his muscles were hard and massive. I was in good shape and I was strong, but I was not sure I was a match for this fellow.

Just then a big, fat woman came running up with a whiskey bottle that she swung at his head. She kept saying, "Let me hit him in the head!"

I said, "No!" and kept jerking his head back and forth, trying to keep her from smashing the bottle across his skull. Her wild swings threatened me as much as they did the thief, so I didn't know which of us was more frightened of her and her weapon.

Finally I managed to wrestle the thief back to our car. I jerked as hard as I could on his arm in the wrestling hold I had on him, half-hoping I could break his arm and make him somewhat more my physical equal. As I shoved him in the back seat I gave him a kick that sent him sprawling against the far side of the car.

The policeman had caught the man I slammed the car door into, and he shoved him into the back seat with my captive.

Paul Pretty also had captured one of the passengers, and true to his word had given the thief a "knuckle sandwich." This one also was crammed into the back seat with the others.

I told Paul, "The policeman and I are going to take these thugs to the station. You stay here with Dr. Dan's car until we get back, whenever that may be." I swung around in traffic to head out of the *cité* and back downtown.

"My gosh! Did you ever see so much money?" I heard one of the captives say. They had no reason to guess I could understand their language, but I looked around and one of them had opened Paul Pretty's briefcase and was clutching a handful of bills. I made a grab for the money, yanking it all from his hand and shoving it back in the briefcase. Then I yelled at him in his own language, "Oh, you steal our car and now you try to steal our money. You are in big trouble." Then I grabbed the case and pulled it up in the front seat, between my legs and the front of the seat.

The policeman was giving me directions. I thought I knew where the police station was, but the directions he gave me took us deeper into the *cité*. At length we came to what looked like an empty, haunted house in a horror story. It had once been a great two-story colonial home with a circular drive from the street, but now it looked abandoned and totally maltreated. "Turn in here," he ordered.

Driving toward the house, I saw men lying around all along the driveway and all over the porch of the house. Dirty and scroungy, they looked like riff-raff from the streets of the city. I thought, "Oh, my gosh! The policeman is in cahoots with these thieves. It's a gang, and I've been had! I've got to get out of here."

In front of the house I came to a large paved area. I crimped the wheels as I hit the gas full-force to put me into a spin, so I was headed back for the street and out of there. But before the car was fully turned, it was surrounded by about fifty of those men. I couldn't believe how fast they came to life.

One particularly disreputable-looking man poked his ugly face through the window. "What's the trouble?"

The policeman with me answered, "We've caught some car thieves and we've got them in the back seat."

Then a lieutenant came out of the house, his sharp military uniform dispelling my fears. The lieutenant looked at the prisoners in the back seat, then turned and started screaming in Lingala, most of which I could not follow. But his shouting brought the *Commissar du Police* running out of the house. He looked in the back seat and said, "Oh, My God!"

I thought, "Why are they making such a big deal over car thieves? There are thousands of them in Kinshasa."

The *Commissar* directed me to drive alongside what proved to be a huge cell block. The cell held about fifty men, all of whom the *Commissar* ordered out, making them sit down along the side of the building. The police took the man I had caught and shoved him into the cell. They slammed the door, then pulled another big, heavy steel door up against it. A man with a machine gun was stationed at the door, his weapon pointed through the bars at the prisoner.

The *Commissar* took me into his office and started questioning me about everything that had happened. At last he said, "That man you brought in is the most wanted man in Zaire. He killed three women and two policemen. We've been trying to get him for the last year. He is the head of a big gang, so it would be prudent of you not to say too much about having caught him. He is quite famous in his way and has many friends you would not want to get acquainted with."

I absorbed his advice, then said, "So you got what you want. Now what I want is to get back to where I left my buddy and pick up the car they stole from us."

He said, "We have to impound that car. You can't have it because we have to do some work on it first." He could read the frustration in my face. "We'd tow it in, but we don't have any vehicles. You go back to the car and take three detectives with you."

I said, "I can't do that now because I have to go out to our mission compound and get the head of the mission, whose name is Phil Uhlinger."

"That's all right," the *Commissar* said. "Take the detectives with you and you can go pick him up."

So I went out to my now-battered car and loaded up the detectives, three of the roughest-looking men I had first seen lounging along the drive. Now I understood why they looked like bums: they were in perfect disguise to go unnoticed in the streets of Kinshasa.

Our house was located near the entrance to the mission compound, so I stopped there first to tell Dolores that I was all right and that we had caught the thieves. She came out when she heard the car drive up, and I said, "Well, honey, it's all over. We caught the thugs who stole the car."

She came around the car and looked in the window. "Oh, my gosh, Scotty. Don't they look horrible!"

I said, "Honey, these are not the thieves. This is Dick Tracy and his two best cohorts."

Then I got Phil and we transferred to his big station wagon. We loaded in a spare tire and tools to fix the Volkswagen, then Phil drove us back to where Paul Pretty and the car were waiting.

Paul was a sight to behold. He was seated in a large red, overstuffed chair brought from someone's house nearby, in the shade of a great overhanging tree. People were sitting around staring at him as though he were some kind of a god, or at least a chief who had won their enduring respect. When I walked up to him he hung his head and put his hands over his face. "Oh, Scotty," he said, "I'm so ashamed. I'm so ashamed I'll never live this down."

I said, "Live what down, Paul?"

He said, "All morning long I talked about giving somebody a knuckle sandwich, and then when I did, I didn't know that was a girl until I hit her about the third time."

"That's OK, Paul," I said. "She had on a raincoat just like the rest of them and she had short hair just like the rest of them. There is no way you could have known."

We fixed Dr. Dan's car enough to tow it behind the station wagon, then pulled it back to the haunted house. The *Commissar* was waiting for us. "We've been interrogating this girl," he told us. "There are three others who got away and she told us who they are. We want to pick them up before they know we're on to them, but of course we don't have a car. Will you take us out to a couple of addresses?" We did, and they picked up one girl who had been with them, though the other two eluded capture.

We found out the girls were prostitutes and the addresses to which we had taken the police were houses of prostitution. The three thieves had stolen the car the night before, then driven to the house of a white man, where they broke in, beat the man badly and stole all the valuables they could find. Then they had picked up the three prostitutes and spent the night with them. They were just cruising around, having fun, when I caught up with them that morning on the Dag Hammarskjold bridge.

The next issue of the local newspaper, *The Journal*, had a picture of the man I had tackled. The brief story said he had been captured and executed.

What a way to end a term of missionary service!

CHAPTER 21

Zaire—1970-1971

Our third furlough had been anticipated with the feelings of a doctoral candidate approaching graduation: great satisfaction with the work that led up to that point, mixed with overwhelming relief that a respite is in sight.

As with our other furloughs, we faced a constant demand to speak in churches and at conferences all across the nation. We wanted to accommodate as many of these requests as possible, because we truly felt a partnership with those in America whose contributions to our mission program made our work possible. Yet we also needed to have time with family, and especially with Sharan, Jerry and our three grandchildren. We settled on Hutchinson, Kansas, as the best location to meet all our needs: John was enrolled at nearby Ottawa (Kansas) University; Mom, Pop and Granny were only a few hours' drive away and Dolores' parents were even closer; my brother Leon lived a few blocks from us; Sharan and her family just a couple hours' drive; we loved the church in Hutchinson and felt completely at home in it. Wichita offered adequate air connections, so necessary for us to meet our travel obligations. It proved to be a wise choice. We cuddled, coddled and spoiled our grandchildren at every opportunity.

John found in Hutchinson the young lady with whom he wanted to spend the rest of his life. He and Susan Pankratz were married the summer before our return to Zaire.

The Hutchinson church embraced us with open arms and hearts. In fact, the pastor, without my knowledge, initiated a program to purchase a new airplane for us for our next term. When I learned of his plans, I was aghast. The generosity motivating him and the church was overwhelming, but I had been having second thoughts about having my own plane on the mission field.

I loved to fly, and having my own plane allowed me to accomplish more than seemed possible. But there were nagging thoughts that I could not shake. How much did having my own plane feed my ego? Was I rationalizing my own self-centeredness for the joy of flying? Was having a plane placing more non-building demands on me than I should allow? How long could I fly over the jungle before I crashed through its beautiful but deadly canopy? With MAF now so well-established in Zaire, couldn't they meet all my genuine travel needs?

My only answer to those questions was that if it was God's will for me to fly a plane in Zaire, it must be the property of the Zairian church, and church officials themselves must assign the plane to me because they felt it necessary. When I sold "Charlie Sierra Sierra" at the end of the last term, I decided not to have a plane of my own again in Zaire.

I tried to explain this to our pastor.

"But Scotty, we've already started the fund-raising for this project," he told me.

"Don't think I'm not grateful," I said. "But there is absolutely no way I could accept a plane under these conditions. I may be stubborn, but I have to do what I think is God's will."

"Don't make up your mind until you see this," he said, spreading a colored brochure out on the desk between us. "This is the plane we want to get for you."

"Oh, man, it's beautiful!" I sighed and had a momentary temptation to reverse myself on the spot. Pictured was a sleek blue-and-white Cessna 182.

"Here's the equipment we're going to have in it." He pulled out a sheet of paper listing optional equipment that included everything I would have wanted had I made out the list myself.

"It is absolutely perfect," I said. "There is only one thing wrong with it."

"What's that?" the pastor asked.

"I can not...must not...will not accept it." There must have been a finality in my words that got through to him.

"But we've already raised over ten thousand dollars toward this plane. What are we going to do with that money?" He mused more to himself than to me, "We can't very well give it back to all the people who contributed. They gave it for a plane and I don't think we can arbitrarily use it for something else."

"You'll find something," I assured him.

Turning down the possibility of flying my "dream plane" seemed a hefty price to pay for a conviction that even I could not fully justify at the time, but I left with my heart overflowing with appreciation for these people, whose love and commitment had so motivated them.

Love given to and received from people dear to us refreshed our spirits and renewed our commitment. As our furlough ended, we carried the warmth of that love back across the Atlantic and into the continuing chaos of Zaire.

When I built the hostel in Kinshasa, I also added a large storeroom building with a second floor consisting of a room I intended to use as an office. During our absence this "Upper Room," as I called it, had served as a guest room for visitors. Now that we were back in Kinshasa, the "Upper Room" was the only available space for Dolores and me to live. I had installed a shower and sink in the room and had a stool under the stairs. It was a far cry from the palatial homes we had occupied during our "house-sitting" days, but we were together and happy. We appreciated the other missionaries who invited us to their meals, but we knew how much of a burden it was for them to prepare "extras" for us.

We called it our "cozy nest," and the description was apt. We were up among the trees and the birds. Just outside our window grew a flamboyant tree, its nearly solid-red flowers looked like millions of red orchids. Outside the opposite window a huge mango tree offered its bumper crop of ripe and delicious fruit. At night enormous bats flew in, took a chunk out of the fruit and dropped the rest to the ground, leaving the morning sun to find hundreds of partially eaten mangos littering the ground. Beside the front steps the grapefruit tree bore early, immature fruit. The tastes and odors of Zaire mingled with the barrage of colors assaulting the senses. We were home again.

A quick inspection trip to the scattered mission stations was in order to see just where the building program was at each. Bob Pearson had done an excellent job at Vanga during my absence, but the Kikongo station had a serious problem. Pierre Kumbi, our head workman there, died, leaving four buildings standing in early stages of construction. We had a project there to build a complete school for the wives of the pastors-in-training. Four personnel houses awaited finishing. Kimpese was preparing for the major project of building a maternity hospital. At every station work was waiting and needed to be done. But that would have to wait for five weeks while we built four trucks.

We didn't exactly build the trucks, but it was the next thing to it. We had ordered four trucks—two three-quarter-ton pickups and two seven-ton flatbeds. They arrived all broken down in four large crates weighing eleven tons. All we had to do was load the crates, transport them from the dock to Kinshasa, sort out all the pieces and store them securely from thieves, then put the trucks together piece by piece. We were making good progress on this job when an emergency interrupted us.

That morning in a small village in Central Congo, a group of men left long before daylight to hunt the buffalo or antelope or wild pig. An overload of powder or a clogged barrel in an old muzzleloader exploded into the face of one of the hunters. It was a quick end to the joyous event. The blast destroyed one eye and a large part of the face, but the hunter was alive. The only hope was the Baptist Mission station at Mulundu, miles away, but it was a hope. A flurry of activity followed: A hastily built litter. Men running with the litter for miles. A dugout across a swift river and strong men paddling with all their might. On to the mission while there is yet time, but time and life are running out. A frantic call on the radio of the inter-mission network, which finally reached MAF with the question, "Can you save this man?"

Missionary Aviation Fellowship had one plane at the time, a Cessna 206 that had flown three thousand hours in the last five years. That plane was torn down for a complete inspection and it would take many hours to reassemble it. At eight o'clock MAF called Jack Rumohr, who was helping me assemble the trucks, and asked if he could fly this medical emergency.

Jack had never made that flight from Kinshasa, and he wanted me as copilot. After a hurried trip to the airport, flight plans filed, gas tanks topped off, by 9:30 we were airborne in Jack's Maul 220, headed down "Thunder Boom Alley." The name for this area was more than apt. Rain beat a staccato against the plane and wild fingers of lightning threatened us, as memories of hundreds of such flights in the last ten years raced through my mind.

We slipped onto the tiny grass strip at noon, had a hurried bite to eat while our critically injured passenger was loaded aboard the plane, and minutes later were again airborne.

A gold plaque on the panel of Jack's plane read, "In memory of Christopher Lyons." I didn't know Christopher Lyons before he died in Vietnam, but I know the love of a mother and father for a wonderful son. That love made this trip, this day possible. It was a love so strong I heard it resonating in the engine. I saw it in the sky. I felt it as I held the hand of our passenger and it passed between us.

We reached our destination in time—a fine modern hospital where operations were done by the best of surgeons—and the patient lived to return to his family and friends.

I went to bed that night too tired to pick up all the threads that had woven the fabric of that day. Where did each one start and where did it lead? The hunger and the joy that initiated the hunt. The torn body that shared the small cabin of the plane. The torn body of a boy in Viet Nam whose loving memory was etched into a gold plaque on the plane...the plane...the plane.

The next morning, I was called before the executive committee of CBZO, the governing body of the church in Zaire.

"Tata Scott, we have received a letter which concerns you." The men seated around the table gave no hint as to what lay in store for me.

I waited with as much patience as I could muster and finally said, "Oh?"

"This letter informs us that there is a man in America who wants to donate an airplane for our work. We have deliberated and prayed over the matter and decided we will accept the plane with certain conditions." He paused momentarily for emphasis. "First, we accept the plane as the property of CBZO. We believe it better for the plane to belong to the church than to an individual. Second, we have assigned the plane to you. You are to use it as you have used the others. And third, of course, we don't have the rest of the money the letter says we need."

"May I see the letter?" I asked.

He handed me the letter and I scanned it hurriedly. The plane was the anonymous gift of a couple in New York state who had originally bought it for their son. I was hardly shocked to read that the plane was a practically new blue-and-white Cessna 182, fully equipped with a list of options that duplicated the list I had seen on the pastor's desk back in Kansas. All that was needed was to find a source of funding to get the plane from America to Africa at a cost of several thousand dollars—just about the amount in the Hutchinson project fund. (Subsequently, the Hutchinson church was happy to have that money used to have the plane flown to Zaire.)

As I studied the faces of these men with whom I had worked so long and shared so much, a strange thought crossed my mind: Someday, somewhere I will tell the story of this plane and how it came to be, and someone will say, "Nah! God doesn't work that way!"

But there are also times when God brings us up short.

There were almost seventeen hundred people in Makala Prison at that time, but the plight of the children especially touched us. So on the day after Christmas, four of us missionary couples took drinks and sandwiches for more than a hundred of the children, some of them as young as six years old.

Shortly after we arrived they hurried me off, around walls and through steel doors. Suddenly I found myself in front of more than two hundred men gathered for worship. Two choirs set the tone for the service and it was time for the sermon. Then I learned I was the preacher for that day. After the service was over, a hundred men came up to shake my hand. One young man had waited until the last, and he held my hand in both of his. Then he asked, "Tata Scott, how is Johnny and how is Nsonaka?" He was referring to one of the Congolese boys we had "adopted."

"Our son Nsonaka is in his third year of studies at Kisangani and our son John is living in the States," I answered. "But how do you know them?"

"I am Ibanda. My father worked for you when you built the mission station at Boko. Both Nsonaka and John were my playmates when we were children."

I studied the hard features of his face, trying in vain to recall the innocent little boy playing with his friends on the sandy soil of those faraway years. "What are you charged with, that you are here?" I asked.

"I am charged with many things, but the most serious one is murder." he said.

That night I was grateful for what God had done through Dolores and me, but remorseful as well. God doesn't always use kid gloves. Sometimes he says, "You failed me, didn't you?"

But some of the day-to-day events held as much humor as frustration.

One day I sent a workman to purchase some six-centimeter nails. He returned with nine-centimeter nails. I took a ruler and showed him the difference between six centimeters and nine centimeters his only reply was, "But Tata Scott, these were the only six-centimeter nails they had."

Potluck, or covered-dish, dinners where each person prepares and brings a dish of food are not unique to America; the Zairians have their own counterpart. One such memorable meal featured luku, greens, beans, goat and palm-oil sauce. When a goat is butchered, the stomach and intestines are saved as a delicacy to be served to the guest of honor. Since I was the senior missionary at this particular meal, I had the privilege of partaking of this dubious treat. To refuse such an honor would be unthinkable. Unfortunately, neither my palate nor the culinary skills of the Mama who prepared this dish were up to par, and I suffered a long and miserable night. No permanent damage resulted, though I lost much of my enthusiasm at being so honored.

Our work finished at Kikongo, we were reassigned to Kimpese. Kimpese was the home of the *Institut Medical Evangélique*, or IME as it was generally known, a cooperative effort among many denominations and nationalities. Americans, Swedes, Canadians, English, Dutch and Africans from other countries as well as Zaire made up a multicultural and multilingual team.

We were to undertake one of the most extensive building programs of our career. The first priority was a twenty-eight-thousand-square-foot, two-story pediatrics unit. Later we would add laboratories, a surgical unit, upgraded maternity unit, apartment houses, and a variety of other ancillary buildings. All this while we continued building programs across our field. During July we had to convert a part of the former American School in Kinshasa into four residences, and before September we had to complete two residences and two classrooms at Kikongo. At least one project was under way at every station.

Kimpese was already the largest hospital in Zaire with more than a hundred and thirty buildings scattered over several square miles. Our largest pastor-training school, as well as a growing agricultural and public health training facility, were also located at Kimpese. The station placed heavy demands on maintenance, which would be my responsibility along with the building program and continuing supervision of the building program for all of our mission stations.

It seemed a totally impossible task, but it would be eased when "Charley Papa Echo," the designation for our new plane, finally cleared customs. There was a new hangar and a three thousand-foot runway at Cico, a nearby cement plant, in which we could house our plane and enjoy a luxurious takeoff and landing area.

Our house there was large and roomy with a spectacular view of the Bangu, large, verdant, flat-topped mountains that dominated the horizon and seemed constantly to be calling out an invitation, "Come and explore, climb and relax, and be renewed." There is a spectacular two-hundred-foot waterfall cascading into a lovely, but insufferably cold, pool for swimming. Air currents created by the falling water whip up white caps on the surface, while the mixed chorus of bird songs lulls one into tranquility.

The great bonus for us was that this house had running water and electricity twenty-four hours a day.

One touch of progress was not such a blessing, however. The road from Matadi to Kinshasa had recently been rebuilt and blacktopped, allowing drivers to attain speeds much higher than they were accustomed to. Most drivers in Zaire pull into a village, stop their truck in the middle of the road, turn off all the lights, and leave the vehicle unattended. On this new road that custom, combined with the speed, resulted in tragedy after tragedy, and the hospital at Kimpese received a constant flow of broken bodies. Often I was called to provide ambulance service, since my vehicles were generally the most available and dependable on the station.

Two highlights occurred almost simultaneously. The most wonderful one was that Johnny and his new wife, Susan, came to spend the summer with us. Not only did we have many picnics, reunions and side trips, but they both found a place to use their skills. Susan worked with the children in both the physical therapy unit and the orthopedic unit. Johnny laid Formica on the counter tops in the pediatrics unit, supervised the building of a house, and lent a hand on other construction projects. As marvelously as they fit in, one could imagine they were full-fledged missionaries rather than guests. It was painful to see them board the plane for home at the end of the summer, but our hearts swelled with pride at the wonderful young adults and the love so obvious between them.

The other highlight was the release of "Charlie Papa Echo" after three months in customs. For those three months, we had been going to the international airport in Kinshasa to clean this beautiful plane and dust the spider webs off it. Then on that wonderful day, after the usual thorough preflight check, I ran the engine up, cleared with the tower, and moments later we were airborne. "Charlie Papa Echo" was ready to undertake the work God had sent her to do. And what a varied ministry that little plane performed!

We flew through the hot, clear air of dry season, through the mountains of smoke as the grasslands were burned off, and into the rainy season, threading our way around the storms. We were able to supervise the scattered construction projects, but found that every trip seemed to involve much more than was planned. Stranded by a storm at Vanga, we laid a long-anticipated vinyl floor in one of the missionary residences. The storm had torn the roof off a church, and that had to be replaced immediately. Always there seemed to be some local leader who *had* to make a quick trip to another location.

And there were always medical emergencies in which our plane was called to evacuate the desperately ill to the hospital at Kimpese. In one week, I made three such flights. One lady had a partially born child; the child was dead but the woman was saved. One mother was brought in with her seven-month-old child, a pitiful thing who weighed less than three pounds, but both of them recovered and did fine. A man with blocked lungs and blocked kidneys screamed his pain during the half-hour flight, but the doctors saved his life. None of them could have survived the twelve-hour (or longer) drive over the rugged roads to the hospital. One flight went the opposite direction: a young teacher with incurable cancer begged with tears in his eyes to be taken back to his own village to die. Unknown to anyone at the time, these medical flights were the prelude to one of the most exciting and satisfying parts of our missionary service.

CHAPTER 22

Kimpese—1972-1974

Perhaps the closest friends we had in Zaire were a Dutch couple, the Swens. Jost and his wife, Irene, were about the age of our Sharan, and their two young children became surrogate grandchildren for us. Irene was a musician, an artist and a linguist who became my French teacher. Jost was a physician working at IME, but he was also responsible for the medical work in Manianga, an area across the Zaire River from Kimpese where the Swedish missionaries had established five mission stations. The clinic-hospitals at these stations were staffed by nurses, but had no resident doctors. Unless Dr. Swen happened to be there, critical cases had to be transported over the worst terrain imaginable on roads that only the bravest souls and strongest vehicles could survive.

When Dr. Swen drove to the nearest hospital in his Land Rover, it was a thirty-six-hour trip. In one week he could visit, at most, two of the hospitals and would come home utterly exhausted.

"Jost," I said to him one day, "this is the only place I have seen in Zaire where what takes an hour by road can be covered in one minute by air."

"Ya, and every hour on the road seems like a day," he said. "I came here to be a physician, but I swear it seems I'm more of a Land Rover jockey."

"If we had landing strips at those hospitals, I could fly you there."

"You'd spend all day flying me around?" he asked.

"Of course not," I said. "I could take off after my work starts. I get everybody working at 7:00 and I can leave at 7:15. I can drop you off at any of the hospitals you want, and be back here to supervise things within an hour. Then I could leave here at 4:00 and pick you up and bring you back home."

"Scotty, you can't imagine what that would mean to me," he said.

"So what about landing strips?" I asked.

"Karl Backman built landing strips at three of the stations last year: Kibunzi, Kinkenge and Sundi Lutete," he said. "Luozi has a place near the river where a strip could be cleared. But I don't know that there is any place in those hills." I knew what he meant, having flown over much of that area—to my judgment the most rugged and mountainous in all Zaire.

Before our conversation ended that day, we had mapped out a rough schedule, which our mission enthusiastically approved. They did not lift any of my workload, but thought it wonderful to add this as an extra.

Dr. Wayne Meyers was in charge of Kivuvu, a leper colony, and soon he and one of his helpers, Dr. Kvernes, was added to the team to treat leprosy patients there. A landing strip was built at Luozi, running perpendicular to the Zaire River with a slight rise from the river inland.

In the first year "Charlie Papa Echo" made 217 flights into this area: 55 business trips, 79 doctor's visits and 83 medical emergencies. God alone knows how many lives were saved and changed by this program, which the MAF later took over as a priority of its own.

This program came nearer to costing my life than anything that happened during all our time in Zaire.

A call came from Sundi Lutete: a woman who had been in labor for many hours had started a transverse birth but could not deliver. A hand and arm of the baby were out, but all attempts to turn the child had failed. The doctors at Kimpese agreed that no child could have a natural birth under those conditions, and a C-section was called for immediately. I was asked to fly over and pick up the patient while the doctors prepared for surgery.

At 2:25 "Charlie Papa Echo" departed Kimpese for a 35-minute flight to Sundi Lutete, 360 degrees due north. At 3:00 we touched down and the patient was waiting on the airstrip. A Swedish missionary had driven her the three miles from the clinic to the air field. We strapped the patient on a stretcher in such a fashion that she could turn and sit up, but not move forward. Her husband and a twelve-year-old girl were buckled in the rear seats, and we were airborne twelve minutes after landing.

Six minutes out of Sundi Lutete, the man in the back seat tapped me on the shoulder and asked, "Is that normal?" He pointed out the right window: gasoline from my right fuel tank was pouring down, squirting across the window and running back.

"Not to worry," I assured him in his native language. Then I carried on a silent conversation with myself. "This is the first real emergency I've had flying in Zaire. I have to think this through carefully and rationally. There is no chance that I can make it to Kimpese; that is out. The best bet would be to turn and fly down the Zaire River to Luozi, where we just finished the strip."

I called Dolores on the radio. "I have developed a serious fuel leak in the right tank. I don't know what to do about it, but I'm going to turn off the electrical system because of the danger of fire. I am going to land at Luozi. I'll call you when I'm on the ground."

"OK, I copied that," answered Dolores. "I'll be standing by." Her voice showed no more sign of tension than if I had told her there was a small storm cloud way, way off in the west.

"Charlie Papa Echo" banked smoothly right as I began to follow the mighty river toward Luozi. A familiar bend in the river appeared before me, and I knew the field was just moments away. I resumed my silent conversation with myself. "The leaking fuel cell is directly over the exhaust pipe, and the gas will drip straight down when I stop, instead of being blown backward. Any backfire from the engine and this plane will blow sky-high. I have to kill the engine and come in dead-stick. I can't use my flaps because they are electrically operated. Get your altitude right, Scotty, and cut your air speed now as you make that final turn over the river. Good easy bank...Six hundred feet above field elevation...Good air speed...Kill the engine...Pull the fuel mixture all the way out...Get it right because there won't be another chance on this landing."

An ear-splitting scream tore through the cabin just then, and I turned to see that the woman on the stretcher beside me had reached down, grabbed the arm of her baby and delivered there in the cabin.

Practicing a dead-stick landing is vastly different than the real thing; in practice you know that you can fire up the engine and correct any misjudgment. This was not practice, but I seemed to be on a near-perfect glide path when the woman began pounding on my shoulder. "Tata Scott. Tata Scott. Look! It's a girl!"

A glance told me she had the baby lying on the stretcher between her legs. "Oh, great!" I thought. "Now I can't use the brakes or I'll slide the baby off the stretcher and onto the right-hand pedals."

Fortunately, the Luozi strip runs slightly uphill from the river, and miraculously the plane touched down almost at the very beginning of the runway. Still, our run-out used the entire strip, and we came to rest just short of disaster.

The father and I used our tow-bar to pull the plane to the other end of the strip, where a Zairian nurse from the mission was waiting with a car. He took the family to the dispensary and returned soon afterward with two bits of information: the mother and perfectly normal daughter were both doing fine, and the mother had named her daughter *Matondo Ndeke*, "Thank You Little Bird."

As soon as the car left for the hospital, I called Dolores. "I'm on the ground at Luozi. My patient delivered on final approach over the Zaire River. Both the mother and baby seem to be fine and have been taken to the dispensary. Would you see if you can get MAF on the network?"

"MAF Kinshasa," I heard her call.

"This is MAF," came the immediate response.

"Have you been reading Charlie Papa Echo?" Dolores asked.

"We've followed it all." I recognized the voice of Roy Parsons.

"Roy, I've got a problem," I said into the microphone. "My right fuel cell developed a leak and is now drained dry."

"What is your flying time to Kimpese?"

"Twenty minutes," I answered. "What do you think of mixing five gallons of auto gas with the gas in the left tank?"

There was a pause that seemed much longer than it really was. "How much gas do you have in your left tank?"

"Seven gallons, as near as I can tell," I said.

"The auto gas should be all right, but keep it on the left tank only. Don't lean your mixture, and when you get home flush out all of it."

"Anything else, Roy?" I asked.

"Pull your spark plugs when you get home and check them for carbon," Roy said. "And one other thing. Good luck, Scotty."

For the first and only time in my life, I put gas in the plane without filtering it. I tried to use a paper coffee filter, the only thing available, but it didn't work so I just dumped the gas directly into the wing tank.

The plane started and ran up to normal. I didn't want to call Dolores until I was certain it would work, so I took off and spiraled up to thirty-five-hundred feet, keeping the field directly below me. The engine ran smoothly.

"Charlie Papa Echo to base," I called.

"Go ahead, Charlie Papa Echo."

"I'm thirty-five-hundred feet above Luozi field and I'm on course for Kimpese. ETA is thirty to thirty-five minutes."

"Roger, Charlie Papa Echo. I'll be standing by."

As I winged my way homeward I gave thanks, not only for God's presence through this ordeal, but also for my marvelous wife. Whenever I flew, she kept the radio turned on in her office and I could reach her from anywhere on our mission field. Her voice had often helped me battle the loneliness and boredom of flying. I knew she had to be terribly worried, yet there was never the slightest trace of anxiety in her words over the radio. She gave reassurance and reinforced my own confidence. Through this experience I had felt no fear, only the pressure to do what was needed, to keep cool and not to make any mistakes.

Then the engine died!

I switched the fuel selector to "Both" and the engine caught, but when I switched back to the left tank it died again.

"Charlie Papa Echo to base."

"Go ahead, Charlie Papa Echo."

"I'm having engine trouble, Dolores," I said. "I don't know how long I can keep it flying."

"Roger, Charlie Papa. I'll be standing by."

Two minutes later I called again. "Dolores, I'm trying to make Malanga. The engine is getting worse."

Roy's voice came over my receiver. "Dolores, where is Malanga?"

"Malanga is a lumber mill about five minutes' flight from Kimpese."

I had spent years flying over jungles, hills and grassland, always keeping an eye out for the choicest place to go down. Suddenly there was no good place! A village down below had a garden area nearby and while it was far from satisfactory it appeared infinitely better than the mass of jungle. I circled the plane downwind.

"Dolores, the engine has totally quit and I can't get it started again. I'm going to do a forced landing in a garden near a small village. I will call you when I'm on the ground."

"Roger, Scotty. I'll be standing by."

I peeled off, making some stiff banks to lose altitude and bring my plane down in the garden. But as I neared the open spot I saw termite hills, six to seven feet high, looming up over the area.

Ten seconds before touchdown, the engine started.

Everything in a pilot's training says never, never, never try to abort a landing under these conditions, but the image of plowing through those termite hills held no attraction whatsoever. I pulled the nose up and began spiraling skyward again.

"Dolores, I don't know why, but I'm still flying. I'm going to try to make it in to Malanga."

"Roger, Charlie Papa Echo. I'm standing by."

But all too soon, the engine quit again. "The engine's dead again," I said into the mike.

Wes Eisemann's voice answered. "Scotty, I think you're out of gas. Try slipping the plane. Put it up on one wing and see if you can get the fuel to run toward the cabin." Wes had been monitoring my problem while he was airborne far away.

I kicked the rudder, the plane took a sharp bank, and the engine started. "I think you're right, Wes," I said. "I'm flying again."

The Cessna would run for a bit, then give its dying gasp and quit. I'd rock the wings, and it came back to life. We nursed each other through long moments and tedious miles. Finally I was able to call in, "Malanga is in sight. If I can get another three minutes, we've got it made."

The engine died again and all the rocking and slipping I could do would not coax it back to life.

"One more minute, if I can make it." Then the most wonderful transmission of the entire day, "Charlie Papa Echo base, this is Charlie Papa. I'm on the ground at Malanga, and it feels wonderful."

This was a case of pilot error, pure and simple. The strip at Luozi is on a slope, and I had my plane nosed up. I did not take that into consideration when I checked the gas in the left-hand tank, so what looked to me like seven gallons could not have been more than two. Perhaps the unusual conditions under which I landed at Luozi played a part in my mental lapse, but there had to be something, somewhere beyond myself that allowed me to land safely at Malanga.

Roy later reaffirmed my conviction. "Scotty," he said, "remember when you called in that you were still flying but didn't know why? Well, I know why. As soon as I heard you say you were going to ditch it, I dropped to my knees and prayed. Just as I said 'Amen' I heard you telling Dolores that you were still flying. I know why!"

"And so do I, Roy," I said.

Even in preserving the integrity of the mission, "Charlie Papa Echo" played a pivotal role.

Our Baptist mission, CBZO, had existed in the Congo since the 1880s. Other denominations also established presences there, and much later we joined with the Methodists, Presbyterians and Disciples of Christ to form the Congo Protestant Council. This was a coordinating body between the missions and for years was a valuable asset for all of us. However, an overly ambitious Zairian named Bokeleale had become the head of the Council, and therein lies the story.

Tata Buhika, our general secretary, called me on the radio from

Kinshasa late one night. "Tata Scott," he said, "we have the most grave situation imaginable. CBZO has just twenty-four hours before it will cease to exist."

"I know we have problems, but..." I was at a loss for more words.

"Bokeleale and his colleagues at the Protestant Council have given each of the missions just twenty-four hours to have the leaders of each and every station sign and return a set of papers or lose their *Personnalité Civile*." He did not need to explain the importance of the *Personnalité Civile*; it is the document that gives governmental recognition to an organization, and without it no organization could exist for one day in Zaire. "Is there any possible way for us to get these papers signed and back in Kinshasa by tomorrow evening?"

"Of course there is," I answered automatically. Then I did some fast and heavy thinking as to what that way might be. "You are in Kinshasa now, aren't you?" I asked.

"Yes. I am here in our office with our other leaders."

"Fine. Have them sign the papers there. Then you drive to Kimpese, getting the papers signed at Sona Bata on the way. I will meet you here at 7:30 tomorrow morning. Can you do that?"

"Of course," he said. "But that is only three of our stations."

"So bring all the other papers with you. Now, get on the radio and tell Nsona Mpangu we'll be there at 8:00. Then tell Kikongo we'll be there at 9:15. Then call Vanga and tell them we will arrive at 10:00. Then you can tell Busala we'll be there at eleven-something. Call Moanza and tell them to expect us at a quarter until one. Tell Boko we'll be there at 2:00. And finally, tell your wife you'll be back for lunch at 3:00."

After I finished the radio conversation, I asked the Reverend Emmet Parks, a pastor from California who was visiting us, if he would like to see all of our stations in Zaire.

"Of course," he said. "But we're going to be here only two weeks, and that isn't enough time."

"You be ready to roll by 7:30 tomorrow morning and I'll surprise you."

At sunrise the next morning I explained our itinerary to the Reverend Parks as we were getting the plane gassed and ready for its marathon. "What's the urgency of all this?" he asked.

"It's just a darned dirty deal," I said. "The head of the Protestant Council is trying to squeeze out the denominational missions so he can take over all by himself. He wants to get control of all the property and all the assets."

"Is there that much?" the Reverend Parks asked.

"We've been here for ninety years and have invested millions of dollars. The other denominations have done the same." I twisted a valve under the wing to bleed any water from the gas tank. "Yes, there is plenty at stake. But what's more important is the work itself."

Tata Buhika arrived on the dot and we had the leaders of Kimpese sign the papers.

The weather was ideal and the schedule worked perfectly. At every station the same ritual was repeated: land; taxi to the group of waiting dignitaries; abbreviated greetings followed by the signing ceremony; back in the plane and airborne again to the next stop. At exactly 3:00 that afternoon we landed in Kinshasa, our mission accomplished and the designs of the takeover frustrated.

Of course, the other denominations were able to recover their *Personnalités Civiles* as well, but only after long and complicated litigation.

Not all the service of "Charlie Papa Echo" was designed to benefit humanity; she also served occasionally to provide the Scotts some much-needed recreation. She took us and the Swens to Albert Park in Kivu for a memorable vacation at the fabulous game preserve. And she also carried us across the equator for me to enjoy one of the richest hunting experiences of my life.

The airstrip at Cico, along with the five-plane hangar, was almost mine exclusively. I told my MAF friends what a wonderful layout it was, so they came down to check things out and were genuinely impressed. They organized a "fly-in" at Kimpese for private pilots, a time of training and low-level competition. It was a great success.

When MAF needed to overhaul all their planes in Zaire, they arranged to use the hangar.

John Fairweather and his wife, Marge, were assigned to Kimpese by MAF since John was to do the overhaul. Our home was a duplex, and the Fairweathers shared the other half. We became close friends during the time they spent at Kimpese, but the time came when John had completely overhauled the several planes they had at the time. He was reassigned to Karawa, a mission station far up in the Equatorial Province. School was approaching and they needed to get their sons, Steve and Rick, set for their new school. They also needed to check out their housing for this new assignment. What could make more sense than Dolores and I flying up with the Fairweathers and making a vacation out of it?

We flew across the equator, up the Zaire River, then turned further north and five hours later landed at their future home. It turned out that the station is located near a beautiful lake, where missionaries in that area take their R & R.

We had no more than arrived when Dr. Thorpe, a local medical missionary, greeted us with happy news. "We have heard that Mr. Scott has had success in hunting buffalo," he said. "So we have arranged a hunt for you. Tomorrow you will go to the hunting camp, which is about a hundred miles from here, and the next day you can hunt. The women can spend a wonderful time in one of the cabins at the lake."

"Are there guides available?" I asked.

"Oh, certainly," Dr. Thorpe said. "There is one thing I would ask that would be a great favor. My son, Chuck, has been raised here and enjoys hunting, but in all his seventeen years he has never killed a buffalo. Would you mind taking him with you?"

"Not at all," I said. "But there is no guarantee that we'll even see a buffalo, let alone get a shot at one."

"Oh, Scotty, I hate to see you go," Dolores said when I told her about the trip. "I can't bear the thought of your sleeping on a tarp out in the open, or at best being in a mud hut."

"Hey! I'll manage. I'll manage," I reassured her.

The next day John, Chuck and I flew to the camp. Our hunting camp turned out to be anything but primitive. The lodge had several bedrooms, a modern bathroom, a lovely dining room with wall-to-wall carpeting and a first-class kitchen, along with a houseboy who prepared a delicious steak dinner for us. This was a huge plantation, which also had a herd of five thousand cattle, part of an agricultural development program.

That evening the plantation director came to visit after dinner. He extracted his bottle of schnapps and placed it carefully on the table beside an overstuffed chair. The chair, though large, was barely able to accommodate the mass of his buttocks, while his stomach oozed forward as though trying to escape the confines of his trousers.

"Well, boys, let me tell you about the cape buffalo," he began. "First of all, there's a lot more Africans killed by the buffalo than there are buffalo killed by the Africans. The odds are much in favor of the buffalo. They're a dangerous animal." He paused for a drink of schnapps. "One of the most memorable hunts I had..." and the story he told turned into another story, and then another and another, far into the night. His Van Dyke beard was getting almost as much schnapps as his mouth was before the evening ended, and we recognized in him a loneliness that seemed to demand a nightly stupor. He had come here as a veterinarian to supervise development of the cattle, bringing his young wife with him. Too soon, his wife was dead. He stayed on with the work, but his life was empty except for the schnapps and the occasional chance to visit with guests at the lodge.

The next morning we were up at 4:00, had a monstrous breakfast, and were loaded into a carryall with a chauffeur and two guides. I noticed ears of corn, still in their husks, in the carryall.

"What is the corn for?" I asked.

"The most important part of the hunt," my guide answered. "See the silk at the top of the ear? You toss a bit of corn silk up in the air to see where the wind is from. Sometimes you cannot feel the wind, but the corn silk will tell you."

I knew the importance of being downwind from the buffalo, but thought it wise to let the guide continue for Chuck's benefit.

"If you are upwind of the buffalo, you may as well go back home. The buffalo can catch your scent a mile away." His small frame seemed to swell at this chance to demonstrate his wisdom. He directed our chauffeur to where he was sure the buffalo would be. On the trail, the corn silk told us we were most fortunate: an almost undetectable breeze was facing us. We followed the trail downward toward the lake and soon found ourselves wading through water up to our waists, though the trees were so dense we could not see open water.

The guide gave us a hand signal to proceed even more cautiously. We slogged ahead for a few more yards, until we were at the edge of the tree line and the lake was visible before us. There in the water, about a hundred yards ahead of us, was a female buffalo with her yearling calf. I motioned to Chuck to take his shot, and he braced his .30-06 against the trunk of a tree. Just then I looked across the lake and saw a magnificent bull standing by the water's edge, some 230 yards away. I tapped Chuck on the shoulder and asked him to wait a moment while I got in position. I calculated the distance to the bull, braced my Weatherby against a tree for stability, took aim, and told Chuck to go ahead and fire. As soon as I heard his shot, I squeezed off the Weatherby and saw the bull take one mighty leap and disappear into the thicket. "Well, he's gone," I thought, but I didn't feel too badly to have missed from that distance.

The cow gave a mighty squeal, thrashing around in the water until another shot finished her and still another brought down the calf. The guides came running when they heard our shots, and we went around to a point of land closer to where the cow and calf had gone down. While the others waded in to retrieve the animals, I got one of the guides to go around the lake with me.

"I shot at a bull across the lake. I may have wounded him," I told the guide, remembering past dangers from wounded buffalo. Walking around the lake to find the spot where my buffalo had disappeared reminded me of locating the landmark when I hit a golf ball into the woods. But we found the place, and much to my surprise there lay the bull. My shot, either absolutely perfect or incredibly lucky, had hit him in the backbone, just behind the shoulder. He was still alive, but the shattered spine had paralyzed him. I ended his suffering with a *coup de grâce*.

The villagers started pouring into the area, responding to some unknown communication or sixth sense or whatever—I have no idea why, but there must have been a hundred who assembled. They hauled out the three carcasses and began butchering and chopping with their machetes.

"What part do you want, Tata?" they asked me.

"All I want is the skull and horns of the bull as a trophy," I said. However, John Fairweather wanted a truckload of the meat for the mission, so they called for a truck from the closest station and loaded it with meat, which they divided among three stations. The villagers got the remainder of the meat and, I am sure, enjoyed a feast the likes of which they had not known for a long, long time.

As I reflected on this experience I thought that, as much golf as I had played, I had never had a hole-in-one, and as much hunting as I had done, I had never had another shot like this. Perhaps I should be happy to settle for one out of two.

While we were on this vacation north of the equator, Dolores' younger brother, Jimmy, died in the States of a heart attack. News reached her too late for her to return for the funeral, but within a month her father also passed away from the same cause. She returned to the States for six weeks to be with her mother and family. The loss of her father was made bearable by the joy of being with John and Susan when their son, Aaron, was born.

Meanwhile, life went on in Zaire at its own crazy pace.

As the economic and political situation continued to deteriorate, General Mobutu needed something to divert the people's attention. He put renewed emphasis on his policy of "Authenticity." There was also a decree that neckties were banned and anyone caught wearing one would be fined. The term "Congolese" was no longer to be used anywhere, the new term being "Zairois."

Mobutu also imposed a tax on radios, so important for us to maintain contact with one another across the field. While we were prepared to pay legitimate taxes, this one exceeded the limits of reasons. One denomination got a bill for $500,000. Obviously, such a tax could not long remain in force, but until it was rescinded, our communications were severely interrupted.

Then our dog, Hedi, died. Hedi had been a member of the family for seven years, and her loss was so painful that we decided never again to have such a pet. But then I ran across a black toy poodle puppy I couldn't resist and brought it home for Dolores. We named her Tina after our friend, Tina Workington. Later the Workingtons wrote, "We now have an ugly little puppy we have named Chester."

Tina loved to nibble on our toes when we went to bed and receive our undivided attention when we arose. Once, while we were packing for a trip with our suitcases opened on the bed, Tina ran out of the bedroom, got her rubber bone, brought it back in and dropped it in the suitcase—her way of telling us she did not want to be left behind.

The work continued at an unbroken and hectic pace. I had building projects and maintenance needs at Kimpese that seemed to expand daily. The medical flight program into Manianga was in full swing. In addition to supervising construction across the field, I was still on the executive committee of CBZO and chairman of the Property and Vehicle Committee. We were tired, burned out and homesick; the end of the term could not come too quickly. We were counting the days until we could be with our children, our grandchildren, our parents and our siblings. Turning a page of the calendar each day and realizing that we were one more day closer to home made life bearable.

Then our headquarters in America asked us to postpone our furlough and undertake a two-year project in Jerusalem. It was a difficult decision, in a way, and yet we had served up to this time guided only by what we felt to be God's will. If God wanted us in Jerusalem, who were we to argue?

We hastened to do all those things that must be done to wrap up the work before leaving. Charlie Papa Echo belonged to CBZO, but it was my responsibility to dispose of her. I found a man who was willing to trade a duplex apartment house in Kinshasa for the plane, an arrangement that promised long-term income for CBZO. Headmen were designated to finish up projects under way. Possessions were either stored or given to friends. Farewell parties and goodbyes were regular occurrences with the missionaries when we all left the field at the end of term, but still there was room for a tear or two in parting.

Every Christian wants to see the Holy Land, and we were no exception. Wes Brown, the missionary who was responsible for setting up the center, not only served as our guide but also proved thoroughly knowledgeable in interpreting the deeper meaning and history of all we saw. It was a rich and rewarding experience, yet it soon became evident that the Israeli government would use its laws to prevent us from developing the "Center for the Study of Religions" we envisioned. Every official with whom we met assured us of cooperation and support, then presented us with additional requirements and regulations that left us no possibility of constructing a building, though we could continue to rent facilities.

So we repacked our bags and went to Milano, Italy, to visit my oldest brother and his wife before returning to America for our long-anticipated furlough.

CHAPTER 23

Sona Bata—1975-1978

It seemed that every time we returned to Zaire, conditions that could not get worse, had. This time it was inflation with a capital "I". The limited food available was priced beyond the means of the common people, resulting in almost universal hunger and not a little starvation. As though that were not enough, a severe drought threatened what food could be grown in the gardens, coupled with the emergence of a disease of the manioc plant.

Dolores and I were assigned to Sona Bata, a station some seventy-five kilometers from Kinshasa and located on the main road south. Our building project there was on a smaller scale than what we had done at Kimpese, but it was only slightly less extensive. We were to build a nursing school, which required four dormitories for students, a school building with numerous classrooms, a kitchen and dining room, a social center, a public health building, a maternity unit, a hospital wing for a private clinic, and all the other necessary sanitary and support buildings.

This project was financed by a generous grant from The Netherlands, but how is one to estimate the final cost in the face of such inflation? To deal as honestly as possible with the donors while also protecting the integrity of the project, I built into the estimate what I thought would be a reasonable inflation factor; and it would have worked fine if the inflation itself had been reasonable.

Finding materials was difficult, and paying for them approached the impossible. Between the time we ordered materials and they arrived, the price might double. We refused to pay bribes, so often only half of what we had paid for was actually delivered. Because wages, set by the government, showed practically no increase, even those who had jobs usually lacked either the motivation or strength to be productive. The government sought to divert attention from the economic disaster by declaring frequent holidays on which no one could be required to work. Building under those conditions required great imagination, unparalleled dedication, a lot of luck and total dependence upon God to make it all come together.

Yet, build we did. Not only were we able to stay on schedule with the Sona Bata project, we also continued with other needed projects across the entire field. Only the fantastic dedication of our workmen and the blessings of our Lord offer a clue as to the success of these projects. It was simultaneously maddening and amazing, a cause for both ulcers and praise.

Refugees from Angola poured across the border as the Cuban-backed military brought oppression, slaughter and chaos to those living there. Their presence added to the problem of scarce food, yet the refugees were so elated at escaping the turmoil of their homeland that they made no complaint.

It was at this time that we began to see an alarming number of patients suffering from what was called "Green Monkey Fever." Little did we suspect the havoc and trauma this virus, later known as AIDS, would cause worldwide.

Life at Sona Bata certainly had its rewards. Away from the city the air was clear and fresh, giving us sunsets we will always remember yet can never describe adequately. The kaleidoscope of colors assaulted the senses, and each seemed to try to outdo the previous one. At night the stars grew closer, like myriad diamonds spread just out of reach on a canopy of black velvet.

Dolores made our yard into a veritable park, with dozens of varieties of flowers, including several of her favorite orchids. I built a gazebo and had trees planted at her direction. We acquired a pair of white geese, which enjoyed the "Dolores Park" as much as did the frequent visitors who stopped at our home for refreshment and use of the bathroom, since no other facility was available on the highway.

In the face of such inflation and famine, it is not surprising that the development of reasonable government, fragile to begin with, should suffer a setback. Corruption was commonplace and taking bribes the accepted reward for public service. Justice in Africa had always impressed me as having a brutal element, but now it seemed to become sadistic. Incompetence of government workers, already fed by the cultural demand that those in power provide well for members of their tribe, grew to verge on the ridiculous.

When my new car finally arrived, I had to go to Kinshasa to have it registered and get license plates for it. There was no problem in completing the registration, but the plates were a different matter.

"We don't have any license plates," the clerk told me. "You'll have to make your own. Here are the numbers you are to put on it." He handed me a slip of paper with instructions that the plate should be blue and orange. I had no blue paint at home, so I scoured Kinshasa looking, in vain, for blue paint. Finally I gave up the futile search and returned home to make my plates, substituting black for dark blue, but with bright orange numbers.

Shortly afterward, I was again in Kinshasa when I was stopped by a policeman.

"Where did you get that license plate?" he asked me.

"I made it myself."

"You have made a grave mistake," he informed me. "You used black instead of blue."

"I know," I answered. "There's no blue paint available."

"Oh, it is a grave infraction to have the wrong color on your license plate," he said. It was obvious he wanted a bribe and was exaggerating the magnitude of this offense.

"I don't think it is so bad," I said, "and I am not going to give you a bribe."

My refusal to pay a bribe struck him as a worse offense than having the wrong color paint. "You must come to the police station with me," he said. "You will see how serious a crime this is."

The young lieutenant at police headquarters stared at me before speaking. "This officer tells me you painted your license black instead of blue."

"Yes, I did," I said. "There just isn't any blue paint."

"You are in serious trouble," he said. "For this kind of offense there is a big fine—a really big fine! If you give me some money, I'll see what I can do about it, but if you don't it is really going to cost you a lot."

"Look, I didn't do anything wrong," I said. "I don't pay bribes and I'm not going to give you anything. You just go ahead and do what you have to do."

His jaw muscles tightened and his eyes tried to bore holes through me. "Very well, your fine is going to be one hundred dollars."

"I don't have that much money with me, but I'll get it," I said.

He took my driver's license and automobile registration papers while I called Phil Uhlinger at our mission station. "Phil, I'm in the hoosegow. I used the wrong color paint on my license tag. Would you bring me a hundred dollars to get me out? I'll be waiting for you out in front of the police station."

I sat on the steps of the station, thinking that missionary work probably isn't worth the hassle.

"Tata Scott, what are you doing here?" I raised my glance to the speaker, a young black man immaculately dressed and with vaguely familiar features. Then I recognized him as one of our former students.

"Tata Kiko," I greeted him. "Well, I have made a grave infraction. They told me to make a license plate for my car and I tried to find blue paint but there is no blue paint to be had, so I painted it black. Now Lieutenant Whatever-his-name-is says I have to pay a hundred-dollar fine."

"He did, did he?" Kiko said. "Come with me and I'll have a word with him."

The demeanor of the police changed as we entered the station. Workers who had been slouching stood erect. All eyes followed us across the room. The few who dared to greet my friend did so with the greatest deference.

"Lieutenant, I want to speak with you," Kiko said at the office door.

"Yes, *Commissar*," the lieutenant said. "Do come in. Have a seat. Here, let me move this chair for you."

"I will stand, because we won't be that long," Kiko said, each word broken off as crisply as a palm nut from its cluster. "This man outside the doorway is one of my dear, dear friends. If I ever hear of the police hassling this man again, I'll send you off to the farthest reaches of the interior. You take a good look at that man out there and remember that he is my friend."

"Oh, I'm sorry. I'm sorry," the lieutenant said. "I didn't know that. I'll never make that mistake again. Pardon. Pardon."

"Do you have Tata Scott's papers?" Kiko asked.

"Yes, I have them, and I was just about to give them back when you came in. I certainly wouldn't want to hold Tata Scott's papers."

Kiko was laughing when he rejoined me. "Tata Scott, I'm really sorry," he said. "These guys are just a bunch of clowns. Give them a uniform and a little authority and they go nuts. The government sent me to America for training, and I was just like them before I went to America. I didn't know how a police department was supposed to operate. I thought and acted just like they do. There isn't much I can do about it, but I try."

After the fiasco with the license plates, I had to get my new driver's license. I drove to the nearby center of local government and found the right office with the right official.

"There are new regulations, Tata Scott," he informed me after the paperwork was completed. "You now have to take a driving test."

"Fine," I said. "My car is just outside."

We left the building, but when we got to my car, the official got in the driver's seat. "My, this is a fine car," he said. "It isn't often we see such a fine car." He started the engine and drove us leisurely through the town, repeating over and over again how much he liked the car and how he enjoyed driving it. When he finally returned to his office he stopped the car and congratulated me on passing my driving test.

When a Zairian is accused of a crime, or even is caught in the act, his response is always *"N'est pas moi."* (It isn't me.) One of my colleagues was standing in line at the bank when he felt someone's hand in his pocket. He reached down, grabbed the hand before it could be extracted, and faced the inept pickpocket. Before he could say a word, the owner of the hand protested, *"N'est pas moi! N'est pas moi!"*

The doctor's house at Sona Bata station was almost finished. The walls were up, the roof was on, the windows and doors were installed, and we even had the heavy steel security grills over the windows. The only place the house was open was under the eaves, and another day's work would easily take care of that. Since the house could be closed up securely, I told my workmen to leave their tools in the house to save the time of locking them in the tool shop at night and checking them out again the next morning. I cautioned them to put their tools in the storeroom rather than leave them lying around where they could be seen through the windows.

But the next morning, when we came to work all the tools were gone—hammers, saws, planes, everything.

Upset as I was, I began to investigate. It was obvious that the thief had climbed up the security grill on one of the windows, wedging himself under the eaves and into the attic. Once in the attic, he entered the storeroom through the access hole we had left in the ceiling.

As he swung down into the dark room he kicked his bare foot against the freshly painted wall. A big, dirty footprint was all he left in the storeroom. He had collected the tools and easily unlocked the front door from the inside.

I climbed on a box and grasped the opening in the ceiling, then swung out to see where my own foot would hit the wall. Even at six feet tall, I was not tall enough to make a mark where the thief left his.

Next I examined the footprint more carefully. The little toe was far down on the foot, leaving a big gap between that toe and the one next to it.

Adding up these facts, I knew this much about the thief: he was extremely tall for a Zairian; he had a unique footprint; he knew where the tools were kept.

One of the carpenters hired recently was an exceptionally tall man, and as I moved among the workmen I noticed his foot. The little toe on his right foot was spread, and I said to myself, "There's my culprit right there."

I called for the pastor and the head of the station, Tata Kimpiatu and Tata Dikiefu, to come down to the work site. "Somebody broke into the storeroom last night and stole some really expensive tools," I told them. "The thief was tall and I've got one carpenter that size. Further, it was a man whose toes were spread in a peculiar way." I showed them the footprint. "I want to have several of my workmen step into charcoal and then onto a piece of freshly painted ceiling plaque and make footprints. Is there anything wrong with that?"

"No," they said. "That's a good idea."

I selected six of my workmen, including the suspect, to make footprints, and then I asked Dikiefu and the pastor to compare them with the one on the wall. There couldn't be any mistake. The new carpenter was the thief.

Then I called all my workmen in before Tata Kimpiatu and myself. I dismissed them one by one until only three of my most trusted workmen, the suspect and the leaders remained. I confronted the suspect. "You stole our tools last night."

"Oh, no! No! No! I would never do such a thing."

"Look, here's the footprint on the wall. Here's your footprint you made with charcoal. Can there be any doubt?"

"Everybody has a footprint."

"Yes," I said. "But compare these others; there is no similarity whatsoever. But look at yours, it is identical. And you're the only man tall enough to have reached this far." I pointed to the telltale footprint.

He still protested. "No, it wasn't me. I wouldn't do a thing like that."

"We are trying to reason with you. If you will listen and be reasonable, then you can bring the tools back, we will fire you, and that will be the end of it. But if you don't cooperate, we'll have to get the police, the *Commissar de Police*. When he comes up here and investigates, you're going to be in up to here." I put my hand under my chin.

"You're going to be tied up. He's going to see the evidence and then he's going to put you in the *cachot* and soften you up real good. You can take your choice."

He thought for less than a minute. "OK," he said, "I did it."

"Where are the tools?"

"I took them to Nkisi last night and sold them."

"All right, we'll take you there," I said. "You will go around to all those places and get the tools back."

"They won't give them back."

"Oh, yes, they will. The pastor and I are going with you. You're going to tell those people that you stole the tools and they bought stolen property. Then you have to work out with them about how to give back the money. Anyone who refuses to return stolen property is in as much trouble as you are. They'll give them back."

Celestine drove the thief, the pastor and me to Nkisi, a village about thirty kilometers from Sona Bata. The thief directed us to various places where he had sold the tools. All of them were returned to us, except one exceptionally large and beautiful plane. The man who had bought it was working in his garden and was supposed to return sometime after three.

I left the pastor and Celestine in charge of the thief and told them I would be back after three o'clock.

With the tools in my car, I went home, had lunch, told Dolores what was happening and organized my workmen for the rest of the day. About four o'clock I was back in Nkisi.

When I got there, Celestine rushed up to the car. "He gave us the slip," he said. "He ran away."

"How could he run away?"

"He told us he had to go to the w.c., and we let him go."

I suggested that this was not the most effective way to keep a man in custody, but what's done was done and we should get on with our work. We found the man with the plane, got it back and started home at sunset.

My workmen live in villages around the station, and the thief, as well as many others, lived at Sona Bata village, just a short distance from the mission. As we drove through the village we saw people running and screaming and yelling and carrying firebrands, so I pulled off the road to find out what was going on.

"The thief is back," the people told us. "Somebody saw him and shouted the alarm. He ran off into the forest. Some of our men have gone out to catch him."

I hoped and prayed that he would escape in the dark. I knew what would happen if they caught him: They would kill him.

"Celestine," I said, "I'm going to stay here. You run over to the house and tell Mama Scott that the thief got away and I want to stay here and see what I can do if they catch him. I know Dolores will be worried."

But before he could leave, a commotion at the far end of the village street indicated that the thief had been captured. A circle of a hundred firebrands formed around the captive as he was dragged into the village from the forest. Tata Mbala was nearby and I made him part of our party, along with Celestine and the pastor. Tata Mbala is a large workman on whom I depended a lot, and a man I thought I might need in the next few moments. We got in the car, and with the horn honking constantly I drove right into the center of the circle where all the men of the village were gathered.

I got out of the car and was revolted by what I saw. Two men were holding the thief. The village chief was beating him senseless. The chief was a big burly man with such bulging muscles that he reminded me of Bluto in the old Popeye comic strip. The chief would draw back and hit the thief in the face with all his force, then laugh. The men would hold the victim up and the chief would hit him again. Over and over, the beating continued. The thief's mutilated face was covered with blood. I thought, "I'm already responsible for one man being executed and I certainly don't need another man's death on my conscience. I've got to get this man out of here and get him out fast."

Then an image flashed through my mind. "Probably in all the years in Africa, nobody has ever decked a chief. I wonder what would happen if I decked the chief." The impulse was irresistible. In the flickering light of the firebrands, I threw a punch all the way from the ten-cent seats and hit the chief squarely on the jaw, the kind of swing I'd have dreamed of when I was boxing in the navy. He turned toward me with glazed eyes and fell forward on his face.

It had more of an effect than I could have imagined. Nobody had ever seen anything like that happen, and they were immobilized with shock. The pastor, Celestine and I grabbed the thief, shoved him in the back seat of the car and took off before anyone could recover.

Somehow, through the blood and pulp of his lips the thief managed to tell us where his wife was hiding, so we picked her up as well. I took them to the next junction on the highway, where a taxi-bus was due to stop. I gave them some money for food and said, "I never intended for you to get beaten up this way. I am sorry it happened, but I hope this will be a lesson to you. It's so much easier to follow the ways that are good and honest." I got them on the bus and paid their fares. My parting words to him were, "Don't ever, ever come back here or these men will kill you, and you know they will."

Driving home, I asked Celestine, "Suppose we had not discovered who stole the tools, but the thief told some people in the village what he had done. How would they have treated him?"

Celestine's face broke into a wide grin. "Oh, everyone would have thought him very clever if he had gotten away with it. They think him unworthy only if he gets caught."

Back at our house, Dolores was in a state of near-hysteria. Men had kept running back and forth reporting fragments of the near-riot in the village. I was expected back before dark, but that had been hours ago and she had no idea where I was. She had sent for the pastor, but was told he was still with Tata Scott.

When I finally got home and told Dolores about decking the chief, she said, "Oh, Scotty, this is it! You've really done it now. We might as well start packing." Then, remembering other times when our future was uncertain, she added, "Maybe we should make another tape so people will know what happened to us, just in case..."

I never heard any more about that night. The next morning, Dolores gave my shirt to the washjack to wash. Blood was splattered down the front of it. She heard him laughing and saying, *"Menga ya. Ya mfuma Sona Bata."* (The blood of the Sona Bata chief.)

Oddly enough, the chief and I remained good friends and had many dealings together over the following years. I often wonder if he really knew what happened to him that night. I certainly never mentioned it, and I doubt that anyone in the village had the audacity to tell the chief that he had been KO'd by a sucker punch.

Another thief was caught at Sona Bata by the high school boys. There had been a series of robberies on the station, but we had no clue as to who was the culprit. Then late one night the principal of the high school woke me with the news that the boys had caught the thief and had him tied up on the athletic field.

"Will you take him to the police station for us?" the principal asked.

"Certainly," I said, dressing hastily because I knew that unless we hurried there would be little left of the man for the police to deal with. Sure enough, when we got to the scene we saw the thief bound and bloody. The boys were hitting, kicking and beating him with sticks. It was no easy task to bring the beating to a halt, but we finally managed to get the lacerated body in the back seat of my car and headed for the police station.

239

"No! No!" the thief said. "I don't belong at the police station. I belong at the prison. I am a prisoner, but I got out."

"Whatever turns you on," I said, and turned the car toward the prison.

The gate of the prison had a blockade before it, with sentries posted. I stopped the car at their orders and they peered at us through the windows. When they saw the man in the back seat they became very excited.

"This is big trouble," one of the sentries said. "You had better run and tell the warden about this." He ordered us all from the car while his comrade dashed off into the night. I was struck by the fact that the thief was treated almost as an equal to the sentry, but I did not think it wise at that time to use their language or let them know I understood it.

The warden came puffing down the road, half-dressed, with no shirt on and his belly spilling out over his tattered trousers. He had not yet reached us when he started yelling at the thief. "You idiot! You damned fool! How did you get caught?"

"Well..." the prisoner began.

"Don't you realize how embarrassing this could be for me?" the warden continued. "How could you be such an idiot?"

"You seem to know this man pretty well," I said to the warden. His shock at my use of his language sent a tremor through his rotund body. "He was let out tonight with your permission, wasn't he?"

"I sent him on an errand," the warden said.

"Yes. We know what that errand was. You sent him out to steal for you. How many others do you send out on such errands?"

"Only two others," the warden said. On being discovered, he had lost whatever composure he may have had. I suddenly realized it was his "errand boys" who had stolen Dolores' two white geese.

There was no way I could change the prison system or bring decency and order to this tumultuous time, but at least I could temper the excesses in this one area. I began a recitation of the names of all the high officials I knew in Kinshasa and who I considered my friends, emphasizing those whom I could call *Commissar de Police*. "And if I ever hear of such a thing as this happening again," I concluded, "you know that I will report you to my friends and you will no longer be warden here. You will be lucky if you are not sent to prison yourself. And you know it won't be this prison, where you have friends, but another one far away where you will be just another criminal."

That stopped the robberies at Sona Bata, though I suspect it did little more at the prison than redirect them to other targets.

While we were trying desperately to maintain our schedule on the Sona Bata project, we received word that Germany was interested in investing a million dollars at Vanga for extensive enlargement of the medical facilities there. Sweden also had $600,000 for a laboratory technical school at Kimpese.

In America we have channeled untold millions of dollars around the world through such government programs as AID, VISTA, and a hundred other such agencies. The strong wall of separation between church and state written into our constitution precludes tax money being distributed through church agencies. European countries are not so limited, however.

Those nations with a long history of an established religion distribute a part of their tax revenue to the churches. The churches, in turn, have a national inter-church committee that decides on worthy projects to be funded from the money set aside for foreign aid. The Netherlands was funding the Sona Bata project in this way, and similar systems were the source of the funds now available from Germany and Sweden for expanding the ministries at Vanga and Kimpese.

Even with inflation, a million dollars was far more than we had ever had available for any building program. The opportunity to build a truly modern hospital in this strategic area appealed to us as much as to the Germans. Dr. Fountain and the others had worked under often-impossible conditions, and the thought of giving them the kind of hospital now possible was a dream come true for me. But there were problems I could not ignore.

Time had taken its toll on me physically. A recent recurrence of malaria emphasized my vulnerability. Just keeping up with what was already in progress taxed me to the limit, and I knew it would be foolhardy for me to accept another project of this magnitude.

I worked out designs for the buildings, but the only possible way for these wonderful and needed projects to get off the ground was for another qualified builder to be appointed and take over the responsibility. With much regret I told the executive committee of CBZO of my decision. Without hesitation, they decided to ask our board in America to appoint someone to help. Tata Nlandu, the general secretary of CBZO, drew me aside after the meeting.

"Tata Scott," he said, "I know of the perfect man to come to Zaire to be a builder. It is your son, John. He knows the language, he knows the people, he knows his way around, and he has demonstrated that you have taught him well."

"I couldn't agree with you more," I told him.

"Good. Then will you speak to John about this?" he asked.

"No," I answered. "I could not do that."

Nlandu's expression reflected his puzzlement. "But you said you agree that he is the person we need. Why not ask him?"

"Dear friend," I said, "I came to the Congo many years ago because God spoke to me. I served all these years because I know without a shadow of a doubt that this is where God wants me to be. Without that certainty I could not have lasted a week ... no, I could not have lasted a day."

"Yes, I see," he said.

"Many years ago the missionaries prayed that God would send the needed workers. God spoke to me and to twenty-one others and we came. We must pray that God will send the person He wants and has prepared, whomever that may be." I paused in thought, remembering all that had gone into my own call and the calls of my colleagues. "If Johnny should happen to be that person, I will be the happiest man in the whole world. But I do not want him here unless he has the same certainty that has sustained me."

Only days later we received a package from America, containing a tape recording that John and Sue had made for us. We listened as loving parents as our children told us of how Johnny was progressing in his work, having been made foreman at an *International Harvester* shop though he was years younger than any of the men working for him. They described their new home in Tulsa, their joy in the church they were attending, and of course all the cute things our newest grandchildren, Aaron and his baby sister Robin, did and said. Then at the end of the tape, Johnny got more serious.

"Dad," his voice said, "I have a wonderful life here, but somehow it doesn't seem enough. I don't know what I should be doing with my life, but surely it must be more than I'm doing now. If there is ever a time when I'm needed out there, I'm ready to come in a minute."

Years ago God had spoken clearly to me, saying, "Prepare yourself. I am going to call you to serve me." Now He was speaking much the same words to my son.

CHAPTER 24

Sona Bata—1978-1979

Johnny's call, his response, the decisions made by our board, and the way in which his life had prepared him for this task is a book for Johnny to write. Suffice it to say here that his call and service manifested again how marvelously God prepares and calls His servants. Johnny and Susan were blessed with the same certainty that sustained Dolores and me over our entire career in Africa. They were appointed by our board in January, 1978, but would not be on the field until a year later. Procedures such as medical examinations, orientation, and winding up life in America and packing for a life in Zaire, as well as undergoing language study and orientation in Belgium, were necessary, but they made the days drag slowly for us as we anticipated their arrival.

Meanwhile, our work and life continued.

Missionary work began in the Belgian Congo in 1878, and this centennial year was marked with many observances, both large and small. For Dolores and me, the most memorable was the one at Palabala.

Palabala is the site of the first missionary work in the Belgian Congo. Matadi, the only port city for the entire nation, is situated on the Zaire River about one hundred miles from the mouth of the river, which is navigable from the Atlantic to Matadi.

This is where our first missionaries came, white men who sought nothing for themselves, except to minister to those in need. Like the slavers before them, they landed at Matadi. Little wonder that no red carpet was rolled out for them by the great Bakongo nation.

The Bakongo was an enormous tribe inhabiting the lower Congo and much of what is now Angola. Later, boundaries drawn by white men far across the ocean cut through the middle of this tribe, as if a white man's map could supersede thousands of years of cultural heritage. It did not happen then and it has not happened today!

But the Bakongo were a disciplined nation, having selected three great chiefs to rule concurrently. These three chiefs resided on the top of a flat mountain near Matadi, a mountain called Palabala. The missionaries came to the chiefs, asking permission to live among them, to bring medicine and education to the people, and to share their faith in Christ.

This was a difficult and weighty decision for these men who were charged with the welfare of their nation. The white man had come before with lies and deceptions. What assurance could these newcomers give that they were any different? Should the chiefs risk their people again by opening their doors to these men? They deliberated long and carefully before giving permission for the missionaries to begin their work.

Thus began the ministry celebrated at Palabala a hundred years later.

Of course, when such a celebration is planned a lot of work has to be done in preparation. The roof of the Palabala church needed repairs, paint would brighten things up, broken windows needed to be replaced, and the influx of visitors would need lots of pews or benches. Dolores and I had to go there a week beforehand to take care of such matters. I had my workmen build the benches at Sona Bata in such a way that Dolores and I could assemble them on site, and we loaded them on the flatbed truck along with the rest of our supplies and set off for Palabala mountain. By Saturday morning of that week we were well ahead of schedule for the next day's ceremonies, when we noticed a great number of Zairians arriving. We were assembling the last of the benches when a delegation of Zairians approached.

"Tata Scott, we wish you and Mama to come with us," their spokesman said.

"Where are we going?" I asked.

"If you come with us, you will see," he answered.

The delegation led us further across the mountain, winding along a rutted dirt road until we came to a half-visible path wandering off to the side. The path led through the grasses and around great outcroppings of rock until it came to open space. Two chairs had been placed there, each draped with red cloth symbolizing the greatest respect.

"For you and Mama," the spokesman said, motioning us to take the seats. "We are honoring the three chiefs who welcomed the first missionaries. We revere them because of their wisdom. They were brave men to take the chance they did, but they made the right decision."

"Without their foresight, we might never have been here," I said.

"Tomorrow, all the *mindele* will come for a great celebration in the church, honoring the early missionaries, and that is good. But today, we honor these three chiefs in our own way." He paused for a moment of deliberation. "We thought you and Mama Scott should be a part of our ceremony. Some of the other *mindele* might not understand."

"We thank you," I said.

The ceremony began with a witch doctor in full regalia doing one of the most exotic and expressive dances I have ever seen. Several times during his dance he threw himself to the ground, crawled up to my feet, reached out and touched my shoes, gave me the sign for "God Bless You," then resumed his dance. I realized that far more than being honored individually, I symbolized the entire missionary presence that had been affecting these lives for a century.

While the witch doctor danced, a chief led the people in a litany of praise and remembrance. For this reenactment and recitation of their history, no one carried or needed a prayer book to come in at the proper place. This, their oral history, had been taught and learned around countless campfires over the years in every village.

When the dance ended, we set out again on another trek to the grave of one of the three chiefs, the litany continuing all the while. At the grave the litany intensified until it reached a climax. The current chiefs sprinkled palm wine over the grave and then all the *bambuta* (elder statesmen) drank palm wine in honor of the dead leader. I was a *bambuta* that day, so, of course, I was also given the wine. Then we went to the grave of the next chief, where the whole ceremony was repeated, and then to the grave of the last chief for a final performance. At that point I was glad there were only three chiefs to be so honored, else I might not have made it back to the village on my own.

"Tata Scott," the village chief said as we walked back through the evening dusk, "we celebrate a miracle of trust here. It was nothing short of a miracle that our chiefs trusted these men who came asking for nothing more than to work with us, to work for us, to take nothing but to give everything."

"And many of them gave just that, everything," I said, motioning to the cemetery where those first missionaries were buried. I had read their tragic histories, carved into the rough headstones. Many had served for two weeks or less before tropical disease ended their lives. The rare ones lived for two or three years. But with each loss a new missionary came, an endless procession of saints who had planted what we were now reaping.

That Saturday night was one we shall long remember. We made our beds in one corner of an otherwise empty church building, pulling two benches up against our cots as our only semblance of privacy. When the meetings ended at 1:30 a.m. we went to bed. Minutes later, hundreds of people literally flooded the church, forming a solid covering of wall-to-wall humanity. At 3:00 a.m. two men crowded past our cots, looked at us and lay down on the narrow bench with their feet on our beds. The next morning two old pastors, friends from Vanga, greeted us and informed us that they were the ones who had come in so late and so tired and had slept on "our" bench. They said, "We saw it was white people, then we looked at your faces and saw it was the Scotts so we knew it would be OK." Probably we have never received a better compliment.

The celebration at the church the next day was wonderful, majestic and inspiring. Delegates came from nearby churches, as well as from all the denominations doing missionary work in Zaire. Choirs sang, sermons were delivered, prayers were offered; everything was as it should be. In November, fifty thousand Protestants from all over the country gathered at the stadium in Kinshasa to celebrate the same centennial. That, too, was spectacular and inspiring.

But Dolores and I experienced our greatest sense of awe early on, at the top of Palabala mountain, as we joined in a time of worship few *mindele* have been privileged to share.

I remembered an occasion when I first came to Congo and an old missionary had asked me if I wanted new nails or used nails and how many I needed. Now, as prices continued to skyrocket and materials grew ever harder to procure, I found myself more akin to him than I could have imagined. Trusses required new nails, but window casings accepted used ones just as well. Even when it was available, fuel cost too much for a vehicle to be used to less than its capacity. The big truck broke down and no parts could be found to repair it. We ordered a new engine from overseas and were informed that we could expect delivery in somewhat less than six months.

To complicate things even further, Dolores suffered a severe case of sciatica and I had surgery for a hernia. It was time for us to take a break and regain perspective.

That break came in midsummer in the form of a vacation with Dr. and Mrs. Swen and their two children, Raoul and Odeal. We flew to

Nairobi, Kenya, and from there took off for a tour of game preserves and natural wonders.

On the long drive to the Mara Serena Lodge in the Masai Mara Game Reserve, we saw wild animals by the thousands. Five elephants were helping themselves to the trees and shrubbery on the hotel lawn. A curious little animal parked on our porch that night and seemed indifferent to us. At least, it didn't know what "Shoo" and "Shoo away, already" meant. The next day we learned it was a hydrax, strangely enough a member of the elephant family.

We crossed the Sand River into Tanzania and were in the Serengeti National Park where 11 million animals live. They all came out to the road to see us drive by: lions, cheetahs, zebras, giraffes, buffalo, wildebeests, hartebeests, water buck, gazelles and impalas.

At Ol Duvai Gorge we saw where Louis and Mary Leakey discovered Zinjanthropus, our 1.75-million-year-old ancestor, better known as "Nutcracker Man." Then on to Ngorongoro crater, which has to be the most amazing thing we have ever seen. From the rim of the crater to its floor is a nearly vertical drop-off of 2,000 feet. At the rim of the crater, one can view all 102 square miles of its interior. Taking a four-wheel-drive vehicle to the floor of the crater allowed us to enjoy lunch not thirty feet from lolling hippos and thirsty zebras.

At Lake Manyara we saw millions of pink flamingos take off like a cloud and settle again on the edge of the lake. And finally at Mombasa, on the Indian Ocean, we enjoyed the sun, the sand and the food.

It was a marvelous vacation. This respite with people whom we loved so dearly was everything we could have asked for, and we flew back home, ready again to face the stark reality of Zaire and the months of work awaiting us.

Christmas arrived on time that year, but our greatest present did not arrive on the twenty-fifth. At 7:00 a.m. on the thirtieth, we heard Johnny on the radio hookup from Kinshasa. He had sent a telegram advising us to meet them at 9:00 p.m. on the twenty-ninth and it arrived in Kinshasa at 6:00 p.m., just in time for the Emmerts to meet their plane.

Immediately we drove to Kinshasa, where we found our family strolling along the mighty Zaire River fronting our mission station. Words can never express our joy and relief at seeing them. Dolores greeted Aaron in French and Aaron said, "Let's not start *that* stuff!"

The grandchildren were as lovable with us as if we had been together all their lives. They made an immediate hit with the older missionaries, with whom they were open and friendly. They were perfect children, as any grandparents can understand.

We all returned to Sona Bata for a few days of getting reacquainted, when we were notified that the new engine for the truck had arrived. John and I spent several days installing the engine, our work under the mango tree that served as our hoist frequently interrupted by torrential rains. But at last the truck was operational. We loaded it with freight and supplies, and John and his family left in it to get settled at Vanga.

Gasoline cost four dollars a gallon in Kinshasa and six dollars a gallon at Vanga, so we did all we could to switch our vehicles to diesel, which cost only one-sixth as much. The government's handling of the economy was a farce at best and a tragedy at worst. Attempts to regulate prices only led to longer lines and fewer goods. Social problems received no better treatment. When students at the university staged a protest rally, government troops came in and shot several demonstrators and immediately inducted the rest of the students into the army.

I am somewhat competitive and hate to come in second in almost anything. I lost one contest, however, in which I didn't know I was engaged and which gave me far greater pleasure in losing than I could otherwise have known.

One of my European friends said of Johnny, "He speaks far better French than you do, Scotty."

John helped me lay out one of the buildings at Sona Bata and my workmen said, "He speaks Kikongo better than you do, Tata Scott."

Celestine, my chauffeur for years, worked with John for only a short time when he informed me, "He is a much better mechanic that you are, Tata Scott."

I had not been able to buy a single piece of reinforcing steel for more than six months, but John went into Kinshasa and found reinforcing steel and nails enough to do the entire Vanga project at half the price I had been quoted.

He took the plans for the Vanga hospital and drew up a materials list for everything in the project. He made a detailed outline for constructing and financing the project over the next three-and-a-half years. The German representatives in charge of the funding were thrilled and amazed at his work and, of course, had to remind me, "This is more detailed planning than we ever received before, Mr. Scott."

Any father would be delighted to come in a distant second in such comparisons.

At long last our new truck arrived. I went to Matadi to get it, filled with joyful anticipation at finally seeing my bright, spotless vehicle: but what I saw was hardly a thing of beauty. The windshield and tail lights, the windshield wiper, the jack and the door lock were all stolen or broken. The battery was gone and the cab smashed in two places. It was all repairable or replaceable, given enough time, effort, good fortune and patience. I could have cried, except that it seemed somehow a fitting climax to our next-to-last term of service, now coming to an end.

CHAPTER 25

Sona Bata—1980-1984

Like the seasons of the year, each term of service during our missionary career had its own unique rhythm and tempo, each so very different from any other, even though the work of building continued unbroken. This term was unique in several ways.

Johnny was so accomplished that his presence on the field both gave me an added resource in my own work and reduced my responsibility up-country. Of course, having our grandchildren in Zaire was a new and wonderful experience for us.

During this term I began to see myself more clearly than ever before as first a missionary and secondarily a builder. Not that the building program diminished to any degree; it didn't. Throughout my career I had put the building first and foremost. Now I found myself assigning more emphasis to people, their needs, hopes, fears and potential.

Finally, I suppose it is only natural to become more introspective near the end of an important phase of one's life. Certainly this was true for me, and the physical problems that surfaced in these final years intensified it.

Angela, John and Susan's third child, arrived on March 20, 1980, at the Vanga hospital, just before we returned from furlough. Requirements of our work took us to Vanga rather often, and John's trips to Kinshasa usually included some time at Sona Bata. We took advantage of these times to assist with one another's projects, as well as to enjoy being a family. I remember particularly well the bridge I had built between Vanga and Milundu, and which had deteriorated over the years to become a bane for Johnny.

We went to Vanga to spend Christmas, and John and I redesigned the bridge. Two days before Christmas we spent eight hours in his shop cutting lumber and making forms, cutting and forming all the steel. On the day before Christmas we trucked it all to the river and to the concrete abutments he had built. We worked another hard eight hours installing all the steel and the forms. Then on the day after Christmas we took rock, cement and twenty workers to the site and with another eight hours' work we had mixed and poured ten cubic meters of concrete. That doesn't seem like much by American standards, where one simply orders "Ready-mix," but it is a lot when the concrete is mixed by hand a shovelful at a time. That night the bridge was completed and a happy father and son returned to the family circle.

We had planned to leave Vanga three days after Christmas, but Susan wanted a better place to conduct school for the five missionary children at Vanga. She had been using one of the children's bedrooms. I designed an octagonal building behind their house, and we spent another week completing the construction.

Likewise, when Johnny and his family came to Sona Bata there was always some project of mine to which he turned his hand. Not only did we get some needed work accomplished, we also reveled in the sheer joy of working together.

God still blessed our work and our lives, though I sometimes wondered if the problems of Zaire could be resolved with less than His direct intervention. President Mobutu summarily announced that all five- and ten-zaire notes were invalid and had to be exchanged for new bills before a given date. The surprise measure was designed to catch hoarders who were not allowing their money to circulate. Unfortunately, not enough new bills were available to cover the exchange, and the result was confusion, frozen bank accounts, many losses, and cash in very short supply.

At the same time, inflation and famine continued unchecked. Dolores and I splurged on a lunch at our favorite restaurant in Kinshasa and the bill came to 335 zaires. Just a few years earlier I had bought a new automobile for 600 z's.

We found it necessary to provide our workers with one meal a day; otherwise they did not have the strength to do their jobs.

The fuel shortage complicated life for everyone, small units of the military often eased their immediate problem by coming to me and demanding fuel for their vehicles. Of course, there was never any payment for such "contributions."

Under these circumstances, it was not surprising that witchcraft made a strong reemergence, offering the people some sense that events could be influenced if not controlled.

Yet God was with us in marvelous ways. Even under the most trying circumstances, construction continued uninterrupted. And in our personal lives we continued to witness His hand on us.

A Christian Women's Conference in Kinshasa brought John and Susan, Dolores and me, and missionaries from all our stations to the capital. The three-day conference was a success and ended after church and dinner on Sunday.

Tropical rain was pelting the city as we prepared to start the one-hour trip to Sona Bata. John was driving along the heavily traveled, very narrow, two-lane highway through the residential suburb. Susan, holding ten-month-old Angela, was strapped in the front seat of the VW Rabbit. Seven-year-old Aaron and four-year-old Robbin were in the back seat between Dolores and me.

John had to stop behind a stalled car to let oncoming traffic pass. Just as the road ahead was cleared of traffic, our car was struck in the back by an enormous bus. It was terrible: in less than a second our beautiful car was hurled sixty feet forward and demolished, damaged beyond repair. The bus had hit us at full speed, track marks indicating that the driver made no attempt to apply his brakes.

Our car ended up in our own lane in front of the stalled car, but by some miracle we never touched another car. Inside our car broken glass was everywhere. It had slashed and penetrated our suitcases, yet not one of the seven of us suffered so much as a scratch.

The first car to come along took the women and children to the mission station. Dolores will never forget Trissie Rumohr holding her hand as they prayed together. Gordon Bottemiller, John Allan and Charles Moore organized everything for our needs and in minutes were on their way to help us. They brought the police to make a report, picked up the pieces, and in two hours we were all back at the mission.

Missionary doctor Bill Macpherson came by to check us out. The only injury was some cracked ribs for me. Presbyterian missionary JoAnn Ellington sent her son across town with pain medicine not otherwise available. Canadian Baptist colleague McKenzie loaned us a VW Rabbit until we could arrange other transportation.

We gave thanks to God for seeing our family through this accident relatively unscathed. We thanked Him again for the support of our colleagues and the privilege of sharing our lives and work with such people. And we did not fail to thank Him for those back in America who continued to remember us in their prayers. Moments like this remind us again of the peace and power that can be found only through His love and presence.

Not long after, we were again thrown back on our faith, as we thought we would lose our beautiful Angela.

Dolores and I were scheduled to leave for the States for a vacation in just over a week when we heard Johnny calling us over the radio from Vanga. "Angela has some kind of infection that has come up very suddenly. Apparently she had been bitten by a mosquito or insect of some sort and she is running a high fever."

"Is Dr. Fountain on the station now?" I asked.

"Yes," he answered. "Dr. Dan is here and also a German pediatrician who is working here. They are both treating her. They think it is some sort of staph infection and apparently Angela's immune system can't handle it on her own."

"It sounds like she's in the best of hands," I said.

"They aren't so sure themselves," John said. "They think she may need to go to the States. Susan and the children may have to go back home with you."

"You know that won't be any problem for us," I assured him. "Just keep us posted."

Within two hours, we heard them calling over the radio for a plane to come to Vanga and take them to Kinshasa; the infection had gone that badly and that quickly. There happened to be a plane in the area that could be diverted to them. Before the plane left Vanga, we were in our car and headed to the capital.

We were not prepared for the sight little Angela presented when the plane landed. Her eyes were distended and bulged from their sockets like Ping-Pong balls. She was burning with fever and her pale skin emphasized her fragile condition. I had the sinking feeling that there was little hope for her, and that if she should survive she certainly would be blind. We hustled the family into our car and headed for Mama Yemo hospital.

Susan held Angela while John guarded a carefully wrapped parcel. "Dr. Dan sent medications he is sure won't be available at Mama Yemo," he said. "He also sent a supply of needles because he knows that sterilized needles just don't exist at Mama Yemo."

Mama Yemo is a huge hospital, in fact the only large hospital in

Kinshasa. Built by President Mobutu and named for his mother, the structure is far more impressive than its reputation for medical care is. People said, "If you want to die, go to Mama Yemo." Still, it was the best Kinshasa had to offer.

"We can work around the hospital problems," I said with more enthusiasm than conviction. "And besides, Bill Macpherson is there. He's a wonderful physician." Dr. Macpherson had been appointed as one of our missionary doctors a few years earlier, and he left his practice in Los Angeles to work at Vanga. After a few years at Vanga, he decided he could do more good for the people by working at Mama Yemo. He was appointed to the staff and the board of the hospital, but soon found that his lone voice could do little to attain the positive impact he wanted to make on that monstrous institution.

"Give us the details," Dolores said. "How did this develop?"

"We first saw a small red place on the tip of her nose," Susan said. "We thought it was a bug bite and treated it as such. For about three days she was fussy and ran a bit of a fever, but we assumed she was cutting a new tooth. Then, last Friday she woke up with a very swollen right eye. We took her to Dr. Dan immediately to be examined. He started her on megacillin. On Saturday her eye was worse, and we gave her penicillin and ampillicin. Sunday her swelling had gone down some and her temperature was normal. Monday the swelling continued to go down and she felt like playing."

"That's why you didn't call us then," I offered.

"Of course," Susan said. "It looked as though it was rather minor. But Tuesday morning the temperature was back, along with a marked increase in the swelling and redness of both eyes. We treated her with medication to reduce the swelling and fever and waited. By eleven o'clock the swelling was worse and the left eye was seriously involved, too. At one o'clock Dr. Dan and Dr. Reinhart, the German pediatrician, examined her again. The blood vessels in the nose had broken and she was draining from the mouth and nose."

"What about the eyes?" Dolores asked.

"Her right eye was extended beyond the tip of her nose. There was no movement in the right eye and no response to light. The left eye was swollen completely shut and the right side of her face was distorted. She was in a great deal of pain. Then she became nauseated and they found that there was pressure on the brain from all the accumulated fluids. That's when Dr. Dan decided the treatment available at Vanga wasn't enough."

The oppressive edifice of Mama Yemo loomed before us, and Dr. Macpherson was there to meet us. "I've got a private room for Angela," he said. "There are only a few in the whole hospital, but I managed one. Now, let's have a look at our little patient."

"We'll be taking her back to the States with us," Dolores said as Bill examined our granddaughter.

The doctor turned to Dolores with a look that held no room for optimism. "Transporting her is out of the question," he said. "Just getting her here..." He didn't finish that sentence; but then he didn't need to. "We'll get her on i.v.'s immediately and start her medication. We may be able to stabilize her enough to go to South Africa, but to America...no way!"

The private room that awaited us was appalling. It was little more than a five-foot-by-nine-foot cell, located just behind the intensive care unit. A narrow frame held a stained and dirty mattress. A screen at the window managed to keep the swarm of flies from escaping. The tropical heat seemed trapped in the room along with the flies, and the air hung as motionless as our tiny patient. The drab and peeling walls merged with the dirty floor to emphasize the gloom. Outside the window passed a seemingly endless procession of families taking the remains of their loved ones from the hospital to the morgue.

"Sit here and hold the baby," I told Susan. "Dolores and I will be back soon."

We went to the mission station and got a supply of fresh, clean linen, pillows and pillowcases, a cot on which John and Susan could rest, boiled water to drink, and a cooler with ice cubes frozen from previously boiled water, and on the way back to the hospital I bought a large electric fan for the room. It was no substitute for air conditioning, but it made a great difference in the suffocating atmosphere.

One of us had to be with Angela twenty-four hours a day. We saw immediately that we could not trust the best medical help at the hospital. She was receiving an infusion, and the help had no idea of the importance of the continued flow or the need to maintain the proper drip.

I spent most of my time killing flies. Each time the door to the room was opened, flies swarmed in from the rest of the hospital to be trapped against our window screen. Then, at night, the same thing happened with mosquitoes.

It was depressing to have our beloved Angela dependent upon such a place; it was even more depressing to realize that for the millions of people in Kinshasa, this represented the best medical care they would ever know.

But with the wonderful care of Dr. Macpherson, Angela's condition stabilized. Within three days he said she could be transported to

South Africa, only a five-hour flight away, where she could receive the best of care. John and Susan were able to get tickets and reservations for the next flight.

"Scotty and I will stay here and take care of the children," Dolores offered. But Johnny and I conferred and decided it would be best for Dolores and me to fly home as planned, taking Aaron and Robin with us. At least between South Africa and America we could maintain contact by telephone, an avenue of communication notoriously undependable in Zaire.

South Africa has been much criticized, but it will always hold a cherished place in our hearts. Not only have we thoroughly enjoyed vacationing there, but the support and generosity shown John and Susan during this time was enough to win the hearts of any but the most embittered.

On the flight down, they met a South African who insisted he would take them directly to the hospital, the address of which was listed in the letters they carried. He assured them that his car would be waiting for him at the airport and that it certainly was nothing more than humanity demanded. As it turned out, the wrong hospital had been named in John's instructions, but one of the staff physicians there personally drove them to their proper destination.

Angela had lost all the ground she gained in Kinshasa, but a team of five physicians gave her their utmost care in the modern hospital, first-class by any standards in the world. She was given a private room and twenty-four-hour private nursing. For the first time since the ordeal started, John and Susan could think of getting some rest. Another South African who they met only casually invited them to his beautiful home on a lake, where they were fed, rested and treated like longtime friends.

They had left Zaire in such a rush that there was no time to arrange visas, so John set out to find the proper government office. He asked a policeman for directions, and the officer talked with him long enough to learn why they had come to South Africa. "How are you getting around?" he asked.

"Mostly walking," John answered, "but there is always the bus and taxis."

"That's no good," the policeman said. "No good at all! Look, my wife does not work, she is at home all day. We have a car, and any time you want to go somewhere just give her a call. She will be more than happy to be your chauffeur for as long as you are here."

John conveyed all this to me by telephone within an hour of our arrival at mother's house in Hutchinson. He was also able to report that the doctors were encouraged about Angela's response to treatment, but guarded about what permanent effects she might suffer. One of her doctors had treated a child with the same problem a couple of years earlier, and he had saved her also.

Within two weeks they were able to return to the States, though Angela was still on i.v.'s and heavy medication. The doctors in Hutchinson continued the treatment begun in South Africa, and she continued to improve slowly. To us it was a blessing that she survived at all, and nothing short of a miracle that she had no lasting long-term effects.

Back at Sona Bata, we were awaiting the funds for the next phase of the building project. There is an agony that only a mission builder knows. He has a big expensive crew that uses lots and lots of expensive material. Every day a thousand things go right; only one thing is wrong—the funds for the project are slow in coming through. Sometimes so slow that there are not ten *lukutu* in the house. The builder knows the funds will come, but in the meantime he cries a lot, he has trouble eating, stomach pains, nightmares, and the closer it gets to payday the worse it hurts.

I eased this problem somewhat by working on the mission station in Kinshasa for several weeks. We did a hundred little jobs that taken individually seem unimportant but collectively add up to putting the station in pretty good order. No one had done any real maintenance in years, and every house had come un-glued. Storm damage was evident all over the station: roofs leaked; termites had feasted on some of the houses for years; two houses had no water pressure; four toilet stools were not working, with three needing replacement; three water heaters wouldn't function; painting was needed; kitchen furniture needed to be made; ceramic tile had to be replaced; etc., etc. We worked on every house on the station, making life a little easier for a lot of good families whom we loved dearly. That done, and the funds finally released, we returned to Sona Bata and the hospital project.

The delegation, pastor and lay leaders came from Nselo, just as they had come every year for twelve years.

Nselo is a church post in the Sona Bata area. Dr. Glen Tuttle had started a medical mission there, and it flourished and grew until finally they built a small hospital. The people at Nselo built their own elementary school and their own high school. They became a very independent group, and relations between Nselo and Sona Bata were not always smooth. Sona Bata felt they were the "mother" and should be consulted more than they were. Nselo felt they could make decisions on their own without interference from Sona Bata.

The good people at Nselo began to build their own church. They had the foundation and the walls erected for a good-sized building when they ran out of resources. That is why the delegation came to me to put the roof on their building. It had become an annual event, one which I did not relish but which I could expect with the same certainty as the approach of the dry season.

My response was almost rote by now. "No. I don't have the money to do it. There isn't any money available to do it. It can't be done without money. It takes a lot of money to buy lumber for a church that size and it takes a lot of money to buy roofing materials. There is no way I can do it."

"But Tata Scott, you are a builder." Their response was as predictable as mine.

"You people at Nselo absolutely have to do the major part of this yourselves. You have to do something out there that is really indicative of your concern. Something that is sacrificial," had been my closing words for years.

Now the delegation greeted me in the customary Kikongo way: they bowed and said they were happy; they had brought gifts. The gifts were a chicken and some eggs. That meant that I had to give them the time of day. We invited them into the house, and they entered with their gifts and a large bundle tied up in cloth. I told the cook to take the eggs and the chicken, which was pooping on the floor, out to the kitchen.

"Tata Scott, you told us to do something that was significant and that was sacrificial." As the pastor spoke he nodded to the deacon who carried the bundle. The deacon laid the bundle in the middle of the floor, untied the top and let its contents spill over the floor. There was a mountain of filthy, odorous money. It was obvious that each of these bills had spent many hours tucked under the clothing and absorbing the sweat of many people, but the delegation's pride was equally apparent.

"We have put on a drive throughout the entire Nselo region, and we've had our annual *Matondo*, and this is the money we have raised. You've got to believe that this is sacrificial." I did not question the sacrifice these people had made, yet they had accumulated the equivalent of only a thousand dollars. I figured it would take five thousand dollars to complete their roof.

"You wait here a bit," I said. "Mama and I have to go shell peanuts." Dolores and I retreated to the bedroom. We had made a rule—or rather Dolores had made me promise—that we would never undertake a project until we could see light at the end of the tunnel financially. But here was a five-thousand-dollar project with only a thousand dollars on hand. As we talked we decided that we could put in a thousand dollars of our own money, but that still left more than we had in sight. To embark on a building project without the funding in place ran against everything we had tried to teach the Zairians and everything we had practiced ourselves. Yet, I could not ignore the tremendous sacrifice these people had made. So we prayed about it.

"Honey, I think we should do it," I said.

"I think you're right," Dolores answered.

"All right, we're going to put a roof on your church," I said as we returned to the delegation. There was no point in telling them that there was not nearly enough money for the job. We just had to tell ourselves that the Lord blessed the loaves and the fishes and He'll have to bless this. So we had prayer and they went back to Nselo.

I still had no idea of how I was going to keep our promise when an enormous eighteen-wheel, flat-bed truck, loaded with a huge crate, pulled into our yard a few days later. The chauffeur brought me the manifest, written in French, identifying the cargo as "Aluminum roofing toles, six meters long," hundreds and hundreds of feet of it. The total weight was some twenty tons.

"What are you bringing this here for?" I asked. "This manifest doesn't have Sona Bata on it. It isn't mine."

"It's for CBZO in Kinshasa and I took it there and met Mr. Weaver," the chauffeur said. "Mr. Weaver said there was no way they could get the crate off the truck. He said there was only one man in the mission who could remove the crate and that is Tata Scott. So he authorized this truck to go to Sona Bata and said that you would take the crate off."

I collected a crew of my men, and we tore the crate open and began to remove the toles one by one, which of course was the only way we could ever have done it. When all the material was removed, we simply shoved the empty crate off the truck, and the happy chauffeur was again on his way.

The next day I called Johnny on the radio. "A truck came in here last night and brought five hundred pieces of six-meter roofing material. Do you know anything about this?"

"I'm waiting for an order," he said. "But I never ordered anything like six meters long. I have no use for anything that long. Let me look into it."

There were many calls to many places before the situation was clarified. Johnny had ordered aluminum material from Germany, but this came from England. He had written his order in French because he didn't speak German. In French he had described these aluminum toles as *bac auto-portant*, which means "self-supporting." The common abbreviation for this French phrase is "B.A.C." The German who received the order didn't take time to translate and read all the information, but when he saw "B.A.C." he said to himself that this stood for the British Aluminum Company, so he forwarded the order to them.

The British Aluminum Company had no idea what John's order was for, with so many of item number such-and-such (from the German catalogue), but they did have some oversize aluminum toles on hand. They must have said, "They want aluminum and we've got to get rid of this stuff, so ship it out."

"There are several thousand dollars tied up in that," I told Johnny when the facts came out. "Somebody has to pay for it and I certainly don't have the money."

"It sure isn't anything I can use," Johnny said.

"I promised to do a church, and it's really strange that if I would take one six-meter tole on each side of that roof, it would fit exactly from the ridge to overhang the eaves. It would be perfect. I've never seen a six-meter tole before. They are real wide and a heavy gauge, they'd last for a thousand years." I paused to dream of having this material available for Nselo. "I want to see if I can raise some money."

A few days later, we drove into Kinshasa and stopped at the home of Marge and Murray Sharp. "Hey, there's a letter for you that just came today," Marge said.

The letter was from the pastor of a church in Iowa. He informed us that a man in his congregation had recently died, and in his will he had left three thousand dollars for Chester and Dolores Scott. We had received small gifts before, but never anything like this. It had been our practice to encourage people to provide financial support through the Board and not to make specific gifts to individual missionaries. Still, that three thousand dollars, along with the thousand raised by Nselo, plus the thousand that Dolores and I committed, was just what was needed for the new roof.

Jerry Weaver made the necessary arrangements for this money to pay for the number of toles I would use at Nselo, and Dolores and I set off to buy the lumber we would need to build the roof trusses. Usually we cut our own timber and sawed it into the lumber we desired, but this time we decided to purchase lumber from a sawmill run by a Belgian. As soon as the lumber was delivered I had my men paint it with a preservative, and we were ready to get the long-awaited project off the ground.

In the thirty years we had been there, we had never had a serious accident on the job. Some of that has to be attributed to luck, but more instrumental are the precautions I always took and the emphasis I constantly placed on safety. I had inspected each piece of lumber that was to go into the trusses, noticing how well my men had painted each piece with the preservative. Some of the lumber I rejected because I didn't trust it for braces. There is a great deal of stress on a roof, and the trusses must carry not only the weight of the roofing material but also withstand the added pressure of strong winds. The last thing a builder wants is to see his creation falling down on top of people.

The trusses were built and raised in place, one by one, each secured to the next one by braces. The operation went like clockwork, and Dolores and a group of children were inside the church enjoying our progress. They had no more than left the inside of the building when one of the braces broke, allowing that truss to fall, which in turn knocked over the next one, then the next, like a row of dominoes. One of the workers was caught under a falling truss and suffered a broken femur. We were just plain lucky that only one man was injured, but even one is too many.

The first concern was to get medical care for the workman. The nearest adequate hospital was at Kisantu, about thirty kilometers away. We loaded him on the truck, and I went to be sure the doctor took good care of him.

All the way back to the job site I worried. What am I going to tell these people? This terrible thing happened and I don't know how even to begin to explain how. I was the *mbuta* here, so I was responsible for any trouble. But when I got to the church the people were all as happy as could be.

"What gives?" I asked.

"We knew this was going to happen," they said.

"Oh, did you really?"

"Yes, we knew it. There is a curse on Nselo so that every time a roof is put up it falls and somebody gets hurt. As soon as one is hurt then the rest of us can relax and finish the job, knowing we are safe."

"You didn't tell me about this before," I said.

"Everybody knows about the curse, so we thought you would know, too. When they put the roof on the Catholic church the trusses all fell after they got them standing. The brother of the man who was hurt today had his leg broken, just like today." The narrator grinned as though a great weight had been lifted from his mind. "And when we built the hospital roof, the trusses fell and a man was injured. So you see, we knew. Now, let's get back to work."

Curse or not, I inspected the wood we had bought from the Belgian. Dry rot had been covered by the preservative paint. I was furious at the lumberman and confronted him for selling us such dangerous material.

"Why did you do such a thing?" I demanded.

"I knew it was bad wood, but I thought I could get away with it," he said with a shrug.

Ka diambu ko.

CHAPTER 26

Sona Bata–1984-1986

Several years earlier, I had been working on a school building at a center not far from Sona Bata. I had trusses built at the shop at Sona Bata and loaded on the truck so that we could take them to the building site and have them ready to be erected when the building was ready for roofing. Such trusses are very heavy and require a lot of lifting. After several days of this, my shoulder started hurting. I assumed it was because I had been doing so much lifting and had pulled a muscle. I almost lost the use of my arm because of the pain, but I finally prevailed on a doctor at Kimpese to shoot it full of cortisone and was able to get back to work.

In mid-1984 I developed the same problem in the other shoulder. It was a holiday, and I worked alone until the middle of the afternoon, when I decided I'd had enough. I went to the house, took my shower and started having chills. I thought probably it was another malaria attack, so I went to bed. Then the other arm began to hurt, and I knew it was something other than a muscle pull. As the situation worsened over time, my arm hurt so badly that the only relief I could get was to raise it above my head, and finally I couldn't even do that any more. The only way I could get my arm above my head was to lay it on a table, and then very slowly and carefully try to work my way underneath it so I would be sitting on the floor with my arm on the table. I began to lose weight at the rate of a pound a day. In one month I went from 180 pounds to 150.

Dolores called Dr. Dan on the radio and told him about my problems. He didn't sound overly concerned. "Get all the lab work done and radio back to me what it is," he said.

The Dutch doctors at Sona Bata tested me for everything they could think of, but they found nothing they could treat. Finally, Dolores was at the end of her rope. She called Miriam Fountain at Vanga on the radio.

"Miriam, there is something wrong with Scotty and I'm going to find out what it is. The doctors here can't tell us why he is having so much pain or why he's losing weight. Would you tell Susan to send down the Merck's Manual?" The Merck's Manual is a self-treatment book for people who must take care of themselves. It describes physical problems, their symptoms and what treatment, if any, is recommended. Miriam knew that when Dolores requested the Merck's Manual, something was really serious. She talked to her husband and our children. Susan later told me that Miriam said, "Susan, I'll tell you that your mother wants the manual, but DO NOT sent it!"

Within two hours, Johnny was on the radio to us. "Dad, Dr. Dan and I have arranged for an MAF plane to bring you to Vanga. He wants to run some tests up here."

Dolores and I threw some things in a weekend case and flew to Vanga. The pilot asked if I would like to fly the plane for a while and I tried, but in a matter of minutes found I couldn't maintain course or altitude. We took a thermos of coffee, as we always did, but I was so weak that I could not press the pressure button hard enough to get the liquid out of it.

Dan Fountain tested me for everything that offered even a hint as to what my problem was. X-rays, malaria tests, blood tests—you name it and if it could be done at the Vanga hospital, he did it. None of these tests identified my problem, though we eliminated a lot of possibilities. He treated me for filaria, a disease caused by a parasite that invades the body and often produces symptoms resembling mine. The tests continued.

"Scotty, we can't find it, whatever 'it' is," Dr. Dan said. "Your white cell count is elevated, indicating some infection, but we can't locate any infection. The only recourse now is for you to return to the States for more extensive examination."

"There's no way I can leave now," I said. "The Sona Bata hospital is all done except for the 'penthouse' above the center section, and that has to be put up right away."

"I'll take care of that," Johnny said. He knew what I called the "penthouse." The hospital was designed as a large X, and the area where the wings met was to be covered by a raised structure that would allow in light and ventilation. It was far too large, too heavy and too complex a job for me to leave to my workmen. "I'll go back to

Sona Bata with you and we'll finish it together."

"There's a medicine which I think will give you some relief," Dan said. "It's not a cure by any means, but I believe you'll think it is a miracle pill. It's called prednisone."

A miracle pill it was. From the first tablet I took I began to feel better—so much better, in fact, that I almost refused to obey the order to return to the States for medical attention. I also began to regain some of my weight. But everyone was adamant, so John, Sue, Dolores and I returned to Sona Bata to prepare for the trip.

The "penthouse" for the hospital was built on the ground, then had to be raised above the roof and lowered into place. We built a catwalk around the opening in the roof, where men could stand and work, and we built a ramp up to the opening. Then, with about thirty of my men assisting, we inched the structure up the ramp, levering it up an inch at a time until it was in place. I had a blocking device to keep it from falling through the opening, and when we finally lowered it into its slot it was a perfect fit. With John's help, we built the structure and had it installed in three days.

That done, I had no further excuse to delay our trip home.

Back in the States the doctors used all their technology to diagnose my problem—CAT scans, ultra-sound, X-rays galore, cultures, tests of every sort—but the results remained inconclusive. Only the highly elevated white count emerged clearly as a clue.

"We're not able to give you a 100 percent positive diagnosis," my doctor said. "There are cases where the best we can do is make an informed guess, but my best judgment is that you have an arbovirus, most likely chickungunya."

The remainder of our time in the States allowed me to recuperate further, as well as to begin planning how I should put my affairs in order. Then we returned to Zaire for our final term.

My symptoms eased enough that I resumed work, though I had to face the painful fact that I no longer had the strength, endurance, or drive that had made me an overproducer for all those years. Increasingly, I turned responsibility over to others and was gratified to find that I had trained my men well. I still planned, supervised and accepted personal responsibility for the projects, but my physical participation was greatly reduced. To my surprise and pleasure, this did not seem to diminish either the quality or quantity of the work. Rather, it both allowed and forced me to give more attention to the individuals with whom I worked, though sometimes I felt my usefulness was over. Johnny helped me through those feelings.

One day, as we were working together, I indicated that I was really discouraged because I couldn't be the kind of builder I had been. I wondered whether I should even call myself a missionary any longer.

"Dad, we went into a village two days ago, remember?" John said. "As soon as the people saw who it was they all began to shout, 'Tata Scott! Tata Scott!' Then everybody ran out to see you and talk to you. They didn't do that because you are a builder. They did that because of something far more important." He laid down the tool in his hand and looked at me for a long moment. "They respect you and love you because of the way you have brought Christ into their lives. They know that sooner or later all these buildings will be gone, but you have helped them build on something that is eternal."

As I reflected on the relationships we had with the people, I realized that fewer and fewer of them came to us with problems related to buildings and more and more of them came with problems of a personal nature. There were people waiting to see me at the end of the workday, and I invited them into the house and talked while I relaxed in my easy chair. When we awoke in the morning, there would be people who wanted to talk before I went to work. It seemed that an endless string of searching, dreaming, hurting, needing, hoping people and I found a fulfillment here even greater than I had known before.

I seemed to be on call twenty-four hours a day, whenever there was a need. Dolores often scolded me, saying that I never learned to say "no," but I didn't take her too seriously because she was always ready to open our home at a moment's notice to anywhere from one person to two dozen, as the occasion demanded. And, indeed, our home often resembled an inn as much as it did a residence. She was a delighted and delightful hostess who expressed no surprise when a touring group of twenty Americans would show up without notice.

One relationship that I consciously developed had little to do with spirituality; the implications were much more pragmatic, though I liked the man a lot. We had fun together and he came to our house often.

The local *Commissar du police* had responsibility for an area roughly the same as our counties in America. He cultivated my friendship as much as I did his. I had a vehicle and he didn't. If there was a truck wrecked along the road, or an armed robbery he had to look into, he knew he could send one of his *gendarmes* to ask me to send my vehicle and chauffeur to help him out a bit, and I would do so. If it sounded like something really interesting, I'd often go along.

From my end it was helpful to have people know that the

Commissar and I were good friends. That reduced the likelihood of trouble around the mission. When trouble did arise I'd jump in the car, go pick him up, bring him back to the mission and turn the affair over to him.

On this particular day my friend came and asked me, "Could you go help me? I need the vehicle to go pick someone off the railroad track."

"Oh, really? What happened?"

"There was an old guy at the market yesterday and as he was going home to his village he got run over by a train," the policeman said. "He had been drinking."

I stopped at the hospital and picked up two or three nurses and a stretcher. We drove through the drizzle to where the policeman indicated the accident happened. As we walked down the railroad tracks I saw a man's torso. It was obvious that the man had been spread-eagled along the tracks so that the train would run the length of his body, entering at the groin. However, the body had slipped on the track, and the train had run across the groin and out underneath an arm. But, the head was not attached to the torso. Finally we found the head about ninety meters away.

The minute I saw his head I began to get a very clear picture of what had happened. Somebody had taken a machete and chopped off his face, just as one would chop the bark off a tree. His head had been cut off with a machete, not a train wheel. Then I noticed there was no blood anywhere to be seen.

As the nurses and police were assembling the various pieces of the body I called the *Commissar* over and said, "You know this is not an accident. You told me this man had been drinking and was walking down the railroad tracks."

"It certainly wasn't a robbery," the policeman said. "See, here is a bar of soap he bought at the market yesterday. If it had been a robbery they certainly would have taken the soap."

"Yes," I said, "but how do you account for the fact that his head was cut off before he was laid on the railroad track?"

"Oh, no, no, no!" he answered. "His head was cut off by the train."

"How do you account for the fact that they shaved off his features with a machete so that nobody could recognize him?" I asked.

"That was done when it was dragged along the gravel."

"How do you account that there is no blood?" I persisted.

"Because of the rain," he said.

"It hasn't rained that much. It's only a light drizzle."

"Look," he said, "I've got so much to do. If I start looking into all these dumb questions that you're asking I have to fill out reports and reports and reports. But if I say this guy was drunk and walking down the railroad track then all I have to do is file one report and say, 'I found a drunk who was walking down the railroad track and a train hit him.' It happens two or three times a week on the tracks between Matadi and Kinshasa." Seeing that I was still not buying his reasoning, he concluded, "Besides that, I don't have all those forms and I'd have to go into Kinshasa and try to find all those papers."

We had to keep the remains in our morgue. I had a coffin made. As we spent the mandatory three-day waiting period for someone to identify the victim, I asked around on my own. No one admitted knowing who he was or where he was from. No village reported a man missing. I was told several times, "Quit worrying about it, Tata Scott. He was probably a stranger who came here and got in a fuss with somebody."

That may have been the case, but to me it had all the earmarks of a family head who had been judged guilty of not protecting some member of the family from harm. If that was the case, one or more close relatives would be assigned to carry out the execution. There is a brutality in this culture that the Western mind cannot comprehend, but which is so deeply ingrained that it is seldom questioned by the people. Perhaps that element of the culture is a natural outgrowth of the brutality of life itself that confronts these good people daily.

One step the government has taken to minimize the atrocities is the creation of the *groupement*. This is best described as a local council to which the government gives authority. Thus the officials can say, "Don't carry out your own sentence. When you find a person guilty of an offense, turn them over to us and we will put them in prison." The headman of the village is either blessed by the government or he is replaced. This is understood throughout the village, and the people know that all communication with the government goes through the headman. This is his job, so the people do not consider him a traitor when he gives negative information to the government, an "outsider." Trying to balance the culture of the village against the demands of the government often puts the headman in a difficult position. Matadi was one of my carpenters, a devout Christian and also headman of his village. He anguished over decisions he had to make and spent hours with me talking them over. The system allows a degree of control without attempting to discard the culture.

Tata Nsilu was also one of my carpenters, a man who had worked at Sona Bata for years. I had offered to take him on jobs in other areas, but he always refused. He wanted to stay at Sona Bata because of the hospital. He and his wife never should have married because both of them had the genes for sickle-cell anemia. But, of course, they did marry, and they had twelve children. With this tragic genetic combination it was a certainty that a percentage of the children would develop sickle-cell anemia and some would die at an early age. Dr. Tuttle had examined the children and told Nsilu which of them had the disease and which were likely to die in childhood.

Nsilu was a good man. His Christian faith, along with his natural character, made him a good father and husband. He did his best to raise the children who did not die in infancy and sacrificed for them to have the best he could offer. All the children were in school, a tremendous expense for a laborer.

We had been working on a job outside of Sona Bata, and at the end of the day Tata Nsilu and I were in the truck returning home. I was hungry and stopped to buy a hand of bananas. I took one for myself and pulled a couple from the hand and gave them to him. As I ate my banana I noticed that Nsilu was holding his in his lap and just staring at them. "What's the matter? Don't you like bananas?" I asked.

"Tata Scott, do you know that this is the first banana I have had in a year?" he said.

He never spent money on himself. Every penny had to filter down to feed his family and educate his children. I realized that this skinny little man had practically starved himself to provide for his children.

One day Nsilu came to me and said, "Tata Scott, I need to have a few days off."

"Oh. What's the matter?" I asked.

"My mother is in prison," he said.

"What? Your mother in prison!" I knew his mother, an elderly and feeble woman who lived up on top of the Bangu above Kimpese. "What did your mother do?"

"She is accused of eating the souls of two of my children," he said. "The children died of the disease, but the *groupement* says she ate their souls. I have to go to the village and see if there is anything I can do about it."

Nsilu returned to his village. "My mother is innocent," he said. "I have letters here from Tata Scott and from the doctor at Sona Bata that proves her innocence. They died of a sickness that doesn't have anything to do with my mother."

The trial was reconvened with the headman and the witch doctor jointly presiding.

"You are accused of eating the souls of your grandchildren," the headman said. "Do you acknowledge your guilt?"

The grandmother refused to answer yes or no. Her wrinkled face betrayed no emotion and her fragile frame, though bent, conveyed the message that this was a strong-willed woman.

"Here are the letters from the missionaries. They say there is a certain sickness that the children would have died from anyway. But how much weight can we give these letters?" the witch doctor asked, his headdress bobbing like punctuation marks.

The discussion of the letters shifted the focus to Nsilu and away from his mother. If the cause of the children's deaths was found in Nsilu, then he was the one who should go to prison and have to pay the fine. Not only is Nsilu guilty in that case, but so is his wife's brother, because the wife's brother had allowed Nsilu to damage the children. It was apparent that the verdict was about to be reversed and new culprits named.

The grandmother stepped forward. "It was me. I left in the middle of the night. I went to Sona Bata. I ate the souls of the two children and then I came back here."

"Look at my mother," Nsilu said. "See how old and frail she is. She lives up on the Bangu, many miles from the village. How could she have left her home, come down the mountain, come to our home, eaten the souls of our children, climbed back up the mountain and back to her home, all in one night?"

His mother gave him an angry stare, then faced the court again. "It was me," she repeated.

"Mother, I know what you are doing and I won't allow it," Nsilu said. "You are innocent and you are only trying to protect me."

"I'm an old woman," she said. "What difference does it make to me? I'm ready to die anyway, so what difference does it make if I go to prison?" Nsilu begged and pleaded with her but was unable to shake her determination.

The headman and the witch doctor conferred in hushed tones, then the headman stated the verdict. "This is a grave offense," he began. Turning to Nsilu, he said, "Your family has to buy a big hog. Your wife's family has to buy a big goat. Then your mother has to cut the head off the hog and put it on the goat. Then she must cut the head off the goat and put it on the hog. The goat with the pig's head goes to me and the pig with the goat's head goes to the witch doctor. There is a fine that must be paid, fifteen hundred z's. Then your mother must go to prison, just as we have said."

I suppose that we Americans might consider the animals to be "court costs," but the two presiding judges and their families no doubt considered them good food. To me, it was enough of a tragedy that Nsilu lost two of his beloved children without having the loss compounded. A resolution was brought to the village, but at what a price! There are some things about the African culture that we Westerners do not, will not, cannot understand.

When we first arrived in the Belgian Congo, the forest grew on the outskirts of the Capital. The city people would go into the forest and cut firewood for cooking and heating. As the population of the city grew by the millions, the forest was cut back further and further from the city, until by the time we left there was really no forest left between Kinshasa and Sona Bata.

However, a small bit of forest did grow alongside our house at Sona Bata, with a beautiful spring that ran down the hillside and gave an endless supply of fresh water. We tried to protect this vestige of forest and did all we could to keep its trees from being consumed. Insofar as I was able, I forbade that any firewood would come from this growth. We bought firewood and charcoal and had it brought into Sona Bata as a further means of protecting the forest.

Then one night we had a particularly severe storm, with thunder booming and lightning crashing and rain pouring. When morning came, I saw that an enormous tree had been struck by lightning and had fallen at the edge of the forest. It lay there day after day. At length I talked to the chief of Sona Bata. "Why don't the people at Sona Bata take this tree and use it for firewood?"

"Oh, Tata Scott!" he looked at me quizzically. "You must be crazy. You don't take a tree that's been hit by lightning and use it for firewood. You'd get the itch."

"Is that right?" I said.

"Absolutely," he replied. "That is tabu. You just don't ever use such a tree for firewood."

I told my yard boy, "Go cut the tree up into firewood size and bring it over here."

"Oh, no! We would never do that," he said.

"Oh yes you will," I said.

"No, Tata Scott," he insisted. "If we burn that wood we will get the itch."

"Would you get the itch if you cut it up?" I asked.

"Oh, no. Only if we burn it for firewood," he said.

"OK," I said. "You cut it down and I'll use it for firewood."

The tree was cut up and brought, piece by piece in a wheelbarrow, to the house, where it was stacked into the biggest pile of firewood imaginable. I dug a great pit and began making charcoal. The Africans stood around and I could read their faces saying, "Boy, are you going to be sorry! You just wait."

The firewood and charcoal from that tree seemed to supply just as much heat as any other, and I thought nothing about it.

All those years in Africa, neither Dolores nor I had had any skin problem. But when we returned to the States at the end of our career, both of us suffered itching that almost drove us out of our minds for nearly a year.

As I said, there are some things we just can't understand.

CHAPTER 27

America—1987

The Atlantic stretched from horizon to horizon, a seemingly endless field of blue-gray, looking as endless as time itself. Waves rolled and crested far below the 747, too far away to be seen, but I knew they were there, each a response to a force and power beyond itself. Does one wave last all the way across the ocean, I wondered, or does it flow and merge with others until there is a final cresting on some distant shore? Does it matter whether or not an individual wave is seen and recognized, so long as it responds to The Power?

Thirty-five years earlier, we had crossed this ocean as a young family, heading into a life we knew little about. Now, Dolores and I were returning alone, leaving behind a life's work and a host of friends who had loved us, taught us, nurtured us and allowed us to do the same for them. Leaving behind the physical evidence of our presence: a building for every month we had been on the field. Leaving behind a core of workers, trained and capable. Leaving behind a son and his family to carry on and expand the work we had begun. Leaving behind a nation that still had not found itself. Leaving behind a growing indigenous church with a dynamism we only prayed for at the beginning.

Leaving one thing, though, means entering something else.

It had been a difficult decision to finally accept closure. The CBZO leaders wanted us to stay on, more as missionaries than as builders. President Mobutu had honored us with a gold medal and a lot of flowery phrases for what we had contributed to the country. Our workmen expressed dismay at the thought of separation.

"If you really love us, as you have said, how can you just up and leave us?" was the common question put to us. Finally, I came up with the only response they could understand and accept.

"You have a chief, right?" I asked.

"Oh, yes. We have a chief."

"You do what your chief tells you to do, right?" I said.

"We always do what our chief tells us to do."

"I also have a chief," I said. "My chief is in a big building back in Pennsylvania, and my chief said for me to come home."

"We understand that. You must obey your chief." Then it was all right. I was doing the right thing.

Indeed, my chief, the denominational board, had asked us to return to be missionaries-in-residence at our conference center at Green Lake, Wisconsin, for the summer. It was the perfect opportunity for us. Not only did it allow us to terminate our career in Zaire with good feelings and good wishes from the people there, it also provided us with the opportunity to renew acquaintance with many of the friends we had made across America as we spoke in their churches each time we returned for furlough.

Wispy clouds appeared over the ocean, then became fluffy, and at length we were above solid clouds. From our height we could look down at the clouds, glaring white in the sunlight like fluffy cotton spread graciously over the earth. How many times our little planes had taken us over the clouds covering the jungle, but never at this altitude. Flying from one job to another, from one crisis to the next, from one emergency to safety and healing.

Each flight, like each building, had its conclusion as well as its beginning. At the end of each flight, I thanked my Lord for His presence with me during the flight and for my safe arrival. At every dedication of every building I felt a sense of awe at what was accomplished, a profound religious experience that my minister brother called an Epiphany.

If such was true for a single flight or a single building, how much deeper and richer was the closeness of God at the conclusion of a career.

Ka Diambu Ko

Appendix

In 1885 King Leopold II of Belgium claimed a section of west-central Africa as his personal fiefdom. Known as The Congo Free State, it was administered as the personal property of the king until 1908, when it was annexed by Belgium. But of course, life had gone on in the jungles and the savannas for millennia before Leopold ever heard of the place. Hundreds of tribes had lived there, hunting for food and for each other. The tribes varied in size from a handful of villages to what could legitimately be called kingdoms. Other than their general Bantu genetics, the tribes had few things in common; they shared a primal and primary loyalty to their own tribe and hatred and fear of anyone of another tribe.

When white men in Europe drew lines on a map to define the new countries in Africa, they did so without regard to tribal boundaries or rivalries. The boundaries of the "new country" often bisected the territory of a tribe, leaving half the tribe in one country and half in another. No way was, or ever could be, found to convince the natives they were now citizens of a new nation. Centuries and centuries of oral history made each tribe acutely aware of its own importance. "Congo" existed, and in great measure "Zaire" exists today, as a concept in the minds of a few, never as a "homeland" of the masses.

Leopold and the business interests he involved in the enterprise were less than just in their dealings with the natives. The situation became so flagrant and offensive to the Belgian people that in 1908 the state officially annexed the territory and set up a more orderly government for the Congo. Of all colonial powers, Belgium was certainly one of the most benevolent, though totally paternalistic, in its administration. Decisions were made by white men; work was done by the black. Officers in the military were white; a native could never rise above the rank of sergeant. Industries were owned and managed by whites, manned by blacks. Brussels was the seat of government for the Congo, and no native had the right to vote. Yet, Belgium instituted comprehensive programs of public health to control malaria and encephalitis, uniform compensation for work, and a host of similar programs. Both public education and health care were left to be provided by the missions, though the Belgian government subsidized these.

Following World War II, the move for independence from colonial powers swept the globe. A survey of the membership growth in the United Nations gives a fair index of the proliferation of independent-nation states. The Congo was caught up in this climate, and Belgium was anxious for an orderly transition from colonialism to full independence. The Belgians proposed a schedule of gradualism by which Congo could develop the infrastructures and indigenous leadership necessary to govern. At the time college graduates of native origin could be counted on one's fingers.

A first step in the direction of gradualism was the general elections in 1957, the first time any Congolese had a voice in determining any governmental decision. This election fed the fervor for independence, and the newly elected Congolese demanded immediate action.

In the first two months of 1960, a round-table conference of African leaders, held in Brussels, passed a resolution that full independence be granted on June 30, 1960. The Belgian parliament felt this timetable, while dangerous, held less danger than postponing independence further. It is worth noting that after the conference at least two of those attending, Patrice Lumumba and Pierre Muliele, visited extensively in the Soviet Union.

Elections were held before June, resulting in a popular victory for Patrice Lumumba, who became prime minister. The second strongest party was led by Joseph Kasavubu, who became president. Thus the new country began with a division between the leftist prime minister and the Westward-leaning president.

Independence was a concept not well understood by the rank and file of the Congolese, as numerous anecdotes attest. One such story is of the truckload of missionaries who were stopped by Congolese asking if there was any Independence in the truck and if so, would they please hand it over. One of the missionaries took a bit of paper, wrote "Independence" on it and so satisfied the inquisitors. Other stories involve Congolese who had been told that with Independence they would be rich, that in fact they could bury empty cans in their yards and on the morning after independence the cans would be filled with money. Such misunderstanding of the nature of independence led to false expectations by many of the Congolese.

With Independence, the white officers of the military were summarily dismissed and replaced with whomever could declare himself a colonel and make it stick with the troops. For the most part, however, the military found itself leaderless and so without discipline. Within days the military revolted, or rebelled, or rioted, depending on which accounts one chooses to highlight. In any event the result was a blood bath largely, but not entirely, against whites. Women were raped, men were beaten and killed, property was confiscated and chaos reigned. A degree of order was restored when Joseph Mobutu, newly named colonel, put down the worst of the revolting military. Mobutu was an ally of President Kasavubu and was to rise quickly to commander-in-chief of the army.

In early July, Moise Tshombe, president of the province of Katanga, declared Katanga an independent nation. Katanga contains most of the abundant mineral resources of the Congo: diamonds, uranium, tin, copper, manganese, zinc and cobalt. The Belgian government sent in troops to protect its mining interests, and fighting there was fierce. The United Nations agreed to send troops in to maintain order but, limited by its own charter, it could not interfere in internal affairs. This left Lumumba without aid against the secession of Katanga, so he turned to his friends in the Soviet Union for help. President Kasavubu disapproved of Soviet involvement and subsequently dismissed Lumumba as prime minister. He appointed a man more to his liking for that office.

In mid-September Joseph Mobutu had enough of the conflict, so he seized control, dismissed the president and both contenders for the role of prime minister. Later, he reached an accord with Kasavubu, restoring him to the office of president. Lumumba was arrested in December, sent to Katanga under the protection of Tshombe, and just over two months later it was announced that he had been killed while trying to escape.

There had been an ongoing war between the Baluba and Lulua tribes in southeastern Congo, and the Baluba chieftain, King Kalonji, saw this as an appropriate time to disregard Leopoldville's authority in Kasai province. He was not alone. Antione Gizenga declared himself Lumumba's successor and exercised considerable influence in both Kivu and Orientale provinces. Tshombe continued to head what he insisted was the independent state of Katanga. Congo was even less of a nation than it was before independence.

The military forces across Congo were confused and confusing. The United Nations forces were charged with maintaining order but avoiding engagement. Mobutu's army lacked the size, discipline and training to accomplish major objectives. Each faction had armed forces, most of which could best be described as guerilla groups, though some had truly impressive numbers and found themselves supplied with armaments from major world powers. Gizenga recruited an army of mercenaries to stabilize the situation around Stanleyville, and they proved most effective until the money to pay them ran out and they took over Stanleyville as their compensation. Fighting was sporadic, impulsive and unfocused but nonetheless deadly.

The Congo would have had a most difficult time being born if left on her own—but, of course, she was not. The Congo was too strategic, in both location and resources, to be ignored by Washington or Moscow or Beijing or other competing powers in the world. A face-to-face confrontation between the USA and the USSR over the Congo was narrowly averted by the diplomacy of Dag Hammarskjold, secretary general of the UN, who subsequently was killed in an airplane crash while on his way to mediate the conflict in Katanga.

Katanga remained central to the turmoil through the end of 1962, when UN forces launched an initiative against Katanga. This resulted in some of the bloodiest fighting to date, ending with the Katangan army defeated and Tshombe agreeing to reunification. This eased, but certainly did not resolve, the problems of the central government which faced monumental financial and political difficulties. Not the least of these was the *Jeunesse* movement.

Pierre Muliele had been trained in China in counter-revolutionary techniques. He focused on the youth of the Congo and fed their enthusiasm with outlandish appeals to their superstition. He convinced them that the magic powers he bestowed on his followers would cause bullets to turn to water and drip out of the barrels of their enemies' guns. He opposed anything Western and urged his followers to destroy not only white people but also every Congolese who had adopted anything Western. Bands of *Jeunesse* swept across the country leaving death and destruction behind them until the very word *Jeunesse* caused fear and trembling. The movement sputtered out in Leopoldville Province in mid-1964.

Kasavubu finally turned to Tshombe in July of 1964, asking him to form a government, but Tshombe proved to be no more adept at governing than his predecessors had been. The situation stumbled along until November of 1965, when Joseph Mobutu led a bloodless coup and declared himself head of state.

Mobutu became the virtual dictator of Congo and has been the source of controversy ever since. His detractors brand him as arrogant, brutal and self-serving, criticizing him for nepotism and amassing great personal wealth at the expense of the country. His admirers insist that arrogance, a degree of brutality, nepotism and personal wealth for the chief are so deeply rooted in African culture that no one could rule the Congo effectively at this time without them. Most agree that Mobutu has made great strides in restoring order but has done poorly with the nation's economy. Inflation continues year after year at a staggering pace. A Congolese bureaucracy has replaced the Belgian bureaucracy and proven itself to be less than efficient. The infrastructure is in need of general overhaul, while extravagant expenditures have been made on monumental showplaces.

Index

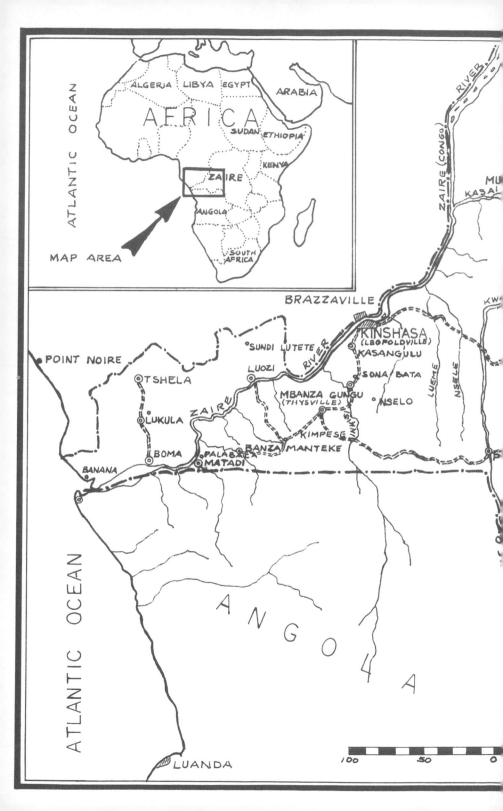